SUSAN BROCK, SUSAN CERASANO, PETER CORBIN, PAUL EDMONSON,
E. A. J. HONIGMANN, GRACE IOPPOLO, J. R. MULRYNE and
ROBERT SMALLWOOD
former editors

SARAH DUSTAGHEER, PETER KIRWAN, DAVID MCINNIS and LUCY MUNRO
general editors

For more than half a century *The Revels Plays* have offered the most authoritative editions of Elizabethan and Jacobean plays by authors other than Shakespeare. The *Companion Library* provides a fuller background to the main series by publishing important dramatic and non-dramatic material that will be essential for the serious student of the period.

To buy or to find out more about the books currently available in this series, please go to: https://manchesteruniversitypress.co.uk/series/revels-plays-companion-library/

John Fletcher's Rome

Manchester University Press

THE REVELS PLAYS COMPANION LIBRARY

John Fletcher's Rome

QUESTIONING THE CLASSICS

Domenico Lovascio

Manchester University Press

Copyright © Domenico Lovascio 2022

The right of Domenico Lovascio to be identified as the author of this work has been asserted by them in accordance with the Copyright, Designs and Patents Act 1988.

Published by Manchester University Press
Oxford Road, Manchester M13 9PL

www.manchesteruniversitypress.co.uk

British Library Cataloguing-in-Publication Data
A catalogue record for this book is available from the British Library

ISBN 9781 5 261 5738 6 hardback

First published 2022

The publisher has no responsibility for the persistence or accuracy of URLs for any external or third-party internet websites referred to in this book, and does not guarantee that any content on such websites is, or will remain, accurate or appropriate.

Typeset
by New Best-set Typesetters Ltd

For Giulia, Cesare, and Juno

CONTENTS

ILLUSTRATIONS	viii
GENERAL EDITORS' PREFACE	ix
PREFACE AND ACKNOWLEDGEMENTS	x
NOTE ON THE TEXT	xviii
INTRODUCTION: THE ROMAN PLAYS IN THE FLETCHER CANON	1
Fletcher's classical settings	1
Ancient Rome and early modern England	2
The Roman plays of John Fletcher	6
The 'Fletcher canon'	12
The contents of this book	15
1 'TAKE YOUR LILY / AND GET YOUR PART READY': FLETCHER AND THE CLASSICS	26
2 'I AM NO ROMAN, / NOR WHAT I AM DO I KNOW': FLETCHER'S ROMAN PLAYS AS *TRAUERSPIELE*	61
3 'HAD LUCRECE E'ER BEEN THOUGHT OF BUT FOR TARQUIN?' THE INADEQUACY OF ROMAN FEMALE *EXEMPLA*	105
4 'TO DO THUS / I LEARNED OF THEE': SHAKESPEARE'S EXEMPLARY ROMAN PLAYS	134
CONCLUSION: QUESTIONING THE CLASSICS	177
BIBLIOGRAPHY	185
INDEX	205

ILLUSTRATIONS

1 Portrait of John Fletcher, from life, about 1620, oil on oak panel, unknown artist (© National Portrait Gallery, London).   28
2 The emperor in agony in the final act of *Valentinian*, in *The Works of Mr. Francis Beaumont and Mr. John Fletcher*, with an introduction by Gerard Langbaine the younger, 7 vols (London: Tonson, 1711), 3:1309 (ULB Bonn, Fb 407). Reproduced by permission of Universitäts und Landesbibliothek Bonn.   64
3 The Egyptians defeated by the Romans at the end of *The False One*, in *The Works of Mr. Francis Beaumont and Mr. John Fletcher*, with an introduction by Gerard Langbaine the younger, 7 vols (London: Tonson, 1711), 3:1149 (ULB Bonn, Fb 407). Reproduced by permission of Universitäts und Landesbibliothek Bonn.   114
4 The Icenian queen and her daughters defy the Romans' siege in *Bonduca*, in *The Works of Mr. Francis Beaumont and Mr. John Fletcher*, with an introduction by Gerard Langbaine the younger, 7 vols (London: Tonson, 1711), 4:2185 (ULB Bonn, Fb 407). Reproduced by permission of Universitäts und Landesbibliothek Bonn.   146
5 Diocles exhibits a boar he has successfully hunted, while Delphia and Drusilla fly on a chariot pulled by dragons, in *The Prophetess*, in *The Works of Mr. Francis Beaumont and Mr. John Fletcher*, with an introduction by Gerard Langbaine the younger, 7 vols (London: Tonson, 1711), 4:2035 (ULB Bonn, Fb 407). Reproduced by permission of Universitäts und Landesbibliothek Bonn.   160

GENERAL EDITORS' PREFACE

Since the late 1950s the series known as The Revels Plays has provided for students of the English Renaissance drama carefully edited texts of the major Elizabethan and Jacobean plays. The series includes some of the best-known drama of the period and has continued to expand, both within its original field and, to a lesser extent, beyond it, to include some important plays from the earlier Tudor and from the Restoration periods. The Revels Plays Companion Library is intended to further this expansion and to allow for new developments.

The aim of the Companion Library is to provide students of the Elizabethan and Jacobean drama with a fuller sense of its background and context. The series includes volumes of a variety of kinds. Small collections of plays, by a single author or concerned with a single theme and edited in accordance with the principles of textual modernisation of The Revels Plays, offer a wider range of drama than the main series can include. Together with editions of masques, pageants and the non-dramatic work of Elizabethan and Jacobean playwrights, these volumes make it possible, within the overall Revels enterprise, to examine the achievements of the major dramatists from a broader perspective. Other volumes provide a fuller context for the plays of the period by offering new collections of documentary evidence on Elizabethan theatrical conditions and on the performance of plays during that period and later. A third aim of the series is to offer modern critical interpretation, in the form of collections of essays or of monographs, of the dramatic achievement of the English Renaissance.

So wide a range of material necessarily precludes the standard format and uniform general editorial control which is possible in the original series of Revels Plays. To a considerable extent, therefore, treatment and approach are determined by the needs and intentions of individual volume editors. Within this rather ampler area, however, we hope that the Companion Library maintains the standards of scholarship that have for so long characterised The Revels Plays, and that it offers a useful enlargement of the work of the series in preserving, illuminating and celebrating the drama of Elizabethan and Jacobean England.

S. DUSTAGHEER, P. KIRWAN, D. MCINNIS, L. MUNRO

PREFACE AND ACKNOWLEDGEMENTS

Studies on the reception of the Roman past in early modern English literature and culture have experienced an exponential growth since the turn of the millennium. Predictably enough, Shakespeare's Roman plays remain the most obvious and common objects of study.[1] The last few years have witnessed an impressive proliferation of critical treatments of Shakespeare's Rome and his engagement with the classics, with the publication of edited collections by Maria Del Sapio Garbero and Daniela Guardamagna (both springing from the series of coordinated events devoted to Shakespeare and the resonance of ancient Rome throughout his oeuvre held in Rome from 7 to 20 April 2016 under the collective title 'Shakespeare 2016: Memoria di Roma' to celebrate the quatercentenary of Shakespeare's death), a thematic issue of *Shakespeare Survey* on 'Shakespeare and Rome', and a special issue of *Shakespeare* on 'Shakespeare: Visions of Rome', as well as monographs by Paul Cantor, Patrick Gray, Jonathan Bate, and Curtis Perry.[2] Attempts have been also made towards wider-ranging and more sustained explorations of clusters of non-Shakespearean Roman-themed plays in both the commercial theatre and neo-Senecan drama.[3] *John Fletcher's Rome: Questioning the Classics* both contributes to and offers a corrective to this burgeoning area of research by focusing on a group of Roman plays that have featured only in passing in the critical debate.

Judging from current critical trends, Fletcher is not perhaps an obvious choice as the subject of a monograph. This is, however, at odds with his standing in his own day. As Celia R. Daileader and Gary Taylor point out, 'Fletcher was, without doubt, enormously esteemed in his own time, and was by all objective measures more successful as a dramatist than his senior contemporary, Shakespeare.'[4] In addition, the critical prejudice that hindered for decades a complete appreciation of Fletcher's works – at least since Samuel Taylor Coleridge's famously unfavourable comparison of Fletcher with Shakespeare and resulting critical damnation – has been gradually (albeit not completely) overcome, particularly thanks to such groundbreaking studies as those by Eugene M. Waith, Clifford Leech, Nancy Cotton Pearse, Philip J. Finkelpearl, Sandra Clark, and Gordon

McMullan.⁵ Yet critical surveys of Fletcher's works are still relatively few, especially as regards book-length treatments, with only two monographs published between 1995 and 2019.⁶ Thus, while the situation has slightly improved, what McMullan argued in 1994 still appears to have currency as I write this in 2021:

> The ... plays in which Fletcher was involved form the single most substantial canon of dramatic work to come down to us from the English Renaissance. Yet they remain almost wholly unexplored by critics ... Fletcher occupies a curious position among Renaissance playwrights, managing to be at once central and marginal. He is central for three reasons: he wrote three plays with Shakespeare ... he succeeded Shakespeare as the chief playwright of the King's Company, and he exerted a substantial generic influence over drama for decades both before and after the shutdown of the theaters in the 1640s and 1650s. At the same time, he is almost entirely overshadowed culturally and historically by the phenomenon of Shakespeare.⁷

As a matter of fact, the Fletcher canon still constitutes, to a certain extent, 'the vast unexplored Amazonian jungle of Jacobean drama', as Finkelpearl suggested in 1990, and still exhibits what Clark in 1994 described as an 'extraordinary invisibility'.⁸ The situation is further complicated by the fact that many of the plays in which Fletcher had a hand were the outcome of collaboration with other playwrights, among whom Francis Beaumont and Philip Massinger stand out.

Commendably, the situation now seems to be on the verge of a major change, as suggested by a series of promising initiatives and publications. Pavel Drabek's book *Fletcherian Dramatic Achievement* was published in 2010. Martin Wiggins convened 'The Beaumont and Fletcher Marathon' at the Shakespeare Institute, Stratford-upon-Avon, in June 2013 (the first public reading of the whole canon), which was followed by 'The Massinger Marathon', featuring the plays of Fletcher's other major collaborator, in June 2018. José A. Pérez Díez and Steve Orman organized the 'John Fletcher: A Critical Reappraisal' conference in Canterbury in June 2015. Sarah E. Johnson coordinated the seminar 'Finding Fletcher' at the annual meeting of the Shakespeare Association of America in 2017. Pérez Díez and Wiggins are now assembling a collection of essays for a projected *Oxford Handbook of John Fletcher*. A spate of fully annotated, single-volume, modern-spelling critical editions of plays in the canon have recently appeared in such major series as Arden Early Modern Drama (Beaumont and Fletcher's *Philaster* and Fletcher's *The Island Princess*, as well as Massinger's *The Renegado*), the New Mermaids (Fletcher's *The Tamer Tamed*), and the Revels Student Editions (Fletcher's *The Tamer Tamed*), as well as in *The Routledge Anthology of Early Modern Drama* (Fletcher and Massinger's *The Sea Voyage*).⁹ Others are forthcoming in the

Revels Plays (Fletcher and Massinger's *Love's Cure*, *The False One*, and *Sir John Van Olden Barnavelt*).[10] Besides, *Philaster*, *The Tamer Tamed*, *Love's Cure*, and *The Island Princess* are to appear in the forthcoming RSC edition of the *Plays of the King's Men* in 2023, and the Malone Society plans to publish an edition of the surviving manuscript of Fletcher and Massinger's *The Elder Brother* in 2025 as a way to commemorate the quatercentenary of Fletcher's death.[11] Finally, 2020 witnessed the publication of a monograph by Peter Malin on the modern performance history of plays in the Fletcher canon, excluding his collaborations with Shakespeare, and the same year also saw the first Italian translation of the *Tamer Tamed*, an extraordinary event given that Italian translations of plays in the Fletcher canon other than collaborations with Shakespeare had only previously been available for Beaumont and Fletcher's *Philaster* and *The Maid's Tragedy*.[12] In the wake of such a significant body of initiatives and publications, this book seeks to contribute to a comprehensive re-evaluation of John Fletcher's dramatic achievement.

* * *

For the idea of writing this book I am indebted to José A. Pérez Díez. We first met at the 'John Fletcher: A Critical Reappraisal' conference that he convened with Steve Orman at Christ Church University, Canterbury, on 27 June 2015. About a year later, he asked me to contribute a chapter on 'Fletcher and Classical Antiquity' to a projected collection that would become *The Oxford Handbook of John Fletcher*, on which he is currently working with Martin Wiggins. Ironically enough, the present volume sees the light of day before that collection, but I admit I would have never thought of writing a monograph on this topic had I not set out to investigate Fletcher's Roman plays to prepare that chapter in the first place.

I am grateful to Matthew Frost at Manchester University Press, who considerately and professionally helped the book along its way, and to series editors Sarah Dustagheer, Peter Kirwan, David McInnis, and Lucy Munro for their support and enthusiasm, as well as the valuable insights they provided at the proposal stage. Special thanks go to Andrew Kirk for his meticulous copy-editing.

I owe a particular debt of gratitude to my general editor, Lucy Munro. She proved to be an exceptionally perceptive reader, provided incisive comments, suggestions, and corrections, and was extremely generous in sharing with me her immense knowledge of all things Fletcher. Her painstaking attention to detail, her intellectual rigour, and her illuminating editorial feedback have made this a much better book than it would have been otherwise, and any errors that remain are entirely my responsibility.

The research undertaken in this book has been possible largely thanks to funding made available from the Italian Ministry of Education, University, and Research (MIUR), which supported the project 'Classical Receptions in Early Modern English Drama' as a Research Project of National Interest (PRIN2017XAA3ZF). This monograph is part of that broader research. The Principal Investigator was Silvia Bigliazzi (University of Verona), while the three local units were coordinated by Carlo Maria Bajetta (University of Aosta), Alessandro Grilli (University of Pisa), and me at the University of Genoa. I thank all the participants in the project for many fruitful discussions and stimulating exchanges.

I am grateful for having been able to air my views at various venues, and for the discussion and feedback I have received from critical but invariably helpful audiences. Parts of Chapter 2 were presented at the ninth Italian Association of Shakespearean and Early Modern Studies (IASEMS) conference 'Early Modern Identity: Selves, Others and Life Writing' at the University of Cagliari on 12 June 2018; a shorter version of Chapter 1 at the annual 'Spiritual and Material Renaissances' colloquium at Sheffield Hallam University on 26 June 2018; an abridged version of Chapter 3 at the thirteenth European Shakespeare Research Association (ESRA) conference 'Shakespeare and European Geographies: Centralities and Elsewheres' at Roma Tre University on 10 July 2019; and a short section of Chapter 4 at the 'Virtual Spiritual and Material Renaissances' colloquium that Lisa Hopkins organized via Zoom on 16 June 2020. I thank all the people who provided helpful suggestions and comments on these occasions, namely Alessandra Petrina, Daniela Guardamagna, Donatella Pallotti, Lisa Hopkins, Pavel Drabek, Tom Rutter, Matthew Steggle, Todd Borlik, and Coen Heijes.

I am grateful to a number of friends and colleagues who have commented on single chapters of the book or have kindly provided helpful information or material, namely Luisa Villa, Antonio Giovinazzo, Camilla Caporicci, Fabio Ciambella, Cristiano Ragni, Emanuel Stelzer, Freyja Cox Jensen, and Chris Laoutaris. Special thanks go to Michela Compagnoni, Lisa Hopkins, Cristina Paravano, and Maddalena Repetto, who nobly read the entire typescript before submission to the publisher.

All my colleagues working in English at the Department of Modern Languages and Cultures at Genoa have been splendid to work with: Laura Colombino, Stefania Michelucci, Paola Nardi, Luisa Villa, Annalisa Baicchi, Marco Bagli, Cristiano Broccias, Ilaria Rizzato, Laura Santini, and Elisabetta Zurru.

I owe deep gratitude to the staff of my Department Library. Simone Tallone has been characteristically helpful, diligent, and resourceful, while Franco Reuspi has once more proved to be the most efficient librarian in the world by responding promptly to my book orders and requests for interlibrary loan materials. This book would simply not exist without them. Daniela Lilova and Martina Steden-Papke at the Universitäts- und Landesbibliothek Bonn were also vitally helpful in providing images very quickly during pandemic times.

The Introduction incorporates a little material from Domenico Lovascio and Lisa Hopkins, 'Introduction: Ancient Rome and English Renaissance Drama', in *The Uses of Rome in English Renaissance Drama*, ed. Domenico Lovascio and Lisa Hopkins, *Textus: English Studies in Italy* 29.2 (2016), thematic issue, 9–19. Chapter 2 includes short sections taken from 'Julius Caesar's "just cause" in John Fletcher and Philip Massinger's *The False One*', *Notes and Queries* 62 (2015), 245–7; 'Julius Caesar, *Translatio Imperii* and Tyranny in Jasper Fisher's *Fuimus Troes*', in *The Uses of Rome in English Renaissance Drama*, ed. Domenico Lovascio and Lisa Hopkins, *Textus: English Studies in Italy* 29.2 (2016), thematic issue, 185–212; and 'She-Tragedy: Lust, Luxury and Empire in John Fletcher and Philip Massinger's *The False One*', in *The Genres of Renaissance Tragedy*, ed. Daniel Cadman, Andrew Duxfield, and Lisa Hopkins (Manchester: Manchester University Press, 2019), 166–83. An earlier and much shorter version of Chapter 3 appeared as 'Bawds, Wives, and Foreigners: The Question of Female Agency in the Roman Plays of the Fletcher Canon', in *Roman Women in Shakespeare and His Contemporaries*, ed. Domenico Lovascio (Kalamazoo, MI: Medieval Institute Publications, 2020), 165–84. I am thankful to all the relevant editors and publishers who have granted permission to reproduce previously published material.

My son, Cesare, had not even been born when I decided to write this book but was often sitting on my lap or crawling around my desk as I wrote it, and even walking and jumping around the house as I made the final revisions. His smile, curiosity, and exuberance have been an unfailing source of joy, strength, and enthusiasm. Juno, my adorable dog, will never be able to read this book, but she lay right by my side for much of the time that I wrote it despite having our home garden freely accessible. Her unconditional love, infinite playfulness, and indescribable fluffiness provided welcome distractions and heart-warming cheerfulness. Finally, I owe special gratitude to Giulia. We have been travelling together on the journey of life for over sixteen years now, and she has always been supportive of my personal and academic endeavours. This project was no exception. All along she provided words of encouragement and made sure

I had the necessary quiet to read and write by often taking care of Cesare by herself. She patiently tolerated all the time I subtracted from our family in the early mornings and at the weekends, and I will never thank her enough. This book is dedicated to the three of them.

DOMENICO LOVASCIO
Genoa, 23 April 2021

NOTES

1 See Barbara L. Parker, *Plato's Republic and Shakespeare's Rome: A Political Study of the Roman Works* (Newark, DE: University of Delaware Press, 2004); Maria Del Sapio Garbero (ed.), *Identity, Otherness and Empire in Shakespeare's Rome* (Farnham: Ashgate, 2009); Sarah Hatchuel and Nathalie Vienne-Guerrin (eds), *Shakespeare on Screen: The Roman Plays* (Mont Saint Aignan: Publications des Universités de Rouen et du Havre, 2009); Maria Del Sapio Garbero, Nancy Isenberg, and Maddalena Pennacchia (eds), *Questioning Bodies in Shakespeare's Rome* (Göttingen: V&R Unipress, 2010); Warren Chernaik, *The Myth of Rome in Shakespeare and His Contemporaries* (Cambridge: Cambridge University Press, 2011); Maddalena Pennacchia, *Shakespeare intermediale. I drammi romani* (Spoleto: Editoria & Spettacolo, 2012); Colin Burrow, *Shakespeare and Classical Antiquity* (Oxford: Oxford University Press, 2013); Lisa S. Starks-Estes, *Violence, Trauma and Virtus in Shakespeare's Roman Poems and Plays: Transforming Ovid* (Basingstoke: Palgrave Macmillan, 2014); Paul Innes, *Shakespeare's Roman Plays* (London: Palgrave, 2015).

2 Peter Holland (ed.), *Shakespeare and Rome*, Shakespeare Survey 69 (2016), thematic issue; Paul A. Cantor, *Shakespeare's Roman Trilogy: The Twilight of the Ancient World* (Chicago: University of Chicago Press, 2017); Maria Del Sapio Garbero (ed.), *Rome in Shakespeare's World* (Rome: Storia e Letteratura, 2018); Patrick Gray, *Shakespeare and the Fall of the Roman Republic: Selfhood, Stoicism and Civil War* (Edinburgh: Edinburgh University Press, 2018); Daniela Guardamagna (ed.), *Roman Shakespeare: Intersecting Times, Spaces, Languages* (Bern: Peter Lang, 2018); Jonathan Bate, *How the Classics Made Shakespeare* (Princeton, NJ: Princeton University Press, 2019); Domenico Lovascio (ed.), *Shakespeare: Visions of Rome*, Shakespeare 15.4 (2019), special issue; Curtis Perry, *Shakespeare and Senecan Tragedy* (Cambridge: Cambridge University Press, 2020).

3 See Anthony Miller, *Roman Triumphs and Early Modern English Culture* (Basingstoke: Palgrave Macmillan, 2001); Andrew Hadfield, *Shakespeare and Republicanism* (Cambridge: Cambridge University Press, rev. edn, 2008); Lisa Hopkins, *The Cultural Uses of the Caesars on the English Renaissance Stage* (Aldershot: Ashgate, 2008); Freyja Cox Jensen, *Reading the Roman Republic in Early Modern England* (Leiden: Brill, 2012); Edward Paleit, *War, Liberty, and Caesar: Responses to Lucan's Bellum Ciuile, ca. 1580–1650* (Oxford: Oxford University Press, 2013); Patrick Cheney and Philip Hardie (eds), *The Oxford History of Classical Reception in English Literature, Volume 2: 1558–1660* (Oxford: Oxford University Press, 2015); Daniel Cadman, *Sovereigns and Subjects in Early Modern Neo-Senecan Drama: Republicanism, Stoicism and Authority* (Farnham: Ashgate, 2015); Domenico Lovascio, *Un nome, mille volti. Giulio Cesare nel teatro inglese della prima età moderna* (Rome: Carocci, 2015); Domenico Lovascio and

Lisa Hopkins (eds), *The Uses of Rome in English Renaissance Drama*, *Textus. English Studies in Italy* 29.2 (2016), thematic issue; Daniel Cadman, Andrew Duxfield, and Lisa Hopkins (eds), *Rome and Home: The Cultural Uses of Rome in Early Modern English Literature*, *Early Modern Literary Studies* 25 (2016), special issue, https://extra.shu.ac.uk/emls/journal/index.php/emls/issue/view/15, accessed 25 February 2021; Lisa Hopkins, *From the Romans to the Normans on the English Renaissance Stage* (Kalamazoo, MI: Medieval Institute Publications, 2017); Domenico Lovascio (ed.), *Roman Women in Shakespeare and His Contemporaries* (Kalamazoo, MI: Medieval Institute Publications, 2020); Paulina Kewes, *Ancient Rome in English Political Culture, ca. 1570–1660*, *Huntington Library Quarterly* 83.3 (2020), special issue; Tania Demetriou and Janice Valls-Russell (eds), *Thomas Heywood and the Classical Tradition* (Manchester: Manchester University Press, 2021).

4 Celia R. Daileader and Gary Taylor, 'Introduction', in *The Tamer Tamed or, The Woman's Prize* by John Fletcher (Manchester: Manchester University Press, 2006), 1–41 (31).

5 Eugene M. Waith, *The Pattern of Tragicomedy in Beaumont and Fletcher* (New Haven, CT: Yale University Press, 1952); Clifford Leech, *The John Fletcher Plays* (Cambridge, MA: Harvard University Press, 1962); Nancy Cotton Pearse, *John Fletcher's Chastity Plays: Mirrors of Modesty* (Lewisburg, PA: Bucknell University Press, 1973); Philip J. Finkelpearl, *Court and Country Politics in the Plays of Beaumont and Fletcher* (Princeton, NJ: Princeton University Press, 1990); Sandra Clark, *The Plays of Beaumont and Fletcher: Sexual Themes and Dramatic Representation* (Hemel Hempstead: Harvester Wheatsheaf, 1994); Gordon McMullan, *The Politics of Unease in the Plays of John Fletcher* (Amherst, MA: University of Massachusetts Press, 1994). Clark, *Plays of Beaumont and Fletcher*, 2–10, offers a concise survey of the critical reception of Fletcher's work from Coleridge to the 1990s.

6 Marie H. Loughlin, *Hymeneutics: Interpreting Virginity on the Early Modern Stage* (Lewisburg, PA: Bucknell University Press, 1997); Pavel Drabek, *Fletcherian Dramatic Achievement: A Study in the Mature Plays of John Fletcher (1579–1625)* (Brno: Masarykova univerzita, 2010).

7 McMullan, *Politics of Unease*, ix.

8 Finkelpearl, *Court and Country Politics*, 245; Clark, *Plays of Beaumont and Fletcher*, 2.

9 Francis Beaumont and John Fletcher, *Philaster*, ed. Suzanne Gossett (London: Methuen for Arden Shakespeare, 2009); John Fletcher, *The Tamer Tamed*, ed. Lucy Munro (London: Methuen, 2010); John Fletcher, *The Tamer Tamed or, The Woman's Prize*, ed. Celia R. Daileader and Gary Taylor (Manchester: Manchester University Press, 2006); Philip Massinger, *The Renegado*, ed. Michael Neill (London: Methuen for Arden Shakespeare, 2010); John Fletcher, *The Island Princess*, ed. Clare McManus (London: Methuen for Arden Shakespeare, 2012); John Fletcher and Philip Massinger, *The Sea Voyage*, ed. Claire M. L. Bourne, in *The Routledge Anthology of Early Modern Drama*, ed. Jeremy Lopez (London: Routledge, 2020), 1017–78.

10 John Fletcher and Philip Massinger, *Love's Cure, or The Martial Maid*, ed. José A. Pérez Díez (Manchester: Manchester University Press, 2022); John Fletcher and Philip Massinger, *The False One*, ed. Domenico Lovascio (Manchester: Manchester University Press, forthcoming 2022); John Fletcher and Philip Massinger, *Sir John Van Olden Barnavelt*, ed. Andrew Fleck (Manchester: Manchester University Press, forthcoming).

11 John Fletcher and Philip Massinger, *The Elder Brother*, ed. José A. Pérez Díez (Manchester: Manchester University Press for Malone Society Reprints, forthcoming).
12 Peter Malin, *Revived with Care: John Fletcher's Plays on the British Stage, 1885–2020* (London: Routledge, 2020); John Fletcher, *Il domatore domato*, trans. Cristina Longo and Marco Ghelardi (Spoleto: Editoria & Spettacolo, 2020); Francis Beaumont and John Fletcher, *Filastro: azione drammatica in 5 atti*, trans. Luigi Gamberale (Agnone: Sanmartino-Ricci, 1923); Francis Beaumont and John Fletcher, *La tragedia della fanciulla*, ed. and trans. Giuliano Pellegrini (Florence: Sansoni, 1948); Francis Beaumont and John Fletcher, *La tragedia della fanciulla*, trans. Lorenzo Salveti and Aldo Trionfo (Bologna: Cappelli/Associazione Teatri Emilia Romagna, 1979).

NOTE ON THE TEXT

Quotations from all early modern English texts are modernized in spelling and punctuation according to the Guidelines of the Revels Plays series or are taken from modernized editions. Translations, unless otherwise stated, are my own.

The date limits for all the plays mentioned in the book are those provided by Martin Wiggins, in association with Catherine Richardson, *British Drama, 1533–1642: A Catalogue*, 9 vols (Oxford: Oxford University Press, 2012–18).

For ease of reference and for consistency's sake, the names of all *dramatis personae* drawn from history have been regularized to their most common present-day spelling. Hence, Dioclesian has become Diocletian; Aecius, Aëtius; Swetonius, Suetonius; Penyus, Poenius; Maximinian, Maximian; and so on. However, I have retained the forms Caratach rather than Caratacus and Bonduca rather than Boudicca or Boadicea to avoid unnecessary confusion.

INTRODUCTION
THE ROMAN PLAYS IN THE FLETCHER CANON

FLETCHER'S CLASSICAL SETTINGS

At first blush, the plays in the Fletcher canon are not likely to strike audiences and readers as the work of a particularly classically minded playwright. John Fletcher is no Ben Jonson: nothing suggests that he shared either the latter's obsession with the painstaking study of ancient texts and self-conscious effort to imitate the style and form of Greek and Roman writers or his aspiration to be hailed as the early modern English successor of the illustrious authors of classical antiquity. Nor do Fletcher's writings seem to be informed by that sense of profound reverence for the classical heritage that can be appreciated in Philip Massinger's plays based on classical sources. At the same time, Fletcher's engagement with ancient history and literature seems by no means as deeply ingrained, vibrantly pervasive, and in constant evolution as that we are accustomed to perceiving in William Shakespeare's oeuvre.

Admittedly, this looks like one of those cases in which first impressions prove to be largely accurate. For one thing, Fletcher was not particularly keen on setting his plays in the classical world. He set them far more frequently in more or less contemporary continental Europe: less than one sixth of the plays in his canon are set in ancient times, a statistic that may be at least partly connected with the prominence of comedy and tragicomedy over tragedy in his oeuvre. Moreover, when Fletcher did set his plays in the ancient world, those settings were not always classically credible. This notably appears to be the case with the Greek setting of such plays as *The Maid's Tragedy* (1610–11, with Francis Beaumont), *The Queen of Corinth* (1616–19, with Massinger and Nathan Field), and *The Humorous Lieutenant* (1619–23), which do not seem to exhibit a very solid grounding in classical antiquity – their atmospheres feel, if anything, redolent of ancient Greek romance rather than ancient Greek theatre or historiography.[1]

Things are different, however, when it comes to Fletcher's Roman plays. Arguably, the most immediate association that the phrase 'Roman plays' would arouse at a gathering of early modernists would be with Shakespeare and his *Titus Andronicus* (1584–94), *Julius Caesar* (1599), *Antony and Cleopatra* (1606–07), *Coriolanus* (1607–09), and *Cymbeline* (1609–11). Then, someone would be likely to think of Jonson and his *Poetaster, or His Arraignment* (1601), *Sejanus His Fall* (1603), and *Catiline His Conspiracy* (1611). Very few people, if any, would think of Fletcher. As it happens, his name has very infrequently appeared in print in connection with said phrase.[2] Gordon McMullan mentions that 'Fletcher wrote a series of "Roman" plays'; Coppélia Kahn remarks that 'Fletcher wrote Roman plays for the public theatre'; Claire Jowitt and Lisa Hopkins both deploy the exact same phrase, 'John Fletcher's Roman play *Bonduca*'; and John E. Curran, Jr, discusses the 'Roman plays of Fletcher and Massinger'.[3]

Nevertheless, Fletcher did pen as many as four plays that can be classified as 'Roman', namely *Bonduca* (1613–14), *Valentinian* (1610–14), *The False One* (1619–23, with Massinger), and *The Prophetess* (1622, with Massinger) – even though *Bonduca* and *The False One* respectively portray the Romans in Britain and Egypt, while the action of *The Prophetess* is divided across Rome, Persia, and Lombardy. When one thinks about it, four Roman plays are actually more than Jonson ever wrote. Yet even though *Bonduca*, *Valentinian*, and – to a lesser extent – *The False One* have been individually subjected to significant critical scrutiny, *The Prophetess* has been neglected in scholarly discussions. Even more strikingly, these four plays have never been examined together *as a group* in a scholarly monograph. Before spelling out in detail the contents and aims of the present volume, however, it seems expedient to offer a brief survey of the broader understanding of ancient Rome in early modern English culture.

ANCIENT ROME AND EARLY MODERN ENGLAND

Largely conceived of as supreme ideal of military, political, artistic, and cultural excellence, towards which the present invariably tended in an unflagging striving for emulation, ancient Rome penetrated the early modern English imagination with incredible pervasiveness.[4] The adjective 'Roman' primarily stood for a complex of values variously subsumed under the broader notion of *virtus*: *dignitas*, *integritas*, *constantia*, *fides*, *pietas*, *gravitas*, *sobrietas*.[5] Rome, however, arguably also represented evils such as *superbia*, brutality, sadism, ingratitude, destruction, tyranny, horror, blasphemy, fratricide, and human sacrifice. This ambiguity was a crucial aspect of *Romanitas* that early moderns could still penetrate with a higher sense of immediacy than we can today. Their notion of ancient Rome had not yet been encroached upon by the rigid conceptual framework later imposed by neoclassicism, which focused on harmony and restraint while striving to hide disharmony and violence.[6] In addition, Rome to the early modern mind could never mean simply the capital city of the Roman Empire: it also meant the home of the Vatican, and thus connoted Roman Catholicism, the despised Other that Protestants officially feared and hated, but for which many of the older generation perhaps also felt nostalgia. As a result, Rome had for Protestants a double power: it evoked, with extraordinary emotional power, two separate pasts, both acknowledged as foundational to English national identities, but both now lost. In the case of recusant Catholics, Rome continued to be even more crucial to their identity.

As one of the few uninterrupted extensive historical narratives available to the Renaissance – entirely accessible in the vernacular as early as 1601 through translations of major Roman authorities such as Caesar, Appian, Plutarch, Livy, and Tacitus, as well as English compositions providing narrative links between the latter two authors' accounts[7] – the history of ancient Rome constituted an inescapable touchstone in sociopolitical debate. It was regularly used to comment implicitly on topical and often incendiary issues such as the nature and limits of the sovereign's power, the legitimacy and ethics of tyrannicide, the roles of counsellors and favourites in influencing state policy, and the confessional feuds between Protestant and Catholic. It was also frequently deployed to reflect upon the dangers of internecine strife and political fragmentation, the dire social consequences of the disruption of *concordia* and the enfeeblement of *virtus*, the lawfulness and pitfalls of colonial expansion, and the succession to the throne. For versatility, nothing could equal Rome.

The link between early modern England and ancient Rome was perceived as even more indissoluble and fascinating because of a medieval British legend according to which a certain Brute of Troy, a legendary great grandson of Aeneas, had been the eponymous founder and first king of Britain. The story first appeared in the ninth-century *Historia Brittonum* but was especially known through Geoffrey of Monmouth's twelfth-century *Historia Regum Britanniae*. Even though Polydore Vergil had exposed it as fiction rather than history as early as the 1530s, the legend lingered on in many quarters and still found several unquestioning adherents.[8]

Roman history was familiar to quite a large number of individuals thanks to the Latin-centred curriculum of both grammar schools and universities.[9] The events of the Roman past carried a singular dramatic potential that proved to be decisive in stimulating its transformation into a storehouse of spectacular dramatic plots, with *exempla* and lessons of wisdom from the past being routinely applied to the present – either for moral didacticism and topical application or as guidance to sovereigns and politicians – chiefly from the mid-1590s onwards, a decade that also witnessed an impressive proliferation of English translations and original accounts of Roman history.[10]

In addition, a view of history as largely cyclical was still widespread, encouraging an unflinching and systematic quest for analogies with the past, the ultimate objective of which was often to derive beneficial lessons for the present.[11] The basic assumption was that human nature was immutable; the situations and problems of the past were therefore ineluctably bound to repeat themselves.[12] As a consequence, the past was seen as an invaluable treasury of wisdom and knowledge, the lessons of which were indefinitely applicable to later ages.

Historical plays served a function not dissimilar to that served in the contemporary era by such Hollywood blockbusters as Ridley Scott's *Gladiator* (2000), possibly contributing to shaping the social imagination more significantly and with longer-lasting effects than any other cultural or educational means. As Martin Wiggins points out, one should not be surprised 'that Fabian Fitzdottrel, the fatuous hero of Ben Jonson's *The Devil Is an Ass* (1616), has learned his history from plays because he thinks them more authentic than the chronicles: drama actually showed the people and exploits which history books could only report'.[13] A significant share of the English plays written between 1560 and 1700 dealt with historical matters: many of these were staged in front of wide audiences, making their way into the social memory of Londoners and the national consciousness of English people at large.[14]

In this sense, the case of the repertory of the Queen's Men is illuminating. Scott McMillin and Sally-Beth MacLean persuasively argue that the Queen's Men – who remained 'from the beginning of their career in 1583 to their final year, 1602–3 ... the best known and most widely travelled professional company in the kingdom' – managed to spread across the realm through the staging of their English history plays 'a court-sponsored culture' that was firmly grounded in a vision of history combining 'broad anti-Catholicism with a specifically Protestant style, "truth" and "plainness" intertwined'.[15] By touring the country extensively with their history plays, the Queen's Men significantly contributed to shaping the historical perception and awareness of the English nation well beyond London, thus bringing to outlying areas dramatic representations that 'extend[ed] the queen's influence throughout the nation' and fostered national unity as a result.[16]

Poets were regarded as both historians and political thinkers, insofar as political thought was largely also historical thought. Samuel Daniel, poet, playwright, and historian, stands among Fletcher's contemporaries as a notable illustration of this frame of mind, in particular for his historical poem on the Yorkist-Lancastrian dynastic conflict, *The First Four Books of the Civil Wars* (1594).[17] Poetry was even hailed as superior to history for its higher potential to impart moral precepts, inasmuch as poets were granted ampler freedom to modify and rearrange historical events in order to construct narratives capable of persuasively conveying moral teachings.[18] Historical and dramatic writing were often seen as alternative and complementary means of retrieving the lessons of the past, within a cultural framework fostering a less restricted conception of what is now called historiography.[19]

The interest in the Roman past displayed by early modern English playwrights was fervid, incessant, prodigious: if one takes into account the Roman-themed dramatic works written in England between 1567 and 1642 that are still extant together with those that are lost and of which only the titles are known, one is faced with a figure around one hundred, and, as Clifford J. Ronan argues, 'there is good reason to believe that during most years in the Renaissance, the output of Roman plays was at least 10 percent of the total'.[20] Drama proved to be the medium of choice to explore the contradictory duplicity of Rome. Always a synthesis of different polities, cultures, and races, Rome became for early modern English drama the privileged place – at the same time geographic and symbolic, so near and yet so far in both space and time – for the development of a complex series of questions inscribed in a broader range of sociopolitical interests that closely impinged on the British context.[21]

In addition, although the potential to affect the social imagination inherent in any cultural representations of the past predictably and regularly made history plays wind up on the authorities' radar, histories by continental authors were far more frequently scrutinized than those dealing with the classical or British past.[22] This rendered the depiction of events drawn from Roman history particularly expedient for playwrights, as it also enabled them to deny with a certain degree of plausibility the deliberateness of specific parallels with the present if need be. When Massinger submitted a controversial play about the disappearance of King Sebastian of Portugal – who was presumed killed in action in the battle of Alcàcer Quibir in 1578 but was also said by many to have survived and to have spent the ensuing decades wandering the Mediterranean – the Master of the Revels refused to license it. Because Sebastian's absence had paved the way for Spain's annexation of Portugal shortly thereafter, the censor considered the play to be potentially insulting to a Spain with which England had recently signed a peace treaty. Yet when Massinger resubmitted the play with its setting changed to the ancient Mediterranean and with the Portuguese character Sebastian renamed Antiochus, *Believe as You List* (1631) was cleared for staging.

Integrated into such a sensitive and potentially explosive network of negotiations and appropriations between past and present, Roman history and its personalities were variously distorted and manipulated on stage under the influence of powerful sociocultural trends and forces, and inevitably ended up taking on fluid contours and protean features. The result was invariably a complex and enthralling blend of historical actuality and dramatic fiction – a dazzling, captivating and sometimes even disturbing mixture, within which history was shaped anew each time like an amendable palimpsest by the *visio mundi* of whoever staged it. In the process, the past was reactivated by a present that it simultaneously contributed to moulding, which makes the Roman plays of the early modern period particularly compelling objects of inquiry.

THE ROMAN PLAYS OF JOHN FLETCHER

Fletcher's Roman plays, as mentioned above, have not attracted as much attention as either Shakespeare's or Jonson's, nor have they ever been scrutinized together *as a group* in a monograph, despite their considerable potential for insightful critical discussion and fruitful scholarly engagement. The scholar who has come the closest to doing so – in an article-length study – is Curran, who decided to focus, however, on a slightly different cluster of writings, namely 'six Roman plays Fletcher and Massinger wrote, as a team and separately: their coauthored plays *The False One* and *The Prophetess*; the multiauthored *Rollo*; Fletcher's *Valentinian*; and Massinger's *Roman Actor* and *Emperor of the East*'.[23] Curran did not consider *Bonduca*, presumably because it does not feature any characters who may be viewed as tyrants. His 'immediate purpose [wa]s to study this group of plays closely as they ha[d] not been studied before, *as* a group, one which, like Shakespeare's Roman plays, may be fruitfully examined for the interconnections between its members'.[24]

Curran's corpus and mine are different, in that I exclusively concentrate on plays in which Fletcher had a hand (and I therefore exclude Massinger's solo-authored *Believe as You List*, *The Roman Actor*, and *The Emperor of the East*, but I do consider *Bonduca*) and I do not include *Rollo, or The Bloody Brother* (1617–20, with Massinger and an unidentified collaborator) among the Roman plays because – despite being largely based on the history of the Roman emperors Antoninus (better known as Caracalla) and his younger brother Geta as reported by Herodian – its narrative is entirely relocated to medieval France. The scope of our respective explorations is also different, insofar as Curran restricted his analysis – also for obvious reasons of space – to the plays' representation of tyranny, thus identifying in each of them 'an attempt to portray an emperor's unique character, on the foundation of how such psychological factors as the vector of a person's desire and the authenticity and style of a person's outward shows reflect the contours of a specific personality'.[25]

Even so, our larger objectives are partly similar. My primary purpose in subjecting *Bonduca*, *Valentinian*, *The False One*, and *The Prophetess* to comparative critical scrutiny is to shed new light both on each single play and on all of them as a group, while at the same time also seeking more fully to reveal the elaborate network of interrelationships between the Roman plays and the other texts within Fletcher's large dramatic oeuvre. In doing so, I also intend to provide a more accurate assessment of Fletcher's use of classical sources as well as his conception of classical antiquity and history, aspects of his intellectual life that have received limited scholarly treatment. As I therefore want to focus on what *unites* these plays and helps define them as a group, I will not devote any lengthy discussion to the plays' engagement with *localized* topical issues. Fletcher's Roman plays often comment rather frankly upon such touchy Jacobean issues as absolutism and the limits of the monarch's authority; tyranny and the devastating consequences of tyrannicide; rape and its nefarious repercussions on the individual, the family, and society; and empire and the continued, manifold relevance of the Roman conquests to contemporary foreign and domestic policies. These issues have, however, been explored extensively by earlier scholarship.[26]

My decision not to treat these issues in detail does not imply that I shall ignore the plays' firm rootedness in their Jacobean context, nor will I pretend that they were written in a vacuum, as it were; nevertheless, my references to *specific* political events of the period will not be central to my discussion. I will concentrate on how Fletcher realized on stage a distinctive, organic, and peculiarly gripping vision of Rome by using his classical and non-classical sources eclectically; by questioning the classics' monopoly of certain kinds of knowledge and truth; by often discrediting Roman paradigms and models, including the tenets of stoicism; by subtly critiquing exemplary Roman women as exceptionally passive; by treating Shakespeare as a contemporary classic and authoritative historian in his own right; by enacting a dishearteningly cyclical vision of history; and, in more general terms, by sceptically painting a grim, desolating, and unheroic Roman world.[27] I believe that the subtitle chosen for this book, *Questioning the Classics*, manages to capture both Fletcher's sceptical outlook on classical models and his urge to call them into question, while simultaneously asking questions relevant to the Jacobean era, a time in which ideas about the state, individuals, and society were being shaped by a painfully growing scepticism and a momentous transformation of values.

The impression that one gathers from reading *Bonduca*, *Valentinian*, *The False One*, and *The Prophetess* closely together is that the moral and physical integrity of Fletcher's Rome is constantly endangered from both the inside and the outside. Historically speaking, Fletcher does not deviate from the dominant Jacobean trend in being especially interested in dramatizing events belonging to the age of the Roman Empire – Boadicea's revolt and suicide under Nero (61 CE), Diocletian's rise to the imperial throne and ensuing abandonment of power (284–305 CE), and Valentinian III's rape of Lucina and death (455 CE). *The False One* technically deals with the final stage of the Roman Republic (48–47 BCE) but in fact treats Julius Caesar as an emperor in substance (though not in form): he is described as 'Emperor of Rome' in the list of 'The persons represented in the play' in the Second Folio, *Fifty Comedies and Tragedies Written by Francis Beaumont and John Fletcher* (1679).

As a matter of fact, the Renaissance had inherited the medieval misconception that Caesar had been the first Roman emperor, a historical inaccuracy probably stemming from a mistranslation of the Latin noun *imperator* ('commander'). Tellingly, the first two acts of *The False One* deal at length with the decapitation of Pompey. Displaying a severed head on stage in late medieval and early modern English drama, argues Margaret E. Owens, 'serves as a striking, unmistakable icon signifying not only the defeat and demise of the victim but, more crucially, the transfer of political power that is often consolidated through this act of violence'.[28] When Septimius brings Pompey's head on stage at the outset of Act 2, it is clear that it stands to symbolize the death of the Republic and the birth of the Empire.

While it may be true that Fletcher's Roman world does not show the same consistency displayed by Shakespeare's Plutarchan plays because it does not rely on a single main source, it does display a recognizable unity, which is not merely dependent on the fact that in the Roman plays Fletcher seems to be at his least titillating, and that basing his plays in history forces him to stay away from his beloved 'search for the unprecedented hypothesis. What would happen if such-and-such strange situation presented itself?'[29] In fact, the unity of these plays seems especially to lie in their depiction of Rome's confrontation with a crisis of values, its lack of adequate political leaders, its slow degeneration from its glorious past, and its having become a disoriented city that has lost its direction.

This disorientation in the face of a disintegrating reality makes Fletcher's exploration of the Roman world rather distinctive in the early modern period and is one of the several elements that eerily seem to connect his Roman plays with Walter Benjamin's description of the seventeenth-century

German *Trauerspiel*, or mourning play (as distinct from *Tragödie*), in *Ursprung des deutschen Trauerspiels* (1928). *Trauerspiel* is the designation that Benjamin applies to a number of seventeenth-century German dramas not well known outside the German-speaking world. Even though Benjamin never formally describes the *Trauerspiel*, his analysis identifies some defining traits, such as the lack of a focalizing hero, the depiction of history as mechanical and purposeless, and the portrayal of the world as entirely profane and cut off from any possible higher meaning, the immanence of which is heightened by the perceived distance of the divine.

As will be detailed in Chapter 2, the characteristics of the *Trauerspiel* elucidated by Benjamin become a thought-provoking key for examining Fletcher's Roman plays and his conception of history and politics. In looking at the Roman past as it relates to the early seventeenth century not only at the more focused level of potential similarities between past and present events, trends, and behaviours but, more importantly, even bigger-picture questions concerning the disorder and opacity of history, Fletcher seems to have tackled ancient Rome not just as a playmaker but also in the role of the philosopher of history. This contention is particularly significant in terms of helping us more accurately to understand what kind of thinker Fletcher was, what kind of wider perception of history and reality he had, as well as the extent to which his *Weltanschauung* shaped his depiction of ancient Rome. In this book, Fletcher emerges as a writer endowed with a much sharper awareness of the wider mechanisms, processes, and trends influencing history, politics, and human life than has previously been acknowledged.

Do honour and *virtus* still matter? Or has *Romanitas* irreversibly fallen prey to opportunism and base private impulses? Are the ancient *exempla* still viable models? How can you tell enemies from friends? Can rulers be trusted? Can leaders prove to be effective? Is power worth having? Are the gods even watching or listening? Is there any such thing as providence? These are a few of the key questions through which Fletcher seems deeply to probe the events, personalities, and values of ancient Rome. And while *The False One* and *The Prophetess* exhibit tragicomic overtones that give these plays a less serious and grave atmosphere than *Bonduca* or *Valentinian* (the only two tragedies that Fletcher wrote alone), Fletcher's answers to these questions appear to be almost invariably negative.[30]

Broadly speaking, Fletcher seems to look at everything that has to do with classical antiquity with a measure of detachment, suspicion, and scepticism, as though the classical past was no longer able to provide viable models and examples to live by in Jacobean England, when a large share of people felt they had lost their stability and points of reference after the death of Elizabeth I and, disappointed with the new monarch, could not but look forward with anxiety to an as yet unpredictable future. Fletcher's approach to and application of the classics appears therefore somehow akin to McMullan's influential notion of 'unease' as a unifying principle of the works in the Fletcher canon 'in respect of genre, tone, collaboration, gender, politics, and locale'.[31] Fletcher engages with the classics more frequently than one might suppose, but his interaction with them is fraught with doubts, reservations, and aloofness.

Another trait that sets Fletcher's Roman plays apart from those of his contemporaries is that, while one is normally inclined to view early modern Roman plays by Shakespeare and other playwrights as *ideally* addressed to a predominantly male audience, Fletcher writes influential female roles in each of his Roman plays: the eponymous character in *Bonduca*, Lucina in *Valentinian*, Cleopatra in *The False One*, and Delphia in *The Prophetess*. Admittedly, this is in line with his usual practice of attributing relevance to women in his dramatic writings in general. As Andrew Gurr argues, Fletcher appears 'to have been the first writer to show much awareness of the female component in Blackfriars audiences, and took care to cater for it', so much so that his plays 'anticipated the prioritizing of women's roles in the plays that came to prevail in the 1630s'.[32] In addition, Kathleen McLuskie points out that 'Women were addressed directly in both the commendatory verses to the Folio and in prologues and epilogues to the plays themselves. Together these texts address an audience of women who were felt to bring a particular sensibility to the theatre audience.'[33] Though habitual in Fletcher's drama, the presence of non-Roman women such as Bonduca, Cleopatra, and Delphia as protagonists or deuteragonists would have perhaps made his Roman plays more readily palatable to a female audience and does at any rate endow these plays with a distinct feel that renders them immediately distinguishable from those of Shakespeare and his other contemporaries.

In this sense, by focusing on such a noteworthy, though still sadly underappreciated, corpus of plays, *John Fletcher's Rome: Questioning the Classics* seeks to provide a corrective to dominant narratives that all too often equate Shakespeare's Rome with ancient Rome as it was perceived in the early modern imagination at large. It will add to an already significant body of work that has sought to correct the traditional hegemony of Shakespeare in critical discussions of early modern drama by seeing him as one among several dramatists on whom ancient Roman culture exerted a profound fascination. Even though the Shakespearean project is uniquely compelling for its subtlety, a wider and more sustained investigation of the oeuvres of other playwrights of the age can unearth both what unites and what distinguishes the visions of the single playmakers, while at the same time enabling a more precise and engaging assessment of the extent to which Shakespeare is representative of the electrifying and kaleidoscopic ways of negotiating the classics on the early modern stage and page.

While references and allusions to ancient Rome span Fletcher's entire career, his Roman plays – if we rely on Wiggins's 'best guesses' on their dating – are distributed over a timeframe of less than a decade (1614–22), and Fletcher's engagement with Roman history seems therefore to have blossomed at the outset of 'the relatively amorphous five-year period (1614–19)' that Wiggins identifies in his career after he stopped collaborating with Beaumont and Shakespeare.[34] As we shall see in Chapter 3, a focus on the period in which Fletcher's interest in ancient Rome was at its peak even helps to elucidate the views expressed in some of his later plays (even though those plays are not set in Rome), as suggested by the fact that the value systems dramatized and questioned in some of those plays are redolent of the value systems encoded in Fletcher's Roman world.

Curiously, none of the plays that Fletcher wrote with Beaumont was set in ancient Rome, nor did the duo produce any kind of history plays in collaboration. All the dramatic writings dealing with historical matters to which Fletcher contributed are solo works or collaborations with either Shakespeare or Massinger: *All Is True, or King Henry VIII* (1611–13, with Shakespeare); *Rollo, or The Bloody Brother* and *Thierry, King of France, and His Brother Theodoret* (1613–21, with Massinger and an unidentified collaborator); and *Sir John Van Olden Barnavelt* (1619, with Massinger). True, Beaumont's name is associated with 'Madon, King of Britain' (a lost play that must have dramatized events in the life of Maddan, the son of King Locrinus and Queen Gwendolen) in Humphrey Moseley's group entry of twenty-six plays in the Stationers' Register on 29 June 1660. Yet this entry is the only reason for ascribing the play to Beaumont, and Moseley's ascriptions of the other plays in the list tend to be unreliable, which taints the attribution of 'Madon, King of Britain' to Beaumont by association.[35] Besides, even though the setting of *The Maid's Tragedy*, as mentioned above, is the Greek island of Rhodes, the events of the play are not based on history, and no claim to historical accuracy is perceptible. As Lindsay Ann Reid argues, the 'geographical specificity in *The Maid's Tragedy* ... is coupled with a marked sense of atemporality; that is, though the *where* of the action is made abundantly clear to the play's audience, the *when* remains elusive'.[36]

Whereas this cannot but remain informed conjecture, it is tempting to imagine that Beaumont was probably uninterested in – if not even opposed to – dramatizing history, to the point that it was only after Beaumont was out of the picture that Fletcher may have felt at last free to attempt the genre. As a matter of fact, as McMullan observes, 'it was once he had come out from under the influence of Beaumont that Fletcher began to develop his own interests', thereby 'gradually expand[ing] his skills, writing comic prose, poetic tragedies and tragicomedies throughout his career', as Suzanne Gossett points out.[37] Not long after the termination of his partnership with Beaumont, Fletcher would find in Massinger, with his enthusiasm for classical antiquity, the perfect partner for the crafting of Roman plays. Yet notwithstanding the fact that Fletcher made his dramatic ventures into historical territory without the collaboration of Beaumont, throughout this book I will take into account, whenever appropriate, the ways in which the early collaboration with Beaumont oriented Fletcher's later work and outlook.

THE 'FLETCHER CANON'

Wiggins's *Catalogue* lists as many as fifty-five plays associated with Fletcher. In three of these, Fletcher's presence – if any – is faint: *The Laws of Candy*, 1619–23, by John Ford and Massinger, and perhaps Fletcher; *The Nice Valour*, 1622–27, by Thomas Middleton, possibly in collaboration with Fletcher; and *The Fair Maid of the Inn*, 1626, probably by Massinger, John Webster, and Ford, revising Fletcher.[38] Another three plays are now lost: the Holy Grail of Shakespeare scholarship, 'Cardenio', 1612–13; 'The Jeweller of Amsterdam', 1616–17, with Massinger and Nathan Field; and the solo-authored 'The Devil of Dowgate', 1623.[39] All the evidence clearly suggests that Fletcher preferred to collaborate as opposed to working alone.[40] Of the forty-nine surviving plays that *indisputably* include material written by Fletcher, only sixteen can be attributed to him alone (~32%). He wrote eight plays in the company of Beaumont (~16%), two with Shakespeare, one with William Rowley, one with Field, and as many as eighteen with Massinger (~37%, three of them also involving Field and one involving Robert Daborne). Massinger therefore emerges as Fletcher's most important and assiduous collaborator, at least in quantitative terms. Massinger himself and James Shirley also revised (at least) one play each after Fletcher's death.

The collaborative nature of most of Fletcher's output raises the problem of attributing shares of work to each contributing writer when discussing any of the plays that he did not pen alone. Such scholars as Cyrus Hoy, E. H. C. Oliphant, Bertha Hensman, G. E. Bentley, and Jonathan Hope have attempted exactly to apportion sections of the plays between the various collaborators, but the results of these analyses are not entirely reliable because the linguistic methods they employ exhibit certain limitations.[41] The most significant one is perhaps the extent to which these texts as they have come down to us were revised over time by copyists, actors, and compositors, all of them potentially interfering with the 'authorial' text through their linguistic preferences.[42] Besides, given how well trained writers were to memorize texts in their grammar school days and how frequently they must have gone to the playhouse to see and 'hear' plays, it would have been rather easy for them to learn how to mimic and deploy one another's writing style.[43] On top of that, playwrights might have routinely modified their own writing styles in order to endow collaborative plays with as much linguistic unity as possible. Moreover, there could have been cross-revisions, or collaborating playmakers might have composed passages and scenes jointly, thereby decreasing the reliability of any stylometric analyses.[44]

Apart from these linguistic issues, however, another, more fundamental problem is that, as Lois Potter admits,

> we know very little about how [collaboration] was done: whether dramatists worked on their own, submitting their scenes to a 'plotter' who supplied consistency where it was lacking, or whether they worked so closely together that ... it would be impossible to tell who suggested which or what, or how one line sprang full-blown from another.[45]

Potter's remark is especially resonant in the context of what we know regarding Fletcher's collaborative practice. The contributors of commendatory verses to the First Folio, *Comedies and Tragedies Written by Francis Beaumont and John Fletcher* (1647), widely praised the unity of the dramatic works published under the name of Beaumont and Fletcher (though most plays in the volume did not include any contribution by Beaumont) as the result of what they described as a seamless creative process. For instance, Jasper Mayne commends such a 'Great pair of authors', who were 'both so knit / That no man knows where to divide your wit', to the point that 'the press ... / Sends us one poet in a pair of friends', while George Lisle celebrates the playwrights' unique partnership by stating that 'the world never knew / Two potent wits co-operate till you, / For still your fancies are so wov'n and knit / 'Twas FRANCIS FLETCHER or JOHN BEAUMONT writ'.[46]

In addition to the writers of the Folio commendatory poems, other seventeenth-century commentators frequently imagined Beaumont and Fletcher working closely together in the process of composition. Thomas Fuller famously describes them as a couple of twin brothers 'like Castor and Pollux (most happy when in conjunction)' who 'raised the English to equal the Athenian and Roman theatre, Beaumont bringing the ballast of judgement, Fletcher the sail of fantasy, both compounding a poet to admiration'.[47] Fuller then relates an anecdote that is often quoted in scholarship on Beaumont and Fletcher:

> Meeting once in a tavern to contrive the rude draft of a tragedy, Fletcher undertook to kill the king therein, whose words being overheard by a listener (though his loyalty not to be blamed herein), he was accused of high treason till, the mistake soon appearing that the plot was only against a dramatic and scenical king, all wound off in merriment.[48]

The dubious veracity of the anecdote – it even circulated in two versions – is secondary to the fact that stories such as this confirm that the process of early modern dramatic collaboration is extremely difficult to unravel: a play could be conceived anywhere, at any time, in many ways, and its creation would have been often the result of a cooperative effort that would involve a back-and-forth exchange between playmakers bouncing ideas off each other.[49]

As McMullan argues, '[t]he collaborative process – meeting in taverns to agree on plots, writing separate scenes apart and then coming together to edit, handing material to one playwright to finish and copy out – is a hermeneutical nightmare', which turns the Fletcher canon into 'the most substantial early modern challenge to Romantic assumptions about the centrality of individual creativity to the production of art', the plays in the canon being 'irreducibly collaborative, impossible to divide definitively among the various playwrights reported to have been involved', insofar as 'the quest for a stable "fingerprint" which will be applicable to a given playwright, even one which takes into account the social and contextual construction of his "style", conflicts with the basic instabilities and practicalities of the playwriting process in the early modern period'.[50] Although attribution endeavours are crucial to a more accurate understanding of early modern dramatic texts, the aim of establishing the authorial shares in a given play with a 100% level of precision – especially in the case of the Fletcher canon – is an undertaking that unfortunately appears to be fraught with insurmountable difficulties, resistant as the object of analysis proves to be to an excessively divisionist approach.

In general, I concur with Gurr's argument that Fletcher mostly appears to have worked side by side with his various co-writers and then to have revised the completed scripts, thus 'keeping tight control of his collaborative teams'.[51] Such a 'tight control' resulted in what Clifford Leech identifies as 'a certain uniformity of style' across the whole canon, which he attributes

> to the almost continuous presence of Fletcher's hand, now dominant, now merely contributory, yet nearly always bestowing a recognizable touch ... We often use the term 'Beaumont and Fletcher' ... It ... might be more just and more accurate to say 'Fletcher' alone ... in that way we should fitly

recognise the man who exercised perhaps the largest influence on English drama for three-quarters of a century.⁵²

Following in Gurr's and Leech's footsteps, I have decided to use throughout this book the label 'Fletcher canon' rather than 'Beaumont and Fletcher canon', the phrase notoriously used in the title of the edition coordinated by Fredson Bowers. I think of Fletcher, in McMullan's terms, as an 'orchestrator of voices, influences, sources, and contexts'.⁵³ Accordingly, I also often use the adjective 'Fletcherian' as a convenient shorthand term for what pertains to the several plays in the canon. While I shall try to differentiate between Fletcher and Massinger or Beaumont whenever I find it possible and particularly helpful or appropriate, I concur with Lucy Munro's conviction that '[a]pportioning scenes is … a blunt instrument when considering collaborative authorship'.⁵⁴ As McMullan has added, 'to attempt to make a firm crucial distinction between playwrights engaged in the business of the joint writing of a play for a given audience is an even more fraught exercise that [he] had realized when [he] first began to work on the "Fletcher" plays' in the 1990s, especially in light of the significant developments that have since intervened in the study of collaborative production, as well as in the theoretical debate regarding authorship and collaboration, within early modern drama studies.⁵⁵

Accordingly, I will treat the vision of Rome that emerges from the scrutiny of *Bonduca*, *Valentinian*, *The False One*, and *The Prophetess* as belonging more to Fletcher than to Massinger, not only because Fletcher seems to have habitually acted as the lead partner in their collaborative venture and because he wrote a larger share of the works under consideration, but also, and more interestingly, because the choice and use of sources, the overall approach to history and exemplarity, the importance given to women, and the general tone of the depiction of the disoriented Roman world that emerge from these plays are unmistakably Fletcherian, as shall become apparent over the following pages and chapters.

THE CONTENTS OF THIS BOOK

Chapter 1 starts with an account of Fletcher's education and a sweeping survey of his relationship with classical texts, something that has never been done before in such a comprehensive way. This enables the identification of a *modus operandi* that appears to have been distinctive to Fletcher's deployment of classical sources. Fletcher had a predilection for vernacular texts as narrative sources, his resort to the classics for the sake of plot construction being rather sporadic. Even when he did on occasion resort to Latin or Greek writings, little doubt can arise over his preference for working with vernacular translations or adaptations either alone or side by side with the source texts. As there is no reason to assume that he did not share the same familiarity with classical texts as other contemporary playwrights, one gets the impression that Fletcher might have been steering clear of a more pronounced classicist bent in his playwriting. The *modus operandi* that can be identified in his interaction with classical texts can be summarized as follows. First, Fletcher tended to select historians belonging to the period now labelled as Late Antiquity. Second, he favoured historians of Greek origin writing in Greek about Rome, which may have implied some measure of authorial detachment as well as a more distant perspective in the narration. Third, the authors he most frequently selected were not part of the grammar school curriculum. Fourth, Fletcher often turned to vernacular translations despite being able to consult the original texts. Fifth, sometimes the texts to which he resorted were translations of translations, which meant that they presented facts at a double cultural remove, as it were. Finally, Fletcher liked to combine classical with early modern accounts. As the first chapter argues, this choice of unexpected sources seems to have had a role in determining the sense of disorientation that comes across as the cipher of Fletcher's depiction of Rome, especially insofar as those historians generally provided a depiction of the Roman Empire that tended to be more pessimistic than that offered by golden-age writers, as will emerge more fully in Chapter 2.

Chapter 1 then focuses on *The Prophetess* and *Valentinian* as case studies that effectively exemplify the pattern just described, which also characteristically entails what appears to have been a programmatic intention of combining well-known materials with recently published works. For both plays, a discussion of Fletcher's use of character names yields new insights into the plays' construction. Moreover, Otto Ulrich's argument for Nicolas Coeffeteau's *Histoire romaine* as the main source of *The Prophetess* is corroborated with new evidence; as regards *Valentinian*, Fletcher is demonstrated to have relied on a French translation of Procopius' *History of the Wars* (together with Honoré D'Urfé's *L'Astrée*), and verbal echoes from Henry Savile's essay 'The End of Nero and the Beginning of Galba' are identified in the plays for the first time, thus shedding new light on Fletcher's intellectual world and tastes. The chapter finally tackles the unfavourable depiction of education and learning in the Fletcher canon as potentially suggesting the presence of some measure of exasperation or resentment regarding the early modern school system behind Fletcher's overall approach to classical antiquity.

The second chapter explores Fletcher's depiction of the Roman world and values across *Valentinian*, *Bonduca*, *The False One*, and *The Prophetess*, with frequent references to the canon at large. As a close examination suggests, the judgement that the Roman plays seem to pass on Rome is not particularly enthusiastic. Portrayed as a corrupted political reality facing irreversible decay, Fletcher's imperial Rome is shown to be in crisis and profoundly disoriented by the lack of adequate political leaders and the apparent lack of interest on the part of the gods in human affairs. The only area left to the Roman men to prove their *virtus* is the battlefield, but this emerges as insufficient to offset the violence, the opportunism, and the dejection that exude from the plays, which chimes with a more general scepticism as to the dependability of Roman models and *exempla* that pervades the canon. The depiction of the disintegration and decay of the bodies of the Roman emperors in both *The Prophetess* and *Valentinian* is read as a metaphor for the dissolution of the Empire itself. The cruelty and corruption that pervasively taint the Roman world in each of the four plays are indications of Rome's slipping away from the ancient *virtus* of the glorious days of the Roman Republic. The only two Roman leaders who are granted at least a balanced (if ambiguous) depiction are Diocletian and Caesar, who are saved by their martial prowess – military honour emerging as a crucial ingredient of any proper Roman (male) identity in Fletcher's vision of Rome. Consequently, the fact that Valentinian has completely deprived the Roman soldiers of any possibility of asserting their masculinity and enacting their *virtus* through martial exploits is viewed as all the more reprehensible.

The inevitable sense of disorientation that the Roman plays in the Fletcher canon display owing to this lack of dependable leaders – Valentinian, Caesar, and Diocletian all being flawed, though to different extents and in different ways – is compounded by what seems to amount to a generalized detachment of and from the gods, who no longer seem to preside over human events. Whenever they are called upon in desperate situations, the gods provide no significant signs of any interest in human affairs. It is probably in this disorientation that the strongest unifying principle of the reimagining of Rome offered by the Fletcher canon is to be identified. Fletcher's grim outlook on Rome depends in part on his decision to focus on the age of the Empire rather than the Republic. In depicting a dissolving Rome, Fletcher's Roman plays are informed by a pessimistic vision of history and human life that makes them akin in some respects to the seventeenth-century German *Trauerspiel* as discussed by Walter Benjamin.

A fresh examination of Fletcher's depiction of history reveals him as a much sharper observer of reality than is usually recognized, not only in the immediacy of the here and now but also in terms of the larger changes and tendencies that are continually at work in history and politics. In particular, the Roman plays portray what is at best a temporary – though patently precarious – restoration of order at their conclusion, which is presented as almost invariably in danger of being undermined. In this way, Fletcher seems to have been able to channel in his Roman world a disturbing awareness of being caught between an irretrievable past and an unsteady present with no guarantee as to a stable future, which people might have felt during the Jacobean era. The chapter concludes by considering that the pessimistic version of the exemplarity of Rome that these plays voice is consistent with both Fletcher's irreverent approach to classical sources and his grim depiction of a savage, disoriented imperial Rome. In general terms, the impression is that Fletcher does not really believe in anything that might be labelled as 'the myth of Rome'; in fact, he seems actively intent on debunking any such thing and, more generally, on questioning the entire idea of Rome as a model to follow.

Chapter 3 focuses on the contrast between Roman and non-Roman female characters in Fletcher's Roman plays as a trenchant exemplification of his scepticism about the viability and trans-temporal utility of Roman paradigms. The non-Roman women of the canon seem to display more dynamism, assertiveness, and complexity than the Roman women, who remain dependent on patriarchal values and male gazes, their roles being limited to those of wives, widows, or prostitutes. More than examples of chastity, virtue, or corruption, the non-Roman women instead wield actual power and accomplish actions that have a significant bearing upon reality. Such an evident contrast seems to foster the impression that Fletcher and his collaborators found the women of ancient Rome hardly adequate for the development of their ideal 'masculine' female.

Scepticism about the value system encoded by Roman female models also apparently seeps from the allusions and appeals to Roman paragons that recur so frequently across the Fletcher canon, their largest share pointing to *exempla* drawn from the history of the Roman Republic and especially to Lucrece. In particular, the rewritings tend to focus on the issue of Lucrece's consent to sex with Sextus Tarquin, with her resistance being construed as either a sign of coyness or a ruse to increase male desire, in line with early modern assumptions concerning insatiable female sexual voracity. These allusions would cumulatively seem to suggest that, for Fletcher, Roman female *exempla* are no longer untouchable; incorporated as they are in the early modern discourses of misogyny, patriarchy, and politics, any instances of their application to the present should at least be viewed with suspicion.

Among the allusions surveyed in this section, a handful refer to Portia, known to early moderns as an *exemplum* of wifely loyalty to Marcus Junius Brutus, the leader of the conspiracy that killed Julius Caesar. Portia is especially relevant in that she serves as a paragon for Juliana in *The Double Marriage*. To be more precise, however, Fletcher and Massinger do not just refer to the historical *exemplum*; they also have in mind Shakespeare's appropriation of that *exemplum*, which anticipates the broader considerations that will be advanced in the ensuing chapter. That the model of Juliana in *The Double Marriage* is Shakespeare's Portia is clear from the first scene of the play, which re-enacts the well-known orchard conversation between Brutus and Portia in *Julius Caesar*, with Juliana even mentioning Brutus by name to extol the patriotic endeavour to purge one's country of a tyrant. Even though brought to its perfection and lifted out of a more restrictive Roman context, the Roman paradigm in *The Double Marriage* still displays significant limitations: Juliana out-Portias Portia and in so doing explodes the passive Roman paradigmatic ideals of constancy, fortitude, loyalty, and chastity, which plainly emerge as truly admirable and functional only when they are combined with stoicism in order to meet the suffocating demands of a strongly patriarchal society. Impeccable as they are, Juliana's virtues are fundamentally passive.

This negative judgement chimes with the canon's general tendency either to shun or implicitly criticize the tenets of stoicism as they emerge in such plays as *The Little French Lawyer*, *Valentinian*, *The Captain*, and *The Loyal Subject*, which also reinforces the idea that Fletcher's engagement with the Roman past may have influenced his thinking and dramatic craft when writing plays not set in ancient Rome. Just as with his choice of sources, which tends to privilege continental Renaissance publications over the classics and suggests little sense on his part of having found any solemnity in classical texts, these female *exempla* cannot be followed or adopted solely by virtue of their antiquity. In fact, it is their very antiquity that keeps them firmly stuck in the past, thereby making them somewhat unpalatable and, above all, hardly viable as guides for the present and the future.

As the fourth and final chapter seeks to demonstrate, Fletcher seems to regard Shakespeare as a better mentor than classical texts. The chapter first offers a brief survey of the debt of the Fletcher canon to Shakespeare's Roman plays in general and then focuses on *Valentinian*, *Bonduca*, *The False One*, and *The Prophetess* one by one. *Valentinian* is especially in conversation with *Julius Caesar* as regards Maximus' soliloquy in Act 3, scene 3, which reworks material from Brutus' orchard monologue. *Bonduca* is shown to refashion motifs especially from *Cymbeline* and *Antony and Cleopatra*, the most conspicuous similarity being that between the final suicides of Bonduca and her daughters on the one hand and of Cleopatra on the other. *The False One* explicitly draws upon both *Julius Caesar* and *Antony and Cleopatra*, as announced by the Prologue, which frames Fletcher and Massinger's play as a sort of prequel to Shakespeare's. The discussion of *The Prophetess* is the most innovative in the chapter, inasmuch as it sheds light on Fletcher and Massinger's organic, consistent, and flamboyant appropriation of *Julius Caesar* and *Antony and Cleopatra*, particularly as concerns the depiction of Diocletian, who seems to be modelled more after Shakespeare's Antony (as portrayed in both *Julius Caesar* and *Antony and Cleopatra*) than the historical emperor. The crucial elements here are Diocletian's public uncovering of Emperor Numerian's corpse (which re-enacts Antony's unveiling of Caesar's in Shakespeare) and Diocletian's association with Hercules and Mars, who are repeatedly connected with Shakespeare's Antony as well.

Maximus, Bonduca, Caesar, and Diocletian all provide interesting examples of Fletcher's peculiar reworking of material taken from Shakespeare's Roman plays. In all these cases, Fletcher often appears to put Shakespeare's Roman plays on the same level as the accounts of the classical historians, to the point of interweaving Shakespeare's dramatic retellings of Roman history with the actual historical accounts in order to infuse his characters with a heightened awareness of themselves and their historical context, as well as spurring reflections in the audience about the validity of Roman paradigms. The Shakespearean example seems to direct the choices and decisions of the Fletcherian characters by bestowing on them a kind of prescience of future events. On the one hand, this stands as a further exemplification of Fletcher's intense and multifarious engagement with Shakespeare's oeuvre; on the other, it chimes with Fletcher's treatment of ancient sources as surveyed in Chapter 1 and with his view on Roman *exempla* discussed in Chapter 3. When Fletcher's Roman plays are considered in the broader context of the repertory of the King's Men, the possibility arises that the effect of this Shakespearean memory could have been enhanced if the same actors performed different (but connected) roles in different plays, thus coupling textual recollection with the bodily memory of their own previous performances.

While Fletcher's conversation with Shakespeare's Roman plays spans his entire career, it intensifies in the 1619–23 period, which, on closer inspection, in fact seems to exhibit a near obsession with *Julius Caesar* and *Antony and Cleopatra*, ranging from verbal echoes to the re-enactment of theatrical situations. Fletcher seems to have been especially attracted at this time to previously unpublished plays, including *The Tempest*, as already noted by previous scholarship, and *Coriolanus*. Though stage revivals of *Julius Caesar* and *Antony and Cleopatra* might have played a decisive part in reawakening Fletcher's interest in them, it is perhaps not coincidental that this would happen precisely in 1619, when work towards the publication of Shakespeare's First Folio is likely to have started. The chapter ends by wondering whether Fletcher might have had a role – however small – in the preparation of the Folio.

The Conclusion briefly focuses on the recurrence of allusions to the Roman legend of Marcus Curtius in a number of plays in the canon as exemplifying Fletcher's overall approach to classical texts, paradigms, and values as illustrated throughout this book, thereby rehearsing the main claims advanced in the previous chapters. The book argues that Fletcher's predilection for the writings of late antique historians was decisive in shaping his bleak Roman world. The pessimistic vision of a disoriented imperial Rome that Fletcher offers in his dramatic works brings his Roman plays close to the *Trauerspiel*, or mourning play, as described by Benjamin, especially in terms of their grim depiction of a history devoid of purpose and transcendent meaning. This makes Fletcher emerge as a more profound historical and political thinker than has traditionally been acknowledged in scholarship. The book also explores Fletcher's irreverent classicism and his penchant for combining classical and contemporary texts and translations – as well as his fondness for using recently published books – and how his approach to classical sources is connected with his broader attitude towards Roman *exempla*, especially as regards the women of classical antiquity, whose exemplarity he is not inclined to take at face value. Fletcher's scepticism as to the passivity of the Roman women who populate his plays is also mirrored in his overall rejection of the precepts of stoicism, while his consistently de-solemnizing approach to the classics is even more excitingly exemplified by his treatment of Shakespeare as a classic to all intents and purposes.

In touching upon all these issues, this book therefore seeks to contribute to the field of Fletcher studies and the reception of classical materials on the early modern stage by attempting to offer fresh perspectives on the treatment of source materials in early modern drama, to provide correctives to Shakespeare-centric studies of early modern visions of Rome, and to intervene in discussions of early modern historiography, gender, collaboration practices, and the overall place of drama within the larger cultural field.

NOTES

1 Along the same lines, Marco Mincoff, 'Fletcher's Early Tragedies', *Renaissance Drama* 7 (1964), 70–94, remarks that 'Fletcher shows scarcely any contacts' with classical tragedy (81). At the same time, however, he argues that Fletcher's tragedies – especially *Valentinian* – are 'strongly tainted with the spirit of classicism, or rather neo-classicism' (85), as borne out by the characters' 'facile change from one extreme of emotion to the other' (82) and their 'unwilling, passionless submission to a code' imposed by society, which results in 'that frigidity that lies also over French neo-classical tragedy' (80). Even though a few affinities between Fletcher's and French neoclassical tragedies do perhaps exist, Mincoff frankly appears to overstate their relevance.

2 As based on Google searches for the following strings: "john fletcher's roman plays", "john fletcher's roman play", "roman play of john fletcher", "roman plays of john fletcher", "roman play of fletcher", "roman plays of fletcher", and fletcher AROUND(6) "roman plays".
3 McMullan, *Politics of Unease*, 94; Coppélia Kahn, *Roman Shakespeare: Warriors, Wounds and Women* (London: Routledge, 1997), 10; Claire Jowitt, 'Colonialism, Politics, and Romanization in John Fletcher's *Bonduca*', *SEL: Studies in English Literature, 1500–1900* 43 (2003), 475–94 (475); Hopkins, *Cultural Uses of the Caesars*, 59; John E. Curran, Jr, 'Fletcher, Massinger, and Roman Imperial Character', *Comparative Drama* 43 (2009), 317–54 (347).
4 G. K. Hunter, 'A Roman Thought: Renaissance Attitudes to History Exemplified in Shakespeare and Jonson', in *An English Miscellany: Presented to W. S. Mackie*, ed. Brian S. Lee (Cape Town: Oxford University Press, 1977), 93–115. For general discussions on the reception of the Roman past in early modern English drama, see also Vanna Gentili, *La Roma antica degli elisabettiani* (Bologna: il Mulino, 1991), 7–20; Clifford J. Ronan, *'Antike Roman': Power Symbology and the Roman Play in Early Modern England: 1585–1635* (Athens, GA: University of Georgia Press, 1995); Jensen, *Reading the Roman Republic*, 1–21.
5 Ronan, *'Antike Roman'*, 151–4.
6 Ronan, *'Antike Roman'*, 4–5.
7 Paulina Kewes, 'Henry Savile's Tacitus and the Politics of Roman History in Late Elizabethan England', *Huntington Library Quarterly* 74 (2011), 515–51 (518–19).
8 John E. Curran, Jr, *Roman Invasions: The British History, Protestant Anti-Romanism, and the Historical Imagination in England, 1530–1660* (Newark, DE: University of Delaware Press, 2002), 17.
9 Jensen, *Reading the Roman Republic*, 25–44.
10 T. J. B. Spencer, 'Shakespeare and the Elizabethan Romans', *Shakespeare Survey* 10 (1957), 27–38 (29); Kewes 'Henry Savile's Tacitus', 518–21.
11 Paulina Kewes, 'History and Its Uses', in *The Uses of History in Early Modern England*, ed. Paulina Kewes (San Marino, CA: Huntington Library, 2006), 1–30 (2).
12 Blair Worden, 'Historians and Poets', in Kewes (ed.), *Uses of History*, 69–90 (75).
13 Martin Wiggins, *Shakespeare and the Drama of His Time* (Oxford: Oxford University Press, 2000), 24.
14 Worden, 'Historians and Poets', 80.
15 Scott McMillin and Sally-Beth MacLean, *The Queen's Men and Their Plays* (Cambridge: Cambridge University Press, 1998), 67, 34, 36.
16 McMillin and MacLean, *The Queen's Men and Their Plays*, 35.
17 On Daniel, see especially Arthur B. Ferguson, 'The Historical Thought of Samuel Daniel: A Study in Renaissance Ambivalence', *Journal of the History of Ideas* 32 (1971), 185–202; F. J. Levy, 'Hayward, Daniel and the Beginnings of Politic History in England', *Huntington Library Quarterly* 50 (1987), 1–34; Daniel R. Woolf, *The Idea of History in Early Stuart England: Erudition, Ideology, and 'The Light of Truth' from the Accession of James I to the Civil War* (Toronto: University of Toronto Press, 1990), 77–104; Gillian Wright, 'What Daniel Really Did with the *Pharsalia*: The Civil Wars, Lucan, and King James', *Review of English Studies* 55 (2004), 210–32; Paleit, *War, Liberty and Caesar*, 63–77, 258–69.
18 Worden, 'Historians and Poets', 70.
19 Blair Worden, 'Ben Jonson among the Historians', in *Culture and Politics in Early Stuart England*, ed. Kevin M. Sharpe and Peter Lake (Basingstoke: Macmillan, 1994), 67–90 (68); Kewes, 'History and Its Uses', 5. For a broader picture of the evolution

of historical thought in early modern England, see Woolf, *Idea of History*, 9–44; Ivo Kamps, *Historiography and Ideology in Stuart Drama* (Cambridge: Cambridge University Press, 1996), 11–16, 26–50; Daniel R. Woolf, 'From Hystories to the Historical: Five Transitions in Thinking about the Past, 1500–1700', in Kewes (ed.), *Uses of History*, 31–67.

20 Ronan, '*Antike Roman*', 165–85 (174).

21 Maria Del Sapio Garbero, 'Introduction: Shakespeare's Rome and Renaissance Anthropographie', in *Questioning Bodies in Shakespeare's Rome*, ed. Maria Del Sapio Garbero, Nancy Isenberg, and Maddalena Pennacchia (Göttingen: V&R Unipress, 2010), 13–19 (17); Maria Del Sapio Garbero, 'Introduction: Performing "Rome" from the Periphery', in *Identity, Otherness and Empire in Shakespeare's Rome*, ed. Maria Del Sapio Garbero (Farnham: Ashgate, 2009), 1–15 (4).

22 Cyndia Susan Clegg, 'Censorship and the Problems with History in Shakespeare's England', in *A Companion to Shakespeare's Works: Volume II: The Histories*, ed. Richard Dutton and Jean E. Howard (Hoboken, NJ: Wiley-Blackwell, 2003), 48–69 (52–3).

23 Curran, 'Fletcher, Massinger, and Roman Imperial Character', 318.

24 Curran, 'Fletcher, Massinger, and Roman Imperial Character', 318.

25 Curran, 'Fletcher, Massinger, and Roman Imperial Character', 347.

26 For topically inflected readings of these plays, see, among others, Baldwin Maxwell, *Studies in Beaumont, Fletcher, and Massinger* (Chapel Hill, NC: University of North Carolina Press, 1939), 166–76; Robert Y. Turner, 'Responses to Tyranny in John Fletcher's Plays', *Medieval and Renaissance Drama in England* 4 (1989), 123–41; Clark, *Plays of Beaumont and Fletcher*, 85–8, 104–8; McMullan, *Politics of Unease*, 183–96; Julie Crawford, 'Fletcher's *The Tragedie of Bonduca* and the Anxieties of the Masculine Government of James I', *SEL: Studies in English Literature 1500–1900* 39 (1999), 357–81; Miller, *Roman Triumphs*, 140–2; Paulina Kewes, 'Julius Caesar in Jacobean England', *Seventeenth Century* 17 (2002), 155–86; Jowitt, 'Colonialism', 475–94; Marina Hila, 'Dishonourable Peace: Fletcher and Massinger's *The False One* and Jacobean Foreign Policy', *Cahiers Élisabéthains* 72 (2007), 21–30; Marina Hila, '"Justice shall never heare ye, I am justice": Absolutist Rape and Cyclical History in John Fletcher's *The Tragedy of Valentinian*', *Neophilologus* 91 (2007), 745–58; Paleit, *War, Liberty, and Caesar*, 140–51; Samantha Frénée-Hutchins, *Boudica's Odyssey in Early Modern England* (Farnham: Ashgate, 2014), 135–72; William Steffen, 'Grafting and Ecological Imperialism in John Fletcher's *Bonduca*', *Journal for Early Modern Cultural Studies* 17 (2017), 68–96; Domenico Lovascio, 'She-Tragedy: Lust, Luxury and Empire in John Fletcher and Philip Massinger's *The False One*', in *The Genres of Renaissance Tragedy*, ed. Daniel Cadman, Andrew Duxfield, and Lisa Hopkins (Manchester: Manchester University Press, 2019), 166–83.

27 The only (passing) mention of such a sceptical portrayal of ancient Rome on Fletcher's part that I have been able to trace in previous scholarship belongs to Goran Stanivukovic, '"The blushing shame of souldiers": The Eroticism of Heroic Masculinity in John Fletcher's *Bonduca*', in *The Image of Manhood in Early Modern Literature: Viewing the Male*, ed. A. P. Williams (Westport, CT: Greenwood Press, 1999), 41–54 (51), who remarks, with reference to the 'homoerotic symbolism and imagery in *Bonduca*', that 'Fletcher dramatizes in contesting and often ambivalent terms the concepts of a heroic past, of Roman honour, and of masculine virtue'.

28 Margaret E. Owens, *Stages of Dismemberment: The Fragmented Body in Late Medieval and Early Modern Drama* (Newark, DE: University of Delaware Press, 2005), 145.

29 Leech, *The John Fletcher Plays*, 36.

30 Marvin T. Herrick, *Tragicomedy: Its Origin and Development in Italy, France, and England* (Urbana, IL: University of Illinois Press, 1955), 266, describes *The Prophetess* as 'tragical-comical-historical-pastoral'.
31 McMullan, *Politics of Unease*; Gordon McMullan, 'The Strange Case of Susan Brotes: Rhetoric, Gender, and Authorship in John Fletcher's *The Tamer Tamed*, or How (Not) to Identify an Early Modern Playwright', *Renaissance Drama* 47 (2019), 177–200 (194).
32 Andrew Gurr, *The Shakespeare Company 1594–1642* (Cambridge: Cambridge University Press, 2011), 153, 158.
33 Kathleen McLuskie, *Renaissance Dramatists* (Hemel Hempstead: Harvester Wheatsheaf, 1989), 212.
34 Martin Wiggins, in association with Catherine Richardson, *British Drama, 1533–1642: A Catalogue*, 9 vols (Oxford: Oxford University Press, 2012–18), 6:519, #1799.
35 See 'Madon, King of Britain', *Lost Plays Database*, ed. Roslyn L. Knutson, David McInnis, Matthew Steggle, and Misha Teramura (Washington, DC: Folger Shakespeare Library, 2009–), https://lostplays.folger.edu/Madon,_King_of_Britain (accessed 6 July 2020); Wiggins, *Catalogue*, 6.53–4, #1608.
36 Lindsay Ann Reid, 'Beaumont and Fletcher's Rhodes: Early Modern Geopolitics and Mythological Topography in *The Maid's Tragedy*', *Early Modern Literary Studies* 16.2 (2012), 1–28 (1), http://purl.org/emls/16-2/reidrhod.htm (accessed 28 January 2021).
37 McMullan, *Politics of Unease*, 143; Suzanne Gossett, 'Introduction', in *Philaster* by Francis Beaumont and John Fletcher (London: Methuen for Arden Shakespeare, 2009), 1–102 (18).
38 See Wiggins, *Catalogue*, 7.243, #1932; 7.425, #2023; 8.157, #2169.
39 Throughout this volume, extant play titles appear in italics; the titles of lost plays are differentiated using quotation marks.
40 McMullan, *Politics of Unease*, 133–4.
41 Cyrus Hoy, 'The Shares of Fletcher and his Collaborators in the Beaumont and Fletcher Canon', *Studies in Bibliography* 8 (1956), 129–46; 9 (1957), 143–62; 11 (1958), 85–106; 12 (1959), 91–116; 13 (1960), 77–108; 14 (1961), 45–67; 15 (1962), 71–90; E. H. C. Oliphant, *The Plays of Beaumont and Fletcher: An Attempt to Determine their Respective Shares and the Shares of Others* (New Haven, CT: Yale University Press, 1927); Bertha Hensman, *The Shares of Fletcher, Field and Massinger in Twelve Plays of the Beaumont and Fletcher Canon*, 2 vols (Salzburg: Institut für Englische Sprache und Literatur, 1974); G. E. Bentley, *The Jacobean and Caroline Stage*, 7 vols (Oxford: Clarendon Press, 1956–68); Jonathan Hope, *The Authorship of Shakespeare's Plays: A Socio-Linguistic Study* (Cambridge: Cambridge University Press, 1994).
42 See Jeffrey Masten, *Textual Intercourse: Collaboration, Authorship, and Sexualities in Renaissance Drama* (Cambridge: Cambridge University Press, 1997), 17. It must be noted, however, that Hope tries to get around this problem by selecting features that he thinks were less likely to be changed by compositors.
43 See Lois Potter, 'Introduction', in *The Two Noble Kinsmen* by John Fletcher and William Shakespeare (London: Bloomsbury Arden Shakespeare, rev. edn, 2015), 1–170 (23).
44 See Will Sharpe, 'Authorship and Attribution', in *William Shakespeare and Others: Collaborative Plays*, ed. Jonathan Bate and Eric Rasmussen, with Jan Sewell and Will Sharpe (Basingstoke: Palgrave Macmillan, 2013), 641–745 (648).
45 Potter, 'Introduction', 27.

46 *Comedies and Tragedies Written by Francis Beaumont and John Fletcher* (London, 1647), fol. dr–dv, br.
47 Thomas Fuller, *The History of the Worthies of England* (London, 1662), 288.
48 Fuller, *History of the Worthies of England*, 288.
49 The other version of the anecdote was published a few years later in the jestbook *Poor Robin's Jests* (London, 1667), which relocates the conference about the 'plot' from a tavern to the countryside. See Lucy Munro, 'Plotting, Ambiguity and Community in the Plays of Beaumont and Fletcher', in *Community-Making in Early Stuart Theatres: Stage and Audience*, ed. Anthony W. Johnson, Roger D. Sell, and Helen Wilcox (London: Routledge, 2017), 255–74 (255–6).
50 McMullan, *Politics of Unease*, 134–5; Gordon McMullan, 'Fletcher, John (1579–1625), playwright', *Oxford Dictionary of National Biography* (Oxford: Oxford University Press, 2004), https://www.oxforddnb.com/view/10.1093/ref:odnb/9780198614128.001.0001/odnb-9780198614128-e-9730 (accessed 3 November 2019); Gordon McMullan, 'Introduction', in *King Henry VIII (All Is True)* by William Shakespeare and John Fletcher (London: Methuen for Arden Shakespeare, 2000), 1–199 (196).
51 Gurr, *Shakespeare Company*, 152.
52 Leech, *John Fletcher Plays*, 2–3.
53 McMullan, *Politics of Unease*, 155.
54 Lucy Munro, 'Beaumont's Lives', *Early Theatre* 20 (2017), 141–58 (149).
55 McMullan, 'The Strange Case of Susan Brotes', 178.

CHAPTER 1
'TAKE YOUR LILY / AND GET YOUR PART READY': FLETCHER AND THE CLASSICS

Fletcher's favourite narrative sources were vernacular texts. Even though verbal echoes from such authors as Ovid, Juvenal, Horace, and Virgil are far from infrequent in his plays – as are references to events and personalities in Greek and Roman history and mentions of Greek and Roman writers or their works – Fletcher's resort to classical texts for the sake of plot construction is less frequent. It was to English, Spanish, and French texts, rather than Latin or Greek ones, that Fletcher generally chose to turn for inspiration. Even when he did on occasion resort to Latin or Greek writings, little doubt can arise over his preference for working with translations or adaptations either alone or side by side with the source texts.

In general terms, when dealing with classical themes and accounts, Fletcher's interest seems to have been stirred up not only by the possible topical applications of ancient history and its potential to impart authoritative lessons to the present, but also – and perhaps more crucially – by the riveting refractory game generated through the transition and filtering of historical accounts from one age to another, from one language to another, from one culture to another. His Latin was undoubtedly sufficient to avoid the use of vernacular translations, and time pressure in such a competitive business as writing for the stage does not appear sufficient by itself to account satisfactorily for Fletcher's practice.

Fletcher's discontinuous relationship with the classics offers no evidence to suggest that he might have had any particularly favourite classical author to whom he enjoyed returning at various junctures in his career. This sets him apart from Jonson and Shakespeare – the former's clear liking for Horace and Tacitus, and the latter's for Plutarch and Ovid, have been repeatedly emphasized in scholarly discussions.[1] The one Latin text to which Fletcher turned more than once as a narrative source is Seneca the Elder's *Oratorum et rhetorum sententiae divisiones colores* (first century CE), a collection of arguments for oratorical instruction divided into two parts: *Controversiae* and *Suasoriae*. A number of these imaginary debates constitute the foundations of *The Queen of Corinth*, *The Double Marriage* (1620–23, with Massinger), and possibly *The Loyal Subject* (1618).[2]

Arguably, using the same text for three plays out of around fifty hardly signals a marked preference. In addition, and perhaps more significantly, Seneca the Elder's work might be considered a sort of school workbook, insofar as it provided a plentiful storehouse of ideas for the so-called *quaestiones*, those *argumenta in utramque partem* through which early modern grammar school pupils practised arguing both sides of a question, and which were accordingly crucial to the training of future lawyers, judges, clergymen, and diplomats.[3] As it happens, they also inadvertently made a decisive contribution to the rise of a generation of uniquely gifted playmakers by fostering in students a habit of imagining different perspectives around the same issue and of putting themselves, as it were, in other people's shoes, which would later make it easier for them successfully to delineate compelling characters for the stage.[4]

This chapter begins by providing an account of Fletcher's education and then offers a thorough and systematic analysis of the ways in which he selected and approached his classical sources in the context of his writing practice. This leads to the identification of a *modus operandi* that appears to have been distinctive to Fletcher's deployment of the classics. In particular, Fletcher seems to have been fond of consulting works by historians of Late Antiquity (especially Greek ones) rather than those belonging to the 'golden age' of Latin historiography. This choice of unexpected sources seems to have had a role in determining the sense of disorientation that comes across as the cipher of Fletcher's portrayal of Rome, especially insofar as those historians generally provided a depiction of Rome that tended to be more pessimistic than that offered by golden-age writers, as will emerge more fully in Chapter 2. This chapter then considers *Valentinian* and *The Prophetess* in close detail as two case studies that effectively exemplify Fletcher's approach to his classical sources, which also characteristically entails what appears to have been a programmatic intention to combine well-known materials with recently published works. Finally, the chapter attempts to connect Fletcher's *de facto* rejection of the grammar school canon in his dramatic writing with his depiction of schoolmasters and learning in his plays, thereby shedding light on a potential connection between his life experiences and his dramatic portrayal of education.

FLETCHER'S EDUCATION

Fletcher attended the grammar school of the cathedral church in Peterborough, and the survival of a number of documents and statutes relating to the school in the second half of the sixteenth century provides a number of insights into his school experience. The school had to host

1 Portrait of John Fletcher, from life, about 1620, oil on oak panel, unknown artist

'twenty poor boys, with no friends to support them, but of a natural disposition and gift for learning', who 'were to be kept at school for four or five years, until they had obtained some knowledge of the Latin tongue and had learned to speak and write in Latin'.[5] The notion of poverty in this description, however, ought not to be taken literally, since 'poor' was probably to be understood as 'relatively poor'. This is demonstrated by the fact that John's father Richard, who was dean of the cathedral church from 1583 to 1591 and accordingly had the faculty of choosing as many as four boys for enrolment, nominated among the grammar scholars three of his sons.[6]

The dean and chapter of the cathedral were to choose two teachers for the boys, namely a headmaster and an usher. The headmaster had to be 'learned in Greek and Latin, of good character and pious life, with a faculty for teaching', while the usher, though he had to possess 'the same moral qualities and skill in teaching as the headmaster ... needed only to be learned in Latin'.[7] The overall duties of the headmaster were 'to cultivate in religion and adorn with learning alike the twenty boys of our church and all others whatever coming to our school to learn grammar', whereas the usher was especially expected to teach boys the first rudiments of grammar.[8]

Fletcher's headmaster was Simon English, who held the position from 1567 to 1591.[9] He is known to have been a clergyman and was said by his grandson, the historian Simon Gunton, to have been 'of great esteem in his generation for a schoolmaster, under whom the late famous and learned antiquary Sir Robert Cotton and many others of his time and quality received education'.[10] As A. F. Leach points out, however, if Cotton did attend the school in Peterborough, 'it must have been for a limited period, as a "tother school" or preparatory school, since the main part of [Cotton's] school career was passed at Westminster', under William Camden.[11] The ushers of the school at Peterborough in the period in which Fletcher would have attended were Robert Dickinson until 1587, then Henry Thorne.[12] Little seems to be known about either of them.

A detailed description of the school's daily activities in 1561 is preserved, and there is good reason to assume that these would have remained relatively unchanged when Fletcher attended the school in the 1580s. The scholars were required to be at school every working day at 6 a.m. (and under no circumstance later than 6.30 a.m.) both in winter and summer; the usher would be there awaiting them.[13] They would start the day by saying 'some godly prayers; that done, [the usher was] to hear all such as shall be upon his forms such parts as he shall think convenient for them'.[14] Then the boys would have to translate a passage from English into Latin, first orally and in written form.[15] After that, the usher would read to them 'a several lecture either of a poet or prose', and the boys were expected in turn 'to labour the same against one o'clock at afternoon, as well as to expound as to parse every word in the same'.[16] Subsequently, the usher would give the boys 'some good vulgars, some to note phrases, and so to continue among them unto four o'clock'.[17] Finally, 'from four to five, the one scholar [was] to pose [i.e., interrogate] another', and then the usher had 'to command them to commend to memory their Latin against the next day's morning, say prayer and so depart'.[18] This order was to be observed on Mondays, Tuesdays, Wednesdays, and Thursdays.[19]

On Fridays, the scholars were expected 'to render unto him [i.e., the usher] all their Latins by heart made that week and to parse them, and at afternoon to render all their lectures taken that week unto four o'clock'.[20] Finally, on Saturday morning scholars would be assigned a lecture 'both to labour and to expound without the book' the following Monday morning.[21] As this description makes evident, the focus on memorization at the grammar school of the cathedral church in Peterborough seems to have been particularly marked.

The headmaster had to be at school no later than 7 a.m. He was in charge of ministering the scholars 'a theme to be made in prose against four o'clock' and to read them 'a several lecture either of prose or of a poet', so that they could 'render the same again at one o'clock as well in expounding as in parsing the same, with notes of such phrases, adages, and figures as are contained in the same'.[22] The next morning they were required 'to say their lectures given to them the day before without book'.[23] In addition, the schoolmaster was 'to read to them two days, viz. Monday and Tuesday, some Latin author in prose, and Wednesday and Thursday some poet, and in like manner that as upon Monday and Wednesday they shall make their theme in prose, so upon Tuesday and Thursday they shall make their themes in verses'.[24] Then, on Friday they would have to 'render the Monday and Tuesday lectures in prose at the forenoon and their lectures of the poets at afternoon'.[25] Again, the importance bestowed on repetition and rote learning comes across as absolutely overwhelming.

Amid all these activities there was very little time for fun, and by injunctions given by Edmund Scambler, bishop of Peterborough, in 1567, the scholars were to be given 'leave to play but once in a whole week, except it be at the special request of some worshipful person for some urgent cause'.[26] As this was a cathedral church school, supplementary significance was placed on attendance at religious services, so much so that it seems that the boys had to attend cathedral at 5 a.m. before prayers in school at 6.[27] Besides, the scholars

> were ... bound to attend the services with their masters in the choir on festivals at matins, litanies ... mass and vespers, in clean surplices ... On lesser festivals ... they had to be present at mass at the elevation of the Host only, staying till the Agnus Dei was sung, and meanwhile saying in pairs the Penitential Psalms, the Lord's Prayer, and De profundis.[28]

Whereas one can gather a satisfactory glimpse into Fletcher's school years on the basis of the surviving records, this becomes much harder (if not impossible) with regard to his time, if any, at university. It is still widely assumed that Fletcher attended Bene't (now Corpus Christi) College, Cambridge (of which his father Richard had been a fellow), notwithstanding research by Nina Taunton and Arata Ide that convincingly disputes the commonly accepted identification between the playwright and the John Fletcher who appears in the Corpus Christi register as having been set down for 1593 as a Bible clerk and having graduated MA in 1598. Taunton's and Ide's findings are convincing, despite the fact that Corpus Christi has a plaque commemorating both Christopher Marlowe and Fletcher, and that the name of the college's resident drama society is 'The Fletcher Players'.[29]

Hilton Kelliher has even gone so far as to conjecture plausibly that Fletcher might have in fact attended Queens' College, Cambridge, where his brother Nathaniel had been a fellow since 1594, thus potentially restoring the credibility of John Aubrey's statement about Fletcher's attendance at Queens'.[30] A John Fletcher of Sussex (where the playwright was born, more precisely in Rye) enrolled at Queen's on 7 July 1604 and proceeded MA in 1606: the choice of that college, as Kelliher speculates, would have proved particularly fortunate for the 'future dramatist, since alone among colleges it had, ever since 1546, taken the trouble to maintain and store a movable structure for the acting of plays in the Hall'.[31] Kelliher's conjecture may be further corroborated by Charles Cathcart's proposed attribution to John Fletcher of two brief commendatory poems to works by John Weever that appeared in 1600 and 1601 respectively, since Weever had studied at Queens' and was friends with Nathaniel.[32] Interestingly, Richard Fletcher left all his books to his sons John and Nathaniel 'to be divided between them equally' in his will, proved after his death but drawn up in October 1593. The fact that Richard did not leave any of the books to his middle son, Theophilus, might be an indication that he thought that Nathaniel and John were the more promising scholars.[33] At all events, there is as yet no firm, conclusive evidence for Fletcher's having gone to university at all.

However that may be, Fletcher's fluency in Latin is unquestionable given his grammar school curriculum, and he even contributed a short prefatory poem in Latin to James Mabbe's translation of Mateo Alemán's *The Rogue, or, The Life of Guzman de Alfarache* in 1622.[34] Hence, there is no reason to assume that Fletcher did not share the same familiarity with classical – or at least Latin – texts as other contemporary playwrights, even though his oeuvre does not seem to be deeply steeped in classical antiquity. As a matter of fact, not every early modern English playmaker's canon displays a pervasive engagement with the classics. Nor should they be expected to. Yet when considered in the context of such a large corpus of plays as Fletcher's, a more frequent recourse to classical texts becomes somehow notable by its absence and would seem to suggest that Fletcher was perhaps – consciously or otherwise – steering clear of a more pronounced classicist bent in his playwriting.

FLETCHER'S *MODUS OPERANDI*

As mentioned at the outset of this chapter, Fletcher's most intense and enduring literary interest seems to have lain in contemporary continental European writings, and even the choice of those Greek or Latin texts that he every now and then did mine for plot material would seem to signal some form of disregard for the texts that represented the golden age of classical literature and history. To be sure, Fletcher did draw upon such Greek texts as Aristophanes' *Lysistrata* (411 BCE) and Xenophon's *Cyropaedia* (fourth century CE) for constructing the plots of *The Woman's Prize, or the Tamer Tamed* (1607–11) – which famously revives the women's sex-strike trope from *Lysistrata* and is actually, according to Celia R. Daileader and Gary Taylor, 'one of the first English plays based on Aristophanes' – and *A King and No King* (1611, with Beaumont), in which, as Lee Bliss remarks, 'some of the names, relationships, and suggestions for' the central incident come from Xenophon, together with 'the *Cyropaedia*'s two great love stories'.[35] A few names also come from Herodotus and Plutarch.[36] In addition, extensive use of Lucan's *Pharsalia* (first century CE, probably in Thomas Farnaby's 1618 Latin edition) is evident in *The False One* – together with elements from Plutarch's *Lives* (first century CE) in Sir Thomas North's English translation (in one of the early editions published in 1579, 1595, 1603, and 1612), from Suetonius' *Lives of the Caesars* (second century CE), either in Latin or in the 1606 English translation by Philemon Holland, and from Florus' *Epitome of Roman History* (second century CE), possibly in Edmund Bolton's 1619 translation, as shall be discussed below.[37] Plutarch is also the source for a number of anecdotes and incidents in *The Humorous Lieutenant*; *The Maid's Tragedy* makes limited use of Valerius Maximus' *Factorum ac dictorum memorabilium libri IX* (first century CE); and part of the Cuculo-Borachia scenes in *A Very Woman, or The Prince of Tarent* (1621–25, with Massinger) are indebted to Plautus' *Curculio*.[38] Besides, there seem to be echoes of Euripides' *Alcestis* in both *Thierry and Theodoret* and *The Knight of Malta* (1616–19, with Field and Massinger).[39] In any event, notwithstanding the recourse to canonical authors in these relatively few plays in Fletcher's large canon, the verbal echoes mentioned at the beginning of this chapter, and his use of Seneca the Elder's collection, he does seem to have preferred to turn to other kinds of texts when he wanted to carve stories and plots out of ancient history.

The origins of *Rollo* are a case in point. The events depicted in the play are extensively based on the history of the Roman emperors Antoninus (better known as Caracalla) and his younger brother Geta as reported in *The History of Herodian, a Greek Author Treating of the Roman Emperors after Marcus, Translated out of Greek into Latin by Angelus Politianus and out of Latin into English by Nicholas Smyth* (London, [1556]). Yet in adapting this narrative for the stage, Fletcher and his collaborators switched the setting from imperial Rome to medieval France, also changing the name of the two brothers to Rollo and Otho respectively, as well as the names of all other characters, thus curiously pulling the same stunt as Massinger would in *Believe as You List*, though in reverse.[40] The playwrights very probably also consulted the story as narrated in Cassius Dio's *Roman History* (third century CE) – which would have been available to him in Greek, Latin, French, and Italian, but not in English – and in Simon Patrick's translation of Innocent Gentillet's *A Discourse upon the Means of Well Governing and Maintaining in Good Peace a Kingdom or Other Principality* (London, 1602).[41]

Fletcher's choice and handling of classical sources in this specific case prompt a series of considerations. First, he selected Herodian and Cassius Dio, historians writing in the third century CE, that is, at the dawn of the period now labelled as Late Antiquity. Second, he chose historians of Greek origin writing in Greek about Rome, which might have implied some measure of authorial detachment as well as a more distant perspective in the narration. Third, neither author was part of the grammar school curriculum. Fourth, in the case of Herodian, Fletcher turned to an English translation despite being able to consult the Greek text or a Latin translation.[42] Fifth, the text of Herodian to which he resorted advertised itself as the translation of a translation, which meant that it presented facts at a double cultural remove, as it were.[43] Finally, Fletcher combined Herodian's and Cassius Dio's narrations with one contemporary French text (or perhaps two).

Fletcher did something similar, though to a more limited extent, in *The Mad Lover* (1616), in which he mixed some material taken from *The Antiquities of the Jews* by Josephus (a first-century Romano-Jewish historian born in Jerusalem who wrote his works in Greek) as included in *The Famous and Memorable Works of Josephus, a Man of Much Honour and Learning among the Jews, Faithfully Translated out of the Latin and French by Tho[mas] Lodge Doctor in Physic* (London, 1602) and combined it with materials drawn from Honoré D'Urfé's *L'Astrée. Seconde partie* (Paris, 1610).⁴⁴ That Fletcher was frequently attracted to materials in modern European languages such as French and Spanish (and, to a lesser extent, Italian) has been often remarked upon in scholarship, but his habit of combining classical and vernacular texts or translations has gone relatively unnoticed.⁴⁵

Before spelling out the potentially revealing insights into Fletcher's attitude towards the classics at large that these considerations might yield, it seems expedient to scrutinize his Roman plays. Since Fletcher almost certainly relied exclusively on Raphael Holinshed's *Chronicles of England, Scotland, and Ireland* (London, 1587) rather than any Latin sources for *Bonduca*, I will focus my attention on his other three Roman plays, starting with *The False One* and its use of Florus.⁴⁶

THE FALSE ONE AND FLORUS' EPITOME

For penning *The False One* Fletcher and Massinger mainly resorted – as remarked above – to Lucan and Plutarch (with a sprinkle of Suetonius and Florus) perhaps combined with Gentillet (again) and the anonymous *Tragedy of Caesar and Pompey, or Caesar's Revenge* (publ. 1606).⁴⁷ The mention of Florus' *Epitome of Roman History* among the sources of the play requires detailed explanation (and a brief detour) in a chapter devoted to Fletcher's relationship with the classics, as his name does not usually appear in connection with *The False One* despite Otto Ulrich's early twentieth-century intuition, which, however, he did not fully develop.⁴⁸ Fletcher's and Massinger's use of Florus is evident in a number of passages, and some lexical analogies would even seem to indicate that the playwrights used Bolton's translation, which appeared in print in 1619, that is, just one year before the date usually assumed for the play's first performance.⁴⁹ As will become clearer in the rest of this chapter, using recently published books as sources seems to have been another distinctive trait of Fletcher's playwriting.

The affinities between Florus' *Epitome* and *The False One* appear significant. First, like Florus, Fletcher and Massinger identify the renegade Septimius as the sole murderer of Pompey.⁵⁰ This is different from both Lucan's and Plutarch's accounts, which implicate the general Achillas together with Septimius (Plutarch also mentions the centurion Salvius).⁵¹ Second, in *The False One* Pompey's lieutenant Labienus mentions that, after being defeated at Pharsalus, Pompey 'came to Lesbos / And with Cornelia, his wife, and sons / He touched upon [Egypt's] shore' (1.1.250–2). Again, the only source mentioning both sons of Pompey (Gnaeus, also known as Pompey the Younger, and Sextus) in this context is Florus'

Epitome, which highlights the misfortune that 'under the eyes of his wife and children [Pompey] should conclude his days'.⁵²

Third, the priest of Isis Acoreus brands Septimius as 'a fugitive / From Pompey's army' (1.1.152–3), which may recall Florus' description of him as 'Septimius, [Pompey's] fugitive' in Bolton's translation.⁵³ Similarly, when Caesar bewails that he, 'That would not brook great Pompey his superior' (5.2.52), now has to tolerate being insulted by the eunuch Pothinus, his deployment of the verb 'to brook' may signal the playwrights' recourse to Bolton's translation: 'Pompey now was jealous of Caesar's greatness, and Caesar badly endured Pompey's supereminence. The one brooked no equal, the other no superior.'⁵⁴ True, this could also come from Lucan (1.125–6) – which would make Fletcher and Massinger's and Bolton's use of the same verb 'brook' a coincidence – but if that were the case, it would be the only borrowing from Book 1 of *Pharsalia* in the entire play (based on books 6–10), which makes Bolton's Florus more likely as the source of the passage.⁵⁵

Finally, as regards Caesar's decision to 'run the hazard: fire the palace / And the rich magazines that neighbour it, / In which the wealth of Egypt is contained' (5.2.78–80), the play deviates from the sources, none of which relates that Caesar set the palace afire. The closest account, however, is that by Florus, the only authority who at least mentions the neighbouring buildings: 'he [i.e., Caesar], being forthwith beset in the palace royal by the same instruments who murdered Pompey, with wondrous valour and a slender company did bear the brunt of a mighty army. For, by firing the next tenements and the arsenal, he dislodged the enemy, who plied him from thence with shot.'⁵⁶

As Florus was an African writer active in the second century CE, Fletcher and Massinger's recourse to his *Epitome* for the writing of *The False One* would appear *prima facie* to confirm *in toto* the pattern that has been emerging as concerns Fletcher's way of handling classical texts, insofar as the *Epitome* was a text written by a non-Roman author in the imperial era. This is, however, only partially the case, given that Florus' cannot be considered a non-canonical text like Herodian's or Cassius Dio's (or even Josephus'); in fact, as Freyja Cox Jensen argues, 'Florus was a key text in the early modern grammar schools and universities of England.'⁵⁷ Besides, as Daniel R. Woolf points out, it was 'the most readily available synopsis of republican history'.⁵⁸

Nevertheless, Fletcher's *modus operandi* in selecting and utilizing sources, as glimpsed in *Rollo*, *The Mad Lover*, and *The False One*, can be more fully appreciated in *The Prophetess* and *Valentinian*. Here, the extent to which Fletcher tended to privilege vernacular sources (not necessarily translations) over classical historians and loved to mix all those different sources together in an unmistakably characteristic blend of old and new, far and near, foreign and familiar emerges very forcefully.

CASE STUDY: *THE PROPHETESS*

Although scholars usually maintain that Fletcher drew upon *Historia Augusta* – more precisely the chapter 'Carus, Carinus et Numerianus', allegedly written by a certain Flavius Vopiscus – the main source of *The Prophetess* is actually Nicolas Coeffeteau's *Histoire romaine, contenant tout ce qui s'est passé de plus mémorable depuis le commencement de l'empire d'Auguste jusqu'à celui de Constantin le Grand. Avec l'Épitome de Florus depuis la fondation de la ville de Rome jusques à la fin de l'empire d'August* (Paris, 1621), which Fletcher complemented with details he probably found in *The History of Justin, Containing a Narration of Kingdoms from the Beginning of the Assyrian Monarchy unto the Reign of the Emperor Augustus. Whereunto is Newly Added a Brief Collection of the Lives and Manners of all the Emperors Succeeding, unto the Emp[eror] Rodulphus Now Reigning. First Written in Latin by that Famous Historiographer Justin and Now Again Newly Translated into English by G[eorge] W[ilkins]* (London, [1606]).[59] That Coeffeteau's text rather than *Historia Augusta* was the primary source of *The Prophetess* was demonstrated more than a century ago by Ulrich. Yet subsequent scholars appear to have ignored his painstaking work altogether, probably because his 100-page book is written in German.

I do not wish to reproduce Ulrich's argument in its entirety, but it is worth reaffirming that, even though most of what Fletcher could have found in Coeffeteau he could also have found in *Historia Augusta*, there are at least two pieces of evidence that strongly point to the French compilation as his main source. The first is Numerian's brother and co-emperor Carinus' reference to the provost Aper as Numerian's stepfather:

> My brother honoured him:
> Made him, first, captain of his guard, his next friend;
> Then, to my mother (to assure him nearer)
> He made him husband.[60]

All editions of *Historia Augusta* available to Fletcher refer to Aper as Numerian's father-in-law ('Aperi soceri sui'). The only text from which Fletcher could have derived the notion that Aper had married Numerian's mother is Coeffeteau's, which mentions 'Aper, beaupere de ce ieune Prince' and 'Aper beaupere de Numerianus'.[61] In French, *beaupère* can mean either stepfather or father-in-law. Fletcher's misinterpretation therefore seems not only to suggest that he used *Histoire romaine* but that he probably never even looked at *Historia Augusta*; otherwise, he would have corrected his misapprehension about the relationship between Aper and Numerian.

The second piece of evidence is the fact that in Coeffeteau's narrative Diocletian muses about the inconstancy of fortune, abandons the imperial throne, retires to the countryside, and praises the sweetness of his retirement:

> Peut estre que cette consideration luy ietta en l'ame le desir de renoncer à l'Empire qu'il avoit possedé avec tant de gloire. A quoy on aiouste *qu'il se representa sagement l'inconstance & la vanité des grandeurs du monde; qu'il se figura les malheurs qui peuvent arriver aux plus grands Princes, dont Hannibal, Pompée, & Antoine luy estoiet de redoutables exemples* ... Toutes ces pensées firent donç qu'au lieu que l'ambition accompagne les autres Princes iusques au tombeau, il se delibera au milieu des honeurs de renoncer à tout sentiment de sa gloire ... Diocletian ... trouva cette solitude si douce qu'il ne fut point en la puissance des hommes, ny de la fortune de l'en arracher, mais y passa le reste de ses iours, protestant à tout le monde, *qu'il n'avoit iamais gousté les vrais plaisirs de la vie, ny veu luire le Soleil plus doucement que depuis sa solitude.*⁶²

> (Perhaps this consideration instilled in his mind the desire to give up the Empire that he had possessed with so much glory. To which it may be added *that he wisely pictured the inconstancy and the vanity of the greatness of the world, that he imagined the misfortunes that can happen to the greatest princes, of whom Hannibal, Pompey, and Antony stood to him as formidable examples* ... All these thoughts made it so that instead of the ambition that accompanies other princes to the tomb, he decided in the midst of honours to renounce all sense of his own glory ... Diocletian ... found this solitude so sweet that it was not in the power of men or fortune to snatch him from it, but he spent the rest of his days protesting to everyone *that he had never tasted the true pleasures of life, never seen the sun shine more sweetly than since his solitude.*)

Nothing of the sort is to be found in *Historia Augusta*. Yet in *The Prophetess* Diocletian declares:

> I am a man,
> And all these glories, empires heaped upon me
> [...]
> Cannot defend me from a shaking fever
> Or bribe the uncorrupted dart of death
> To spare me one short minute.
> [...]
> Shall I praise my fortune

> Or raise the building of my happiness
> On her uncertain favour? Or presume
> She is my own and sure, that yet was never
> Constant to any? Should my reason fail me
> (As flattery oft corrupts it), here's an example
> To speak how far her smiles are to be trusted:
> The rising sun, this morning, saw this man
> The Persian monarch and those subjects proud
> That had the honour but to kiss his feet;
> And yet, ere his diurnal progress ends,
> He is the scorn of fortune.
> [...]
> No. I will not be plucked out by the ears
> Out of this glorious castle; uncompelled
> I will surrender rather. Let it suffice:
> I have touched the height of human happiness
> And here I fix *nil ultra*. Hitherto
> I have lived a servant to ambitious thoughts
> And fading glories; what remains of life
> I dedicate to virtue. And to keep
> My faith untainted, farewell, pride and pomp,
> And, circumstance of glorious majesty,
> Farewell for ever. (4.6.24–5, 26–9, 37–48, 64–74)

Later on, in their poor grange in Lombardy, Diocletian's newly wed Drusilla tells her husband: 'I am glad ye make this right use of this sweetness, / This sweet retiredness' (5.4.21–2). Despite exact verbal parallels being very few ('cette solitude si douce' becomes 'This sweet retirednesse'), the ideas developed in *The Prophetess* clearly draw on those found in *Histoire romaine* (with also an echo of Shakespeare's Othello's farewell speech).[63] Both texts touch upon the inconstancy and uncertainty of fortune and greatness, Diocletian's desire not to pursue ambition until his death but to renounce the Empire at the height of his honour, and the happiness he finds in his retirement. Hence, there should remain no compelling reason to believe that Fletcher even opened *Historia Augusta*.

Yet in 1620, a year before Coeffeteau's text was published and two years before the play's first performance, Isaac Casaubon's 1603 edition of *Historia Augusta* was republished in Paris with additional comments by Claude Saumaise. No one seems to have noticed that in one of his endnotes to the chapter 'Severus Alexandrus', allegedly written by a certain Aelius Lampridius, Saumaise gives a lengthy description of the 'Dryades', also discussing the story of Diocletian and the Druidess that is at the core of *The Prophetess*. In order to let the reader understand the role of these women, Saumaise writes: 'nominatissimae autem videntur fuisse istae Gallicanae Dryades, ut quae consulerentur in rebus dubiis, non secus atque olim oracula Delphica' ('indeed these Gallic Druidesses seem to have been highly celebrated, as they were consulted on dubious matters, not differently from the way the Delphian oracle used to be').[64] It is true that Fletcher may well have mentally connected by himself the nameless Celtic Druidess who prophesied greatness for Diocletian with the Pythia, the prophetess at Delphi. Yet the possibility is tantalizing that a suggestion regarding the title of the play and the name of its title character, Delphia, might have been provided by this edition of *Historia Augusta*, which had just been published and would have conceivably been advertised and marketed side by side with *Histoire romaine*.

As a matter of fact, name-giving is extremely important in Fletcher's dramatic practice. He seldom seems to have chosen the names of his characters carelessly; in fact, he invariably seems to have had a keen eye for the potential associations that names might evoke in playgoers.[65] *The Prophetess* provides two further examples: Camurius and Geta. Camurius appears in Plutarch's 'Life of Galba' as a soldier rumoured to have murdered the Emperor Galba after the latter had been hurled out of his litter.[66] Hence, it hardly seems coincidental that Camurius appears in *The Prophetess* as one of the soldiers *defending* the emperor's litter. As for Geta, even though the name is the same as that of Caracalla's brother, it is also a name bestowed in a couple of comedies by Terence, *Adelphoe* and *Phormio*, on servants, which ironically tallies with Geta's role as Diocletian's sidekick and comic foil in *The Prophetess*.[67]

CASE STUDY: *VALENTINIAN*

Focusing on names yields even more penetrating insights into *Valentinian*, the narrative sources of which are the 'Histoire d'Eudoxe, Valentinian, et Ursace' in D'Urfé's *L'Astrée. Seconde partie*, and Book III of Procopius of Caesarea's *History of the Wars* (sixth century CE). Even though most of what Fletcher found in D'Urfé he could have found in Procopius as well, it is evident that he used *L'Astrée* from a few verbal echoes and a number of similarities that the play shares with the romance but not with the historical account.[68] My impression is that Fletcher's interest in the story was aroused by D'Urfé's narrative, and that he then turned to *The History of the Wars* for a more solid historical grounding. Ulrich suggests that a 1587 French translation of Procopius by Martin Fumée 'sehr wohl als Vorlage dienen konnte' ('may have very well served as a model') for Fletcher.[69] On closer inspection, this looks like more than a mere possibility. Several scholars have wondered at the spelling of the name of the Roman general Flavius Aëtius in the First Folio, namely 'Aecius'. This spelling is not to be found either in the Greek edition of Procopius, the Latin translation, or *L'Astrée*, and it does not seem sufficiently accounted for 'aus der gleichen Aussprache von c und t vor I + Vokal' ('on the grounds of the same pronunciation of c and t before i + vowel').[70] Robert Kean Turner remarks that 'in the Renaissance medial -c and -t were often confused ... Whether Fletcher, working from memory, misspelled his character's name or whether the scribe misread his -t as a -c there is no way of knowing, but because the -c spelling is uniform in F1 it must be accepted.'[71] According to Marco Mincoff, '[w]here Fletcher got his *c* from is ... a mystery whose solution would no doubt determine the question of his second source'.[72] In fact, this solution appears to have been hiding in plain sight all along. The 'c' spelling actually seems to derive from the French translation of Procopius mentioned above, in which the character is referred to as 'Aece' throughout. Small as it may look, this piece of evidence, which escaped Ulrich's otherwise very scrupulous eye, points to Fumée's translation as the text of Procopius consulted by Fletcher, which again confirms his penchant for using vernacular translations whenever possible.

Anthroponomastics appears to be a good trail to follow in order to uncover further revelations concerning the play. Apart from a handful of names probably taken from Cassiodorus' *Chronica* (sixth century CE), a crucial addition Fletcher made to what he found in the sources is the name of Maximus' wife, Lucina.[73] As often remarked, she is unnamed in Procopius and is Isidore in *L'Astrée*; yet the issue of Fletcher's christening Maximus' wife 'Lucina' has been addressed only in passing.[74] Lucina was a common epithet of the goddess Diana, whose traditional correlation with chastity (as well as the moon and hunting) was fairly well known, especially because of her occasional association with Elizabeth I. As Lucina's chastity is at the core of the play's events, it made sense for Fletcher to associate her with the Graeco-Roman patron of chastity; in addition, the bawd Ardelia metaphorically associates Lucina with the moon while trying to convince her to consent to Valentinian's wishes, when she bids her 'Come, goddess, come, you move too near the earth. / It must not be, a better orb stays for you'.[75]

Yet Diana had several epithets, which prompts the question as to why Fletcher chose 'Lucina' over the others. Through the epithet 'Lucina' – which also appears in *The Tamer Tamed* and *The Knight of Malta* – Diana was specifically connected with childbirth. References to Diana Lucina's role as helper in childbirth could be found in a host of texts available to early modern readers, some of them as well known and widely appreciated as Ovid's *Metamorphoses* or as accessible to Fletcher as Shakespeare's *Cymbeline*, which was written when Fletcher was also writing for the

King's Men.[76] With this in mind, supplementary meanings seem to accrue to the play's crucial grappling with one particular consequence of Lucina's rape, namely the fact that, following the violation of her body by another man, her husband Maximus will no longer be assured of the purity of their issue.[77] Maximus tells Aëtius:

> If she were anything to me but honour …
> Or could the wrong be hers alone, or mine,
> Or both our wrongs, not tied to *after issues*,
> *Not born anew in all our names and kindreds*,
> I would desire her live; nay, more, compel her.
> But since it was not youth, but malice, did it,
> And not her own, nor mine, but both our losses
> (Nor stays it there but that *our names must find it*,
> *Even those to come; and when they read she lived*,
> *Must they not ask how often she was ravished*,
> *And make a doubt she loved that more than wedlock?*),
> Therefore she must not live. (3.1.232–45, my emphasis)

As Marina Hila comments, 'Lucina's survival would contaminate the family line with offspring of doubtful paternity and would cast on her the suspicion that she consented to the emperor's sexual wishes'; hence, she has to die.[78] Though alien to both Procopius' and D'Urfé's accounts, this interpretation effectively spoke to the importance placed in early modern English society on patrilineality and primogeniture, which resulted in husbands' obsessive concern with 'the sexual exclusivity of the chaste married body' of their wives.[79]

Lucina is envisaged as a mother on at least two other occasions. As early as Act 1, scene 2, Ardelia tries to flatter Lucina into accepting Valentinian's advances with the prospect of giving birth to imperial offspring:

> gods give 'em children,
> Such as her virtue's merit, and his zeal.
> I look to see a Numa from this lady,
> Or greater than Octavius. (1.2.81–4)

As Marie H. Loughlin observes, Lucina's 'issue from a liaison with Valentinian, while technically bastards [*sic*], is here presented in mythologically/historically grand terms as the outcome of Lucina's nurturing of the emperor's newly awakened virtue and love'.[80] After the rape, Aëtius' suggestion that Lucina remain alive in order to present the emperor with 'His swoll'n sins at the full' (3.1.214) not so subtly 'implies the swelling of pregnancy'.[81] Naming Lucina after the goddess of childbirth may arguably have struck a grimly ironic note with classically steeped playgoers.

The name of a less prominent character in *Valentinian*, the above-mentioned Ardelia, would seem to suggest something further about Fletcher's penchant for mixing his sources, perhaps even with a view to flattering his auditors with his assumption of their intimate knowledge of contemporary theatre by fostering a sophisticated intellectual game at least with that proportion of 'relatively well-educated and theatrically aware' playgoers who would have attended performances of those plays.[82] An EEBO-TCP search for 'ardelia' reveals that this name is nowhere to be found in books published in England before 1638.[83] Yet Ardelia was an extremely popular name in the late sixteenth- and early seventeenth-century Italian dramatic tradition. Derived from the Italian substantive *ardore* (ardour), it was frequently encountered as the name of nymphs or enamoured maids in the pastoral genre and *commedia dell'arte*.[84] Fletcher's familiarity with the Italian pastoral tradition is well known because of his engagement with Giovanni Battista Guarini's *Il pastor fido* (1590) and *Compendio della poesia tragicomica* (1602) in *The Faithful Shepherdess* (1607–08). The sophisticated irony of applying a name customarily given to pure nymphs to one of Valentinian's bawds, who is especially insistent in trying to persuade Lucina to accept the emperor's amorous offers, would hardly be lost on the most learned and continental-culture-savvy playgoers (and, later, readers), who would relish regarding themselves as capable of recognizing those allusions and would consequently feel particularly *au fait* with contemporary theatrical fashion. This is all the more so because the name is spoken aloud, thus gaining additional resonance, and her character is more individuated with the theatrical audience than would be the case were it only a speech heading.

Fletcher had already provided ample evidence of his willingness to count on audiences' knowledge of names taken from both classical and continental literature to ironic effect in *The Faithful Shepherdess*. In that play, the references to pastoral conventions and names are clearly intended, as Lucy Munro argues, 'to undercut spectators' expectations, to leave them unsettled and inclined to question what they know – or think they know – about dramatic pastoral'.[85] The names of the Fletcherian characters Daphnis and Chloe are especially a case in point, inasmuch as they are also the names of the eponymous lovers in the renowned third-century Greek pastoral romance by Longus.[86] In *The Faithful Shepherdess*, Daphnis becomes a shy boy who is utterly inadequate to Chloe's hilariously over-the-top sex drive: as she herself acknowledges, 'It is impossible to ravish me: / I am so willing'.[87] When they remain alone in a hollow tree, an enthused Daphnis preserves his chastity despite the ardent encouragement of Chloe, who is left unsatisfied. This shows that Fletcher had been preoccupied with the creation of play-worlds that foregrounded allusiveness by combining elements drawn from native, classical, and continental sources since the beginning of his dramatic career, with a view to fusing old and new either with an ironic or unsettling intent, in such a way that classical patterns and conventions might be at least implicitly questioned.

Going back to Fletcher's recourse to historical accounts, no one has ever pointed out that *Valentinian* also makes use of an English vernacular work of historiography dating back to the 1590s. This occurs in Act 4, scene 1, immediately after Valentinian has read the anonymous letter that Maximus has contrived for him to acquire, which falsely suggests that Aëtius is ambitious for the throne. Valentinian meditates over his possible course of action and eventually decides to have Aëtius murdered because he is afraid to lose his power and his life as the fully fledged tyrant that he is – literary tyrants having been traditionally characterized, at least since Xenophon's portrayal of Hiero I of Syracuse (fourth century BCE), as obliged to pay the penalty for their own undisputed power with a life lived in constant concern for their personal safety.[88] This is how Valentinian reacts:

> No name! This may be cunning, yet it seems not,
> For there is nothing in it but is certain,
> Besides my safety. Had not good Germanicus,
> That was as loyal and as straight as he is,
> If not prevented by Tiberius,
> Been by the soldiers forced their emperor?
> He had, and 'tis my wisdom to remember it.
> And was not Corbulo (even that Corbulo,
> That ever fortunate and living Roman
> That broke the heart-strings of the Parthians,
> And brought Arsaces' line upon their knees,
> Chained to the awe of Rome), because he was thought
> (And but in wine once) fit to make a Cesar,
> Cut off by Nero? I must seek my safety,
> For 'tis the same again, if not beyond it.
> I know the soldier loves him more than heaven,
> And will adventure all his gods to raise him.
> Me he hates more than peace. What this may breed,
> If dull security and confidence
> Let him grow up, a fool may find, and laughed at. (4.1.128–47)

While Valentinian's mention of Germanicus might be regarded as predictable enough, his reference to Corbulo strikes one as rather unusual, in that he is not one of the personalities from Roman history most frequently recalled either in early modern English drama or today. A proximity search in EEBO-TCP for a combined allusion to both Germanicus and Corbulo yields the following passage as the most interesting result:

> Even good princes are jealous of sovereign points and, that string being touched, have a quick ear. They have bought it full dear which ignorantly have sat in their chair of estate, that have worn their diadem to keep it from wetting or upon like occasion. Germanicus, as some here may remember, because one or two in the army had only a purpose to salute him Prince, was never well brooked, till by his own death he had paid the price of other men's rashness. Corbulo (even that Corbulo, which had quieted Germany, subdued Armenia, broken the Parthian spirits, brought Arsaces' line on his knees before Nero), after he had so highly deserved at his hands, it cost him his life that some men in secret thought him a man fit to succeed.[89]

This extract comes not from any classical authority but from the essay with which Henry Savile prefaced his translation of the first four books of Tacitus' *Historiae* and *Agricola* (the first English translation of Tacitus), namely 'The End of Nero and the Beginning of Galba', which David Womersley describes as 'a short piece of "archaeological restoration" in which [Savile] narrated the period of Roman history from the time in AD 66 when the *Annales* break off to 1 January 69 when the *Historiae* begin'.[90] As Womersley adds, 'Such textual reparations were not uncommon. But in Savile's case this filling in of the gap between Tacitus' two major works seems to have been, to at least one contemporary, the most notable feature of the volume.'[91] Womersley is referring to Jonson, but the same seems to have been the case for Fletcher.

In the excerpt from Savile's text quoted above, 'Titus Vinius, then lieutenant of the legion and chiefly in favour with Galba', manages to convince the latter, who was then governor of Hispania, that the best course of action (after Nero has heard rumours of a rebellion seeking to put Galba on the imperial seat in his stead) is not to wait but to raise the army and attack Nero immediately, because Nero would otherwise have Galba and his supporters killed on the first possible occasion.[92] Here, Savile is expanding material taken from Plutarch's 'Life of Galba' – one of the sources of his essay together with Suetonius' lives of Nero and Galba, sections of Cassius Dio (largely Book LXIII), and Byzantine chronicler Joannes Zonaras' *Epitome Historiarum* (twelfth century) – which mentions the exchange between Vinius and Galba, but does not feature Vinius' drawing upon two examples of past Roman emperors (Tiberius and Nero) who killed people who they suspected might potentially cause their overthrow (Germanicus and Corbulo) in order to persuade Galba.[93]

The examples are therefore Savile's invention. As is immediately apparent, the examples deployed by Fletcher are the same as those in Savile's essay.

The phrasing is also very similar. In the play, Germanicus is said to have 'Been by the soldiers forced their emperor', which is 'wisdom to remember'; in the essay, Vinius recounts that 'Germanicus, as some here may remember, because one or two in the army had only a purpose to salute him Prince' ended up dead. In *Valentinian*, 'Corbulo (even that Corbulo', Valentinian recalls, 'broke the heart-strings of the Parthians, / And brought Arsaces' line upon their knees', but was later killed by Nero 'because he was thought / (And but in wine once) fit to make a Cesar'; in 'The End of Nero and the Beginning of Galba', Vinius relates that 'Corbulo (even that Corbulo' – a phrase that Fletcher replicates verbatim – had 'broken the Parthian spirits, brought Arsaces' line on his knees' – another almost word-for-word reproduction – and then paid with his life for the fact that 'some men in secret thought him a man fit to succeed': 'in secret' becomes 'in wine', and 'fit to make a Caesar' becomes 'fit to succeed' in *Valentinian*, which look like small variations indeed.[94] Besides, Fletcher draws upon Savile's passage at a moment at which Valentinian is 'jealous of his sovereign points', that is, afraid to lose his prerogative as emperor, and makes his decision with a view to averting the danger of sitting 'ignorantly' in his 'chair of estate' or, as Fletcher has it, of remaining in 'dull security and confidence'.

One of the features of Savile's essay that perhaps particularly attracted Fletcher at such a critical juncture in the play was that Savile explored the psychology of political leaders as a major determining factor in the course of history.[95] Moreover, the use of this source confirms the patterns that I have been delineating so far concerning Fletcher's recurrent mixing of classical, continental, and English elements in his plays, as well as his typical interest in non-grammar-school texts as sources. This consideration potentially yields a number of insightful suggestions regarding a potential connection between Fletcher's school years and the general stance on education and learning that seems to pervade his plays.

STAGING EDUCATION AND LEARNING

Given that Fletcher must have known long passages of grammar school books by heart, those writings would have been a more expedient choice as source texts of his plays considering the pressure to furnish the playhouse rapidly with a steady output of new plays that characterized the early modern theatrical enterprise. Hence, Fletcher's decision to resort to texts other than these might be plausibly construed as signalling a certain degree of impatience at what he had slogged through at school by means of boringly relentless repetition.

As a matter of fact, Fletcher's plays do not portray education and learning in a particularly favourable light, which is no wonder given the repetitive, exhausting, and oppressive daily routine that he had to endure in Peterborough as a schoolboy. Schoolmasters themselves are not spared. For example, *The Sea Voyage* (1622, with Massinger) mentions 'a schoolmaster that in a time of famine / Powdered up all his scholars' and then ate them, presumably; while the Pander in *The Woman-Hater* (1604–07, with Beaumont) confesses he wears black clothing in order to, 'As all solemn professors of settled courses do, cover my knavery with it'.[96] To be sure, the satire on schoolmasters was not exclusive to Fletcher in early modern drama. As Ursula Ann Potter argues,

> By the early 1600s ... schoolmasters had ... become targets of satire on the public stage. Henry Peacham, writing in the early 1620s, claims that because schoolmasters have generally become 'ridiculous and contemptible both in the school and abroad' ... the profession of teaching is mocked on the stage.[97]

The fact that such satire was commonplace on the early modern English stage helps explain why Fletcher would mock schoolmasters even though he had been trained under such an admired headmaster as Simon English.

At any rate, the plays in the Fletcher canon especially make fun of the (alleged) unprofitableness of learning at large, perhaps another reaction to his grammar school (and university?) education. In *The Mad Lover*, learning is said to consist in 'talk[ing] of turnips / And find[ing] the natural cause out why a dog / Turns thrice about ere he lie down' – with an obscene pun on turnip as 'turn-up', meaning whore – a description very similar to that of learning as a useless effort 'to find the natural reason / Why a dog turns twice about before he lie down' offered in *Wit without Money* (1614–15).[98] In the same play, Shorthose describes Francisco as 'A learned beggar, a poor scholar' who lives 'Like worms, he eats old books' (2.3.16, 17), thus further underscoring the lack of real impact of learning on life. Along the same lines, in *A Very Woman*, Borachia expects learned scholars to be able to answer the following momentous question: 'what's the natural reason why a woman longs / To make her husband cuckold?'[99] Furthermore, in *The Tamer Tamed*, as Gordon McMullan has recently argued (thereby also solving an age-old textual crux in the play), during a quick-fire exchange between Petruccio and Tranio, Fletcher has the former call the latter 'Susenbrotus', thus 'mockingly comparing him to a pedantic grammarian' – namely the German humanist and Latin teacher Jo(h)annes (or Hans) Susenbrotus (1485–1542) – 'perhaps one for whose work (we might imagine) they had shared a dislike as schoolboys – a move that could be seen as a tipping of the hat to Fletcher's collaborator Francis Beaumont, whose earliest work is a spoof *Grammar Lecture* written when he was a law student'.[100]

Even more interestingly, Latin itself is identified as the language needed to 'daunt the devil' in *The Night-Walkers* (1613–16, rev. Shirley 1633), while a school curriculum obsessed with rhetorical skills and Latin eloquence is ridiculed in *The Two Noble Kinsmen* (1613–14, with Shakespeare) through the staging of the schoolmaster Gerald's random quoting of common Latin phrases from school textbooks as mere pedantic affectation, and even more pervasively so in *The Elder Brother* (1615–25, with Massinger).[101] Here, Latin learning is playfully mocked in a hilarious exchange between the title character Charles and his subsizar Andrew as they are about to start a class:

> *Charles.* ... take your *Lily*
> And get your part ready.
> *Andrew.* Shall I go home, sir?
> My wife's name is Lily: there my best part lies, sir.
> *Charles.* I mean your grammar, O thou dunderhead!
> Wouldst thou be ever in thy wife's syntaxis?[102]

It is the ambiguity between Latin learning and sex that makes this comic exchange particularly effective, especially by playing on what McMullan describes as 'a long association between grammar and sex expressed by way of the grammarians' emphasis on "male" and "female", "active" and "passive", and the potential *double entendre* value of technical terms such as *coniunctio*'.[103] Charles is referring to William Lily's *Grammar of Latin in English: An Introduction of the Eight Parts of Speech, and the Construction of the Same* (1542). Lily's *Grammar* was a staple of early modern education: it had become the first and only authorized text for the teaching of Latin in grammar schools and would remain so until the first half of the nineteenth century. Andrew mistakes Charles's reference for an allusion to his wife, whose name too is Lily, and accordingly misunderstands 'part' as indicating his genitals rather than one of the 'parts of speech' dealt with in Lily's *Grammar*. Charles's indignant retort to Andrew's slow-wittedness in turn picks up on the latter's clue and uses the word 'syntaxis' to create a further ambiguity. The main reference is patently to the branch of grammar concerned with the set of principles governing the arrangement of words to form sentences. However, 'syntaxis' also contains the noun 'sin' and had at least another additional meaning that may be relevant in this case. In particular, the phrase 'in syntaxis' that Charles uses was synonymous with the grammatical phrasing 'in regimen'. The *OED* glosses the noun 'regimen' as 'The relation of a word, clause, etc., to the word that *governs* it. Also: a case, word, or phrase so *governed* by another word' (my emphasis). By knowledgeably deploying this phrase, Charles would also seem to be wittily commenting on the fact that Andrew is regrettably governed by his wife, and his reason is ruled by his passion.

Spirited criticism of education, however, is not confined to this scene but is developed throughout *The Elder Brother*, mainly through the depiction (in the first half of the play) of Charles as an otherworldly scholar whose only companions are books. Andrew describes Charles's typical day as follows:

> He breaks his fast
> With Aristotle, dines with Tully, takes
> His watering with the Muses, sups with Livy,
> Then walks a turn or two in *via lactea*,
> And, after six hours' conference with the stars,
> Sleeps with old Erra Pater. (1.2.23–8)

Charles is made fun of especially because his 'bookish contemplation' (1.2.123) keeps him so far from 'worldly business' (1.2.122) that he forgets 'to eat and sleep with reading' (2.4.1) and ends up wondering 'Why should we care for anything but knowledge / Or look upon the world but to contemn it?' (2.4.12–13). Charles's incompetence in the affairs of the world is especially foregrounded in the first part of the play. The worst thing, as Ira Clark remarks, seems to be that 'His interest in marriage has been nullified by scholastic misogyny. And his interest in procreating the family line has been supplanted by the dream of promulgating ideas'; the bad examples of antiquity (Clytemnestra and Tullia Minor) have made marriage such a disturbing prospect for him (1.2.153–71) that he has made 'his book his mistress' (3.3.100).[104] It is only after meeting Angelina that Charles's potential starts to flow and gets a concrete outlet, the moment at which he finally starts to apply his intelligence and knowledge to earthly affairs. Eventually, Charles gets the better of his younger brother Eustace (who wanted Angelina for himself), regains his rights of primogeniture, and – the play's ending suggests – will manage to marry Angelina. In this sense, the play seems to reflect on the status of learning in early modern England. As Jean Lambert points out,

> Ideally, the humanist curriculum and methodology aimed, above all, to produce social and moral subjects equipped to apply precept in action within the confines of a well regulated state. However, principle and practice tended to diverge, the reproduction of autonomous learners more often losing sight of its political end.[105]

As a matter of fact, the message of the play seems to be precisely that learning by itself is not enough: only by uniting the contemplative and the active, only by merging the lessons of the past with a sharp awareness of the present can people succeed in the real world. This aptly mirrors Fletcher's own attitude to the classics, which he invariably read side by side with contemporary authors, in a distinctive fusion of tradition and innovation, invariably attentive – as shall become evident in Chapter 2 – to the wider and deeper social, political, and historical implications of reading the present in light of the past and vice versa.

Andrew's description of Charles's typical day quoted above mentions classical authors who were staple fare of the grammar school and university curricula (Aristotle, Cicero, Livy) but are virtually ignored in the plays of the Fletcher canon. While it would be far-fetched to attempt to draw firm conclusions regarding Fletcher himself from such a playful depiction of education and learning in the plays of the canon – all the more so given that the satire on schoolmasters and scholars was a motif with a wide currency in early modern English drama – the evidence would cumulatively seem to suggest that Fletcher does not appear to have retained especially fond memories of his years as a grammar school pupil and, perhaps, as a university student (if he did indeed attend the University of Cambridge). Although I do not want to push at a potential biographical reading of Fletcher's portrayal of scholars too much, it is still worth noting that he had examples of scholars in his family that might have somehow influenced his depiction of learning in his dramatic writings. His brother Nathaniel was a Fellow at Cambridge but gave up his position in 1611, becoming rector of Barking and Darmsden, Suffolk, while his cousin Nathaniel Pownall wrote a book titled *The Young Divine's Apology for His Continuance in the University* (1612), which was prepared for publication by another cousin, Giles Fletcher the Younger.[106]

CONCLUSION

While some measure of exasperation or resentment regarding the early modern school system might plausibly have something to do with Fletcher's approach to the classics, and while his predilection for texts belonging to Late Antiquity might have largely resulted from a general interest in accounts of the age of the Roman Empire rather than the Republic (as mentioned in the introduction), his resorting to Herodian, Cassius Dio, Josephus, *Historia Augusta*, Procopius, and Justin may reveal something more. Keeping in mind the risk of providing an overly generalizing description of works by different authors active over the course of about five centuries, it is perhaps nonetheless possible to identify a few common features in the writings of Late Antiquity historians that distinguish them from more canonical authors such as Sallust, Livy, and Tacitus, and that might have made them especially palatable to Fletcher. Generally speaking, the historical narration in Late Antiquity becomes more fractured and disjointed, its syntactical structure more convoluted, and a taste for gossipy anecdotes is more palpable throughout. Such features look especially suited to Fletcher's dramatic craft: for him, the periphery is often as relevant as the centre; sometimes a single scene looks more important than an entire act; moments that leave a lasting impression occasionally overshadow consistency. Moreover, these historians expressed a bleak view of the Roman Empire and of life in general that was often more pessimistic than that provided by the historians of the golden age, and this is an aspect that appears both to have appealed to Fletcher's vision of imperial Rome as a disoriented space and to have in turn shaped his dramatic depiction thereof, as will be more evident in the ensuing chapter.

As previously remarked, another manifest characteristic of Fletcher's relationship with the classics is his preference for French (and, to a lesser extent, English) translations over Greek or Latin source texts – though he might have sometimes relied on both at the same time – as well as his frequent use of vernacular texts. Moreover, not only did Fletcher frequently mix different classical sources, usually giving more importance to one over the others (Aristophanes' *Lysistrata* and perhaps *Ecclesiazusae* in *The Tamer Tamed*; Xenophon, Herodotus, and Plutarch in *A King and No King*; Lucan, Plutarch, Suetonius, and Florus in *The False One*; Herodian and Cassius Dio in *Rollo*; *Historia Augusta*, Justin, and Plutarch in *The Prophetess*; Procopius and Cassiodorus in *Valentinian*); even more importantly, he seems to have had a propensity for mingling them with contemporary texts that caught his and his collaborators' attention (Gentillet, D'Urfé, Savile, Coeffeteau) and that usefully complemented what he could find in the classical accounts.

All in all, Fletcher seems to have been mainly drawn to the classics via the contemporaries rather than the other way around. Interestingly, he wrote *Valentinian* and *The Mad Lover* not long after *L'Astrée* had been published; he probably authored *The False One* shortly after the issuing of Farnaby's edition of Lucan's *Pharsalia* and Bolton's translation of Florus' *Epitome*; he penned *The Prophetess* soon after the publication of *Historie romaine*: put differently, Fletcher seems to have been fond of using continental and Englished books hot off the press, conceivably as a way to be always ahead of the playmaking competition. Such a pattern can also be observed in the context of the Spanish sources of *The Custom of the Country* (1619–23), for which he and Massinger used an anonymous 1619 English translation of Cervantes's *The Travels of Persiles and*

Sigismunda, and *The Pilgrim* (1619–21), for which Fletcher used a 1621 English translation (possibly the work of William Dutton) of Lope de Vega's *The Pilgrim of Castile*.[107]

How Fletcher had access to all these books is hard to ascertain, as there is neither any specific piece of evidence as to what he had in his library nor any surviving personal accounts, direct or indirect, about his reading tastes, apart from the occasional dedication in a few books and his father's will mentioned above. While writing for the King's Men, Fletcher might have borrowed books from what Sarah Wall-Randell has described as a 'company library', possibly including 'reference books, such as the Bible, Holinshed's *Chronicle*, Plutarch's *Lives*, Ovid's *Metamorphoses*, Painter's *Palace of Pleasures*, and other key texts, that could have been owned by a playing company and made available to playwrights to mine as sources in the writing process'.[108] Munro suggests that some of these books might very well have been those included in an inventory of the household goods of Elizabeth Condell, the widow of long-standing King's Men's member Henry Condell, which features such titles as Edmund Spenser's *The Faerie Queene*, Giovanni Boccaccio's *Decameron*, Geoffrey Chaucer's works, and Richard Knolles's much reprinted *The General History of the Turks* (1603).[109] As a matter of fact, as Munro points out in her discussion of Daborne's correspondence with the impresario Philip Henslowe, it appears probable that 'company managers or financiers may routinely have lent books or other source materials, such as older playbooks, to playwrights'.[110] Finally, Fletcher is also likely to have benefited from the libraries of his literary patron Henry Hastings, fifth Earl of Huntingdon; that of his brother Nathaniel, who was in Italy as chaplain to Henry Wotton in 1604–06; and those of such literary friends as Michael Drayton and Jonson, as well as Mabbe, who had travelled extensively to Spain and France and would have therefore been ideally placed to furnish Fletcher with books recently printed in continental Europe.[111]

On balance, Fletcher does not appear to have been particularly mindful of any solemnity in classical texts but rather to have used them as though they were equal to any other, even preferring 'Dunce Holinshed, / The Englishman that writes of snows and sheriffs' – as Miramont sneeringly describes him in *The Elder Brother* (2.1.119–20) – to Tacitus and Cassius Dio as the source for *Bonduca* and often alluding to classical antiquity with frank playfulness. This is the case, for example, with Vandonck's bragging for having managed 'to march / Like Caesar when he bred his *Commentaries*, / So I, to breed my *Chronicle*, came forth / Caesar Vandonck *et veni, vidi, vici*' in *Beggars' Bush* (1613–22, with Massinger), and with the references to Nero and Caligula in *The Scornful Lady* (1609–12, with Beaumont).[112] Here, when Elder Loveless is thought to have drowned at sea, and Young Loveless has inherited his wealth, the Poet instructs the latter as follows:

> Do what you will: 'tis the noblest course. Then, you may live without the charge of people. Only we four will make a family, ay, and an age that shall beget new *Annals*, in which I'll write thy life, my son of pleasure, equal with Nero or Caligula.[113]

Munro argues that the examples of Nero and Caligula are 'distinctly unpromising', and when Young Loveless asks 'What mean they, captain?' (2.3.112), the Captain, as Finkelpearl remarks, 'glosses this classical allusion by explaining to the uncomprehending, because presumably uneducated' Young Loveless that it refers to 'Two roaring boys of Rome that made all split' (2.3.113).[114] As Munro comments, '[t]he worst of the Roman emperors, Nero and Caligula, are pulled out of the classical past and reframed as contemporary revelers' in a typical instance of Fletcher's often playful and de-solemnizing approach to classical antiquity.[115]

Fletcher's syncretic manner of negotiating the classics, his incessant *contaminatio* of the ancient and the contemporary, his interest in a distant past as already remodulated by early modern French or English eyes make his handling of classical sources shine as an intriguing form of cultural adaptation capable of incorporating differently inflected cultural voices by blending together the past and the present, Rome and home, history and romance, England and the Continent, in an engagingly hybrid, transnational, pan-European perspective.[116] This comprehensive reassessment of Fletcher's classicism thus sheds new light on what Clare McManus describes as 'the multilingual European textual, theatrical and literary cultures of which the dramatist ... was part' and further corroborates the case Alexander Samson makes for 'the multilingual nature of vernacular culture in early modern Europe and practises of working on multiple polyglot versions of given texts' in relation to Fletcher's Spanish sources.[117] In fashioning the classics thus, Fletcher made significant use of them and simultaneously questioned their monopoly of certain kinds of knowledge and truth, which made his engagement with classical antiquity less immediately recognizable, but not an inch less compelling. More specifically, as will become apparent over the following chapters, his attitude to classical sources appears significantly to have shaped his depiction of ancient Roman politics, values, and models, as well as his general conception of history.

NOTES

1 On Jonson and Tacitus, see J. H. M. Salmon, 'Stoicism and Roman Examples: Seneca and Tacitus in Jacobean England', *Journal of the History of Ideas* 50 (1989),

199–225 (219–25); Malcolm R. Smuts, 'Court-Centred Politics and the Uses of Roman Historians, c.1590–1630', in *Culture and Politics in Early Stuart England*, ed. Kevin Sharpe and Peter Lake (Basingstoke: Macmillan, 1994), 21–43 (31–4); Worden, 'Ben Jonson among the Historians', 67–89. On Jonson and Horace, see Colin Burrow, 'Roman Satire in the Sixteenth Century', in *The Cambridge Companion to Roman Satire*, ed. Kirk Freudenburg (Cambridge: Cambridge University Press, 2005), 243–60 (254–6); Victoria Moul, *Jonson, Horace and the Classical Tradition* (Cambridge: Cambridge University Press, 2010); Ian Donaldson, *Ben Jonson: A Life* (Oxford: Oxford University Press, 2011), 16–18. On Shakespeare and Plutarch, see, among others, Mungo William MacCallum, *Shakespeare's Roman Plays and Their Background* (London: Macmillan, 1910); E. A. J. Honigmann, 'Shakespeare's Plutarch', *Shakespeare Quarterly* 10 (1959), 25–33; Burrow, *Shakespeare and Classical Antiquity*, 202–39; Gordon Braden, 'Shakespeare', in *A Companion to Plutarch*, ed. Mark Beck (Malden, MA: Wiley-Blackwell, 2014), 577–91. On Shakespeare and Ovid, see, among others, Jonathan Bate, *Shakespeare and Ovid* (Oxford: Clarendon Press, 1993); A. B. Taylor (ed.), *Shakespeare's Ovid: The Metamorphoses in the Plays and Poems* (Cambridge: Cambridge University Press, 2000); Gordon Braden, 'Ovid and Shakespeare', in *A Companion to Ovid*, ed. Peter E. Knox (Malden, MA: Wiley-Blackwell, 2009), 442–54; Burrow, *Shakespeare and Classical Antiquity*, 92–132; Bate, *How the Classics Made Shakespeare*, 10–11, 194–203.

2 Waith, *Pattern of Tragicomedy*, 86–98, 203–7; Hensman, *Shares of Fletcher, Field and Massinger*, 2:363–4. Seneca's *Controversiae* were also drawn upon for *The Laws of Candy* and *The Fair Maid of the Inn*, on the authorship of which see the introduction to the present volume, 12. John E. Curran, Jr, 'Declamation and Character in the Fletcher-Massinger Plays', *Medieval and Renaissance Drama in England* 23 (2010), 86–113 (87), suggests that the *Controversiae* also determined the crafting of 'personages individualized well beyond stock type' by endowing them with greater 'depth and consistency', inasmuch as 'motives and drives are envisaged, and shaped to make sense, in light of the ethopoeia in or implied in the *Controversiae* and of the *colores* of Seneca's declaimers'.

3 On arguments *in utramque partem*, see Joel B. Altman, *The Tudor Play of Mind: Rhetorical Inquiry and the Development of Elizabethan Drama* (Berkeley, CA: University of California Press, 1978), 31–53.

4 See Burrow, *Shakespeare and Classical Antiquity*, 39–45.

5 W. T. Mellows (ed.), *Peterborough Local Administration: The Foundation of Peterborough Cathedral: A.D. 1541* (Northampton: Northamptonshire Record Society, 1941), liii.

6 Mellows (ed.), *Peterborough Local Administration*, liv.

7 A. F. Leach, 'Schools', in *The Victoria History of the County of Northampton: Volume Two*, ed. R. M. Serjeantson and W. Ryland D. Adkins (London: [Archibald Constable], 1906), 201–88 (204–5).

8 Leach, 'Schools', 205.

9 Mellows (ed.), *Peterborough Local Administration*, liv.

10 Simon Gunton, *The History of the Church of Peterborough, Wherein the Most Remarkable Things Concerning That Place from the First Foundation Thereof, with Other Passages of History Not Unworthy Public View, Are Represented* (London, 1686), 100.

11 Leach, 'Schools', 208.

12 Jane King and Trevor Elliott, *Mortarboards & Mitres: The Headmasters of the King's School, Peterborough, since 4th September 1541* (Peterborough: The

King's School, 2017), 16, https://www.kings.peterborough.sch.uk/attachments/download.asp?file=114&type=pdf (accessed 13 July 2020).
13 Leach, 'Schools', 208.
14 Leach, 'Schools', 208.
15 Leach, 'Schools', 208.
16 Leach, 'Schools', 208.
17 Leach, 'Schools', 208.
18 Leach, 'Schools', 208.
19 Leach, 'Schools', 208.
20 Leach, 'Schools', 209.
21 Leach, 'Schools', 209.
22 Leach, 'Schools', 209.
23 Leach, 'Schools', 209.
24 Leach, 'Schools', 209.
25 Leach, 'Schools', 209.
26 Leach, 'Schools', 209.
27 Leach, 'Schools', 209.
28 Leach, 'Schools', 204.
29 Nina Taunton, 'Did John Fletcher the Playwright Go to University?', *Notes and Queries* 235 (1990), 170–2; Nina Taunton, 'Biography, a University Education, and Playwriting: Fletcher and Marlowe', *Research Opportunities in Renaissance Drama* 33 (1994), 63–97; Arata Ide, 'John Fletcher of Corpus Christi College: New Records of His Early Years', *Early Theatre* 14 (2011), 63–77.
30 Hilton Kelliher, 'Francis Beaumont and Nathan Field: New Records of their Early Years', in *English Manuscript Studies 1100–1700: Volume 8: Seventeenth-Century Poetry, Music and Drama*, ed. Peter Beal (London: British Library, 2000), 1–42; John Aubrey, *'Brief Lives', Chiefly of Contemporaries, Set Down by John Aubrey, between the Years 1669 and 1696*, ed. Andrew Clark, 2 vols (Oxford: Clarendon Press, 1898), 1.95.
31 Kelliher, 'Francis Beaumont and Nathan Field', 28.
32 Charles Cathcart, 'John Fletcher in 1600–1601: Two Early Poems, an Involvement in the "Poets' War", and a Network of Literary Connections', *Philological Quarterly* 81 (2002), 33–51.
33 The National Archives, PROB 11/87; Alexander Dyce, 'Some Account of the Lives and Writings of Beaumont and Fletcher', in *The Works of Beaumont and Fletcher; The Text Formed from a New Collation of the Early Editions. With Notes and a Biographical Memoir*, 11 vols (London: Moxon, 1843–44) 1.v–xc (lxxxviii).
34 Mateo Alemán, *The Rogue, or The Life of Guzman de Alfarache*, trans. James Mabbe (London, 1622), fol. A3v.
35 Daileader and Taylor, 'Introduction', 14–15; Lee Bliss, 'Introduction', in *A King and No King* by Francis Beaumont and John Fletcher (Manchester: Manchester University Press, 2004), 1–55 (5–7). On *A King and No King* and Xenophon, see also Jane Grogan, 'Introduction', in *William Barker, Xenophon's 'Cyropaedia'* (Cambridge: MHRA, 2020), 1–67 (65). Louis E. Lord, *Aristophanes: His Plays and His Influence* (New York: Cooper Square, 1963), 163, identifies in the *Tamer Tamed* 'some reminiscences of the *Ecclesiazusae*' as well.
36 Bliss, 'Introduction', 8.
37 Otto Ulrich, *Die pseudohistorischen Dramen Beaumonts und Fletchers: Thierry and Theodoret, Valentinian, The Prophetess und The False One und ihre Quellen* (Straßburg: Neuesten Nachrichten, 1913), 80–98; Hensman, *Shares of Fletcher, Field and Massinger*, 1:126–45; Paleit, *War, Liberty, and Caesar*, 146–7.

38 Philip Oxley, 'Textual Introduction', in *The Humorous Lieutenant* by John Fletcher (New York: Garland, 1987), 1–80 (30–32); William Dinsmore Briggs, 'On the Sources of *The Maid's Tragedy*', *Modern Language Notes* 31 (1916), 502–3; Roma Gill, 'Collaboration and Revision in Massinger's *A Very Woman*', *Review of English Studies* 70 (1967), 136–48 (144).

39 Pearse, *Fletcher's Chastity Plays*, 170–1, 189, 228.

40 A similar pattern is discernible in the Anglicization of the oft-staged story of Mahomet and the fair Irene at the fall of Constantinople in Antony Brewer's *The Lovesick King* (1611–55), and in the relocation of the love story of Giovanni and Bellaura to Italy in Shirley's *The Gentleman of Venice* (1639), the source of which, Lope de Vega's *El hombre por su palabra* (1625), sets it in the Balkans.

41 Bertha Hensman, 'John Fletcher's *The Bloody Brother; or, Rollo, Duke of Normandy*', unpublished PhD thesis, University of Chicago, 1947, 133–7, and Gary Taylor and John Jowett, *Shakespeare Reshaped, 1606–1623* (Oxford: Clarendon Press, 1993), 260–71 (270), argue that Fletcher's depiction of the title character was also shaped by the gloomy picture of the historical Rollo, 1st Duke of Normandy, as a tyrant painted by André Duchesne in his compilation *Historiae Normannorum Scriptores antiqui* (Paris, 1619). Though possible, this scenario requires the play to have been staged in 1619–20. Wiggins, *Catalogue*, 7.47, #1841, observes that this 'entails some circumstantial implausibility', since if Field was one of the collaborators, 'there is an uncomfortably narrow time-frame for a relatively obscure source-book to cross the Channel and come to the authors' attention, followed by the planning and execution of their play', given that Field died in 1620. However, the date of Field's death cannot be firmly established. The most secure evidence puts it between 19 May 1619, when he was fourth in a livery allowance list, and 2 August 1620, when his sister Dorcas was awarded administration of his estate. See M. E. Williams, 'Field, Nathan (bap. 1587, d. 1619/20)', in *Oxford Dictionary of National Biography* (Oxford: Oxford University Press, 2004), https://doi.org/10.1093/ref:odnb/9391 (accessed 26 January 2021). The fact that Field is not mentioned in the manuscript of *Sir John Van Olden Barnavelt* might indicate that he was dead by August 1619, but only a handful of actors are named in the manuscript. At all events, apart from the problems and uncertainties that surround the dating and the authorship of *Rollo* (Field's contribution to the play cannot be firmly established so far), I cannot see how the absence of negative depictions of Rollo prior to Duchesne's work should necessarily imply that the play's depiction of Rollo as a bloodthirsty tyrant was prompted by Duchesne's account: it may have come from an as yet unacknowledged source (see Wiggins, *Catalogue*, 7.47, #1841), or it may have simply originated from Antoninus' grim portrayal in Herodian and Gentillet and then been transferred on to Rollo by Fletcher and his collaborators.

42 I have found it impossible to ascertain whether Fletcher resorted to Greek, Latin, or French for Cassius Dio.

43 It is perhaps worth remarking that Agnolo Poliziano, mentioned in the title as the first translator of Herodian from Greek, had also authored *Fabula di Orfeo* (1480), a landmark in Italian pastoral drama together with Torquato Tasso's *Aminta* (1573) and Giovanni Battista Guarini's *Il pastor fido* (1590), which had inspired Fletcher's *The Faithful Shepherdess* (1607–08) as well as his theoretical approach to tragicomedy. The conspicuous presence in the title of the name of such a key figure in the development of Renaissance pastoral drama might have represented a further spur for Fletcher to resort to Herodian's *History*.

44 On Lodge's Josephus, see Freyja Cox Jensen, 'What Was Thomas Lodge's Josephus in Early Modern England?', *Sixteenth Century Journal* 49 (2018), 3-24.
45 See, among others, Clare McManus, 'Introduction', in *The Island Princess* by John Fletcher (London: Methuen for Arden Shakespeare, 2012), 1-95 (16-17, 49-57); Carmen Nocentelli, 'Spice Race: *The Island Princess* and the Politics of Transnational Appropriation', *Publications of the Modern Language Association* 125 (2010), 572-88; Alexander Samson, '"Last thought upon a windmill?": Cervantes and Fletcher', in *The Cervantean Heritage: Reception and Influence of Cervantes in Britain*, ed. J. A. G. Ardila (Leeds: Legenda, 2009), 223-33.
46 On *Bonduca*, see Benno Leonhardt, '*Bonduca*', *Englische Studien* 13 (1889), 36-63; Bernard Joseph Nolan, 'A Critical Edition of John Fletcher's *Bonduca*', unpublished MA thesis, University of Liverpool, 1951, 26-33; William W. Appleton, *Beaumont and Fletcher: A Critical Study* (London: Allen and Unwin, 1956), 54-5; and especially Drabek, *Fletcherian Dramatic Achievement*, 81-94.
47 See Domenico Lovascio, 'Introduction', in *The False One* by John Fletcher and Philip Massinger (Manchester: Manchester University Press, forthcoming 2022).
48 Ulrich, *Die pseudohistorischen Dramen*, 80-98.
49 *The Roman Histories of Lucius Julius Florus from the Foundation of Rome, Till Caesar Augustus, for above DCC. Years, & from Thence to Trajan near CC. Years, Divided by Flor[us] into IV. Ages*, trans. Edmund Bolton (London, 1619).
50 *The Roman Histories of Lucius Julius Florus*, 414 (2.13.52).
51 Lucan, *Pharsalia sive De Bello Civili Caesar et Pompeii Libri X*, ed. Thomas Farnaby (London, 1618), 8.618-19, 667-74; Plutarch, 'The Life of Pompey', in *The Lives of the Noble Grecians and Romans Compared Together by That Grave Learned Philosopher and Historiographer, Plutarch of Chaeronea; Translated out of Greek into French by James Amyot ...; and out of French into English by Thomas North* (London, 1579), 717E.
52 *The Roman Histories of Lucius Julius Florus*, 415 (2.13.52).
53 *The Roman Histories of Lucius Julius Florus*, 414 (2.13.52).
54 *The Roman Histories of Lucius Julius Florus*, 396 (2.13.14).
55 Cf. Lucan, *Pharsalia*, 1.125-6: 'nec quemquam iam ferre potest, Caesarve priorem, / Pompeiusve parem' (Caesar could no longer endure a superior, nor Pompey an equal).
56 *The Roman Histories of Lucius Julius Florus*, 416-17 (2.13.58).
57 Freyja Cox Jensen, 'Reading Florus in Early Modern England', *Renaissance Studies* 23 (2009), 659-77 (660).
58 Woolf, *Idea of History*, 173.
59 On Coeffeteau, see Ulrich, *Die pseudohistorischen Dramen*, 58-75; on Justin, see Hensman, *Shares of Fletcher, Field and Massinger*, 2:302-3. The *Historia Augusta* is a collection of thirty imperial biographies that presents itself as having been written by six different historians but was probably written by one man at the close of the fourth century CE.
60 John Fletcher and Philip Massinger, *The Prophetess*, ed. George Walton Williams, in *The Dramatic Works in the Beaumont and Fletcher Canon*, ed. Fredson Bowers, 10 vols (Cambridge: Cambridge University Press, 1966-96), 9.232-306, 1.1.52-5. All references to the play are to this edition. Subsequent references will be incorporated parenthetically into the text.
61 Nicolas Coeffeteau, *Histoire romaine, contenant tout ce qui s'est passé de plus mémorable depuis le commencement de l'empire d'Auguste, jusqu'à celui de*

Constantin le Grand. Avec l'Épitome de Florus depuis la fondation de la ville de Rome jusques à la fin de l'empire d'August (Paris, 1621), III Partie, 270, 271.
62 Coeffeteau, *Histoire romaine*, 274–5, my emphasis.
63 Ulrich also argues that Fletcher drew the idea of Numerian's eye disease as occasioned by excessive crying from *Histoire romaine*, because it was absent in *Historia Augusta*. Yet more than one edition of *Historia Augusta* prior to *The Prophetess* describes Numerian's disease as caused 'nimio fletu', so that this cannot be taken as evidence of Fletcher's resort to Coeffeteau. For Othello's farewell speech, see William Shakespeare, *Othello*, ed. Michael Neill (Oxford: Oxford University Press, 2006), 3.3.349–59.
64 'Claudii Salmasii in Aelium Lampridium Notae', in *Historiae Augustae Scriptores VI. Aelius Spartianus, Vulcatius Gallicanus, Julius Capitolinus, Trebellius Pollio, Aelius Lampridius, Flavius Vopiscus. Claudius Salmasius ex veteribus libris recensuit et librum adiecit notarum ac emendationum. quib[us] adiunctae sunt notae ac emendationes Isaac Casauboni, iam antea editae adiunctae* (Paris, 1620), 237.
65 For example, on Fletcher's allusive use of the classical names Sophocles, Tranio, and Petronius, see John R. Severn, '"Then turn tail to tail and peace be with you": John Fletcher's *The Woman's Prize, or The Tamer Tamed*, Menippean Satire, and Same-Sex Desire', in *New Directions in Early Modern English Drama: Edges, Spaces, Intersections*, ed. Aidan Norrie and Mark Houlahan (Kalamazoo, MI: Medieval Institute Publications, 2020), 199–218.
66 Resi Gielen, *Untersuchungen zur Namengebung bei Beaumont, Fletcher und Massinger* (Quakenbrück: Robert Kleinert, 1929), 11.
67 Gielen, *Untersuchungen zur Namengebung*, 57.
68 Ulrich, *Die pseudohistorischen Dramen*, 36–52.
69 Ulrich, *Die pseudohistorischen Dramen*, 35. The French translation is *Histoire des guerres faictes par l'Empereur Iustinian contre les Vandales, et les Goths. Escrite en Grec par Procope, & Agathias, et mise en François per Mart[in] Fumee* (Paris, 1587). Marco Mincoff, 'Shakespeare, Fletcher and Baroque Tragedy', *Shakespeare Survey* 20 (1967), 1–15 (3), vaguely observes that 'Fletcher had recourse to a French translation of Procopius' but neither mentions Ulrich's study nor elaborates the point. The *editio princeps* of the *History of the Wars* in Greek by David Hoeschel was not published until 1607. Book III had been first translated into Latin (from Greek manuscripts) in 1509 by Raffaele Maffei, whose translation was reprinted in 1516, 1531, 1576, and 1594, and was the only Latin translation available to Fletcher.
70 Gielen, *Untersuchungen zur Namengebung*, 62.
71 Robert Kean Turner, 'The Tragedy of Valentinian: Textual Notes', in Bowers (gen. ed.), *Dramatic Works*, 4.381–92 (382).
72 Mincoff, 'Fletcher's Early Tragedies', 72.
73 Ulrich, *Die pseudohistorischen Dramen*, 52.
74 Gielen, *Untersuchungen zur Namengebung*, 46; Eileen Allman, *Jacobean Revenge Tragedy and the Politics of Virtue* (Newark, DE: University of Delaware Press, 1999), 118.
75 John Fletcher, *The Tragedy of Valentinian*, in *Four Jacobean Sex Tragedies*, ed. Martin Wiggins (Oxford: Oxford University Press, 1998), 1.2.34–5. All references to the play are to this edition. Subsequent references will be incorporated parenthetically into the text.
76 John Fletcher, *The Tamer Tamed*, ed. Lucy Munro (London: Methuen, 2010), 1.2.107; John Fletcher and Philip Massinger, *The Knight of Malta*, ed. George

Walton Williams, in Bowers (gen. ed.), *Dramatic Works*, 8.360–453, 4.3.15–17; William Shakespeare, *Cymbeline*, ed. Valerie Wayne (London: Bloomsbury Arden Shakespeare, 2017), 5.4.37–9. All references to the plays are to these editions. Subsequent references will be incorporated parenthetically into the text.

77 Loughlin, *Hymeneutics*, 154.
78 Hila, '"Justice shall never heare ye, I am justice"', 749.
79 Loughlin, *Hymeneutics*, 139.
80 Loughlin, *Hymeneutics*, 143.
81 Loughlin, *Hymeneutics*, 160.
82 Bliss, 'Introduction', 30. For a detailed discussion of the composition of the audience in indoor playhouses, see Lucy Munro, *Children of the Queen's Revels: A Jacobean Theatre Repertory* (Cambridge: Cambridge University Press, 2005), 61–6.
83 The first occurrence is in James Shirley, *The Duke's Mistress* (London, 1638).
84 Annalisa Agrati, 'Introduzione', in *La commedia Ardelia* (Pisa: Pacini, 1994), 5–61 (7–9).
85 Lucy Munro, *Archaic Style in English Literature, 1590–1674* (Cambridge: Cambridge University Press, 2013), 181–2.
86 The provenance of names in *The Faithful Shepherdess* has been examined in detail by Florence Ada Kirk, 'Introduction', in *The Faithful Shepherdess* by John Fletcher (New York: Garland, 1980), iii–ci (xxvii–xxviii), and Munro, *Archaic Style*, 181–2.
87 John Fletcher, *The Faithful Shepherdess*, ed. Robert Kean Turner, in Bowers (gen. ed.), *Dramatic Works*, 3.489–612, 3.1.312–13.
88 Xenophon's *Hiero*, a dialogue between Hiero and the poet Simonides set in 474 BCE, is the first literary work ever to investigate the tyrant's inner life. Cf. Robert S. Miola, '*Julius Caesar* and the Tyrannicide Debate', *Renaissance Quarterly* 38 (1985), 271–89 (280 n.23); William A. Armstrong, 'The Elizabethan Conception of the Tyrant', *Review of English Studies* 22 (1946), 161–81 (174–6). See also Silvia Bigliazzi, 'Introduction: The Tyrant's Fear', *Comparative Drama* 51 (2017), 434–54; Francesco Dall'Olio, 'Xenophon and Plato in Elizabethan Culture: The Tyrant's Fear Before *Macbeth*', *Comparative Drama* 51 (2017), 476–505; Peter Womack, 'The Tyrant's Vein: Misrule and Popularity in the Elizabethan Playhouse', *Review of English Studies* 72 (2021), 61–84.
89 Henry Savile, *The End of Nero and the Beginning of Galba. Four Books of the Histories of Cornelius Tacitus. The Life of Agricola* (London, 1591), 3.
90 David Womersley, 'Sir Henry Savile's Translation of Tacitus and the Political Interpretation of Elizabethan Texts', *Review of English Studies* 42 (1991), 313–42 (314).
91 Womersley, 'Sir Henry Savile's Translation of Tacitus', 314.
92 Savile, *The End of Nero and the Beginning of Galba*, 3.
93 Plutarch, 'The Life of Galba', in *Lives*, 1110A; Womersley, 'Sir Henry Savile's Translation of Tacitus', 315.
94 Savile, *The End of Nero and the Beginning of Galba*, 3.
95 The fact that Savile's book was reprinted in 1598, 1604, and 1612 seems further to corroborate the argument provided by Wiggins, *Catalogue*, 6.383–4, #1739, that *Valentinian* needs to be dated closer to 1614 than to 1610, as it seems plausible to argue that the new edition issued in 1612 would have been more readily available to Fletcher than the others, all the more so given Fletcher's penchant for recently published books.
96 John Fletcher and Philip Massinger, *The Sea Voyage*, ed. Anthony Parr, in *Three Renaissance Travel Plays* (Manchester: Manchester University Press, 1995), 135–216,

3.3.99–100; Francis Beaumont and John Fletcher, *The Woman-Hater*, ed. George Walton Williams, in Bowers (gen. ed.), *Dramatic Works*, 1.156–237, 2.2.17. Fletcher's role in the composition of *The Woman Hater* has been much debated. See Cyrus Hoy, 'The Shares of Fletcher and His Collaborators in the Beaumont and Fletcher Canon (III)', *Studies in Bibliography* 11 (1958), 85–106 (98); George Walton Williams, '*The Woman Hater*: Textual Introduction', in Bowers (gen. ed.), *Dramatic Works*, 1.147–55 (150–4).

97 Ursula Ann Potter, 'Pedagogy and Parenting in English Drama, 1560–1610: Flogging Schoolmasters and Cockering Mothers', unpublished PhD thesis, University of Sydney, 2011, 36.

98 John Fletcher, *The Mad Lover*, ed. Robert Kean Turner, in Bowers (gen. ed.), *Dramatic Works*, 5.11–98, 3.2.122–4; John Fletcher, *Wit without Money*, ed. Hans Walter Gabler, in Bowers (gen. ed.), *Dramatic Works*, 6.10–92, 2.4.136–7. All references to the plays are to these editions. Subsequent references will be incorporated parenthetically into the text.

99 John Fletcher and Philip Massinger, *A Very Woman*, ed. Hans Walter Gabler, in Bowers (gen. ed.), *Dramatic Works*, 7.639–731, 3.5.174–5. All references to the play are to this edition. Subsequent references will be incorporated parenthetically into the text.

100 McMullan, 'The Strange Case of Susan Brotes', 193.

101 John Fletcher, *The Night-Walkers*, ed. Cyrus Hoy, in Bowers (gen. ed.), *Dramatic Works*, 7.531–611, 2.1.88.

102 John Fletcher and William Shakespeare, *The Two Noble Kinsmen*, ed. Lois Potter (London: Bloomsbury Arden Shakespeare, rev. edn, 2015), 3.5; John Fletcher and Philip Massinger, *The Elder Brother*, ed. Fredson Bowers, in Bowers (gen. ed.), *Dramatic Works*, 9.469–545, 2.4.50–4. All references to the play are to this edition. Subsequent references will be incorporated parenthetically into the text.

103 McMullan, 'The Strange Case of Susan Brotes', 192.

104 Ira Clark, *The Moral Art of Philip Massinger* (Lewisburg, PA: Bucknell University Press, 1993), 252.

105 Jean Lambert, *Teachers in Early Modern English Drama: Pedagogy and Authority* (London: Routledge, 2019), 12.

106 I thank Lucy Munro for bringing these family connections to my attention.

107 See Wiggins, *Catalogue*, 7:207, #1911; 7:375, #1998.

108 Sarah Wall-Randell, 'What Is a Staged Book? Books as "Actors" in the Early Modern English Theatre', in *Rethinking Theatrical Documents in Shakespeare's England*, ed. Tiffany Stern (London: Bloomsbury Arden Shakespeare, 2020), 128–52 (132).

109 John and Isabel Deodati v. Thomas Seaman and John Hatt, Chancery, 1638, The National Archives (TNA), C 3/400/76, quoted in Lucy Munro, 'Writing a Play with Robert Daborne', in Stern (ed.), *Rethinking Theatrical Documents*, 17–32 (19). See also E. A. J. Honigmann and Susan Brock (eds), *Playhouse Wills, 1558–1642: An Edition of Wills by Shakespeare and His Contemporaries in the London Theatre* (Manchester: Manchester University Press, 1993), 184.

110 Munro, 'Writing a Play with Robert Daborne', 19.

111 I am indebted to José A. Pérez Díez for pointing out Mabbe to me as his main suspect for providing books to Fletcher.

112 John Fletcher and Philip Massinger, *Beggars' Bush*, ed. Fredson Bowers, in Bowers (gen. ed.), *Dramatic Works*, 3.246–331, 5.2.141–4.

113 Francis Beaumont and John Fletcher, *The Scornful Lady*, ed. Cyrus Hoy, in Bowers (gen. ed.), *Dramatic Works*, 2.464–545, 2.3.107–11. All references to the play are

to this edition. Subsequent references will be incorporated parenthetically into the text.
114 Munro, 'Beaumont's Lives', 147; Finkelpearl, *Court and Country Politics*, 199.
115 Munro, 'Beaumont's Lives', 147.
116 On Fletcher as a 'European dramatist' and on his 'transnational' approach to contemporary Spanish sources, see McManus, 'Introduction', 16–17, 49–57; Nocentelli, 'Spice Race: *The Island Princess* and the Politics of Transnational Appropriation'.
117 McManus, 'Introduction', 57; Samson, '"Last thought upon a windmill"', 230.

CHAPTER 2
'I AM NO ROMAN, / NOR WHAT I AM DO I KNOW': FLETCHER'S ROMAN PLAYS AS *TRAUERSPIELE*

'Good aunt, where are we?', a bewildered Drusilla asks Delphia as they reach their destination at the end of a Daenerys Targaryen-like journey on dragonback in *The Prophetess* (2.3.7), perhaps a glance at Christopher Marlowe's *Doctor Faustus* (1587–89), in which the title character, as the Chorus reports, flies to Rome 'upon a dragon's back'.[1] Delphia replies as follows:

> Look down, Drusilla, on these lofty towers,
> These spacious streets, where every private house
> Appears a palace to receive a king.
> The site, the wealth, the beauty of the place
> Will soon inform thee 'tis imperious Rome,
> Rome, the great mistress of the conquered world. (2.3.8–13)

Taken by itself, such a description would seem to suggest that the play's portrayal of Rome contributes to confirming the dominant perception of the city as an unparalleled model of magnificence and excellence in the early modern English imagination. Delphia highlights the height of the buildings, the width of the streets, the luxury of the houses, and the overall sumptuousness of the capital of the Empire – 'the world's metropolis' (4.2.14), as Diocletian will later call it – the centrality of which is further underscored by the anadiplosis of 'Rome' (12–13) and by the trochaic foot beginning line 13, which bestows even more intensity on the repetition of the name of the city by interrupting the regular flow of the blank verse.

But it is all façade. The judgement that *The Prophetess* – and, to varying degrees, all Fletcher's Roman plays – seems to pass on Rome is in fact not so enthusiastic. This chapter describes and examines at length the ways in which Fletcher portrays Rome as a corrupted political reality facing irreversible decay, and how he depicts a Rome in crisis and profoundly unsettled by the lack of adequate political leaders and the apparent lack of interest on the part of the gods in human affairs. The only area left to the Roman men to prove their *virtus* is the battlefield, but this emerges as insufficient to offset the violence, the opportunism, and the dejection that exude from the plays, which chimes with the wider scepticism as to the dependability of Roman models and *exempla* that pervades the canon. In general terms, Fletcher's Roman plays depict a dissolving Rome that is prey to a deep sense of disorientation; in doing so, they express a pessimistic vision of history and human life, which makes them resemble in some respects the seventeenth-century German *Trauerspiel* as famously examined by Walter Benjamin. A fresh examination of Fletcher's depiction of classical history reveals him as a much sharper observer of reality than is usually recognized, not only in the immediacy of the here and now but also in terms of the larger changes and tendencies that are continually at work in history and politics.

THE EMPEROR'S BODY

The Prophetess opens with the soldier Niger's report of the assassination of Emperor Numerian to his co-emperor Carinus. Apparently, the Praetorian Prefect Volusius Aper has deceitfully murdered Numerian and is now keeping his corpse hidden from the army while he waits for the right moment to seize power himself. Accordingly, Numerian's body is left to rot until Diocles (the original name of the soldier who goes on to become emperor as Diocletian) uncovers it in the presence of the emperor's guards in Act 2, scene 2. Concealed in his litter, Numerian's body starts to decompose and stink rather badly:

>*Camurius.*   Does not the body
>   Begin to putrefy?
>*Aper.*   That exacts my haste.
>   When, but even now, I feigned obedience to it,
>   As I had some great business to impart,
>   The scent had almost choked me. (2.2.56)

Aper's final statement, 'The scent had almost choked me', appears redolent of Casca's description of the Roman commoners as an indistinct mound of rank sweat and bad breath in Shakespeare's *Julius Caesar*:

> the rabblement hooted and clapped their chapped hands and threw up their sweaty night-caps and uttered such a deal of stinking breath because Caesar refused the crown that it *had almost choked* Caesar – for he swooned and fell down at it. And for mine own part, I durst not laugh for fear of opening my lips and receiving the bad air.[2]

The bad breath of the populace is a recurrent motif in Shakespeare's Roman world – appearing in *Coriolanus* and *Antony and Cleopatra* as well – and is picked up again elsewhere in *The Prophetess* (3.1.69–73).[3] In this case, however, it is the emperor who is rotting and stinking.

Given that the equation of the royal body with the state had been a political commonplace for decades, it can be plausibly argued that the putrefaction of the emperor's body might be taken metaphorically to stand for the decay of the Roman Empire at large: the body natural of the ruler appears here to be coterminous with the body politic, with the state, the corruption of the one slowly encroaching upon the other.[4] True, Numerian has been slain treacherously and unjustly by an ambitious, evil man who has even denied his body proper burial, thereby horribly trampling upon the sacredness of the funeral rites (and rights) that should be due to anyone. Yet the play's dwelling at some length on the putrefaction and the stinking of the corpse would appear at least obliquely to insinuate that 'imperious Rome' is in fact slowly decomposing, just like its emperor's body, a notion that seems to be confirmed, as we shall see, by further evidence in this and other Roman plays in the canon.

There is another Roman emperor the dissolution of whose body Fletcher makes a point of exhibiting conspicuously on stage, namely Valentinian. In the final act of the eponymous play, as Aspasia Velissariou remarks, 'Fletcher invites the spectators to relish in the spectacle of the tyrant's prolonged agony, the terrible suffering inflicted by the poison and his tortuous corporeal disintegration.'[5] In a masterful *coup de théâtre*, Valentinian's painful degeneration and pangs of death are even raised to the second power by the fact that his poisoner Aretus has earlier himself taken a dose of the same poison in order to exhibit his torments to Valentinian as he takes his time enumerating the emperor's crimes. Such a spectacular duplication further foregrounds the coming apart of the emperor's body and power. The poison administered by Aretus deprives Valentinian of strength, authority, and masculinity. As depicted in Figure 2, Valentinian is symbolically *'carried on, sick in a Chair, with Eudoxa the Empress, Physicians, Attendants'* (5.2.12SD). 'When we see him for the first time as husband', Eileen Allman argues,

> he is emphatically unable to function as a man in that role. Lust, even mobility, is gone. He is equally impotent as Emperor. Although he can still speak, he cannot command. The chilly waters of the Danube and the Volga will not flow through his body to cool it; his physician countermands his desire to drink ... his murderer cannot be tortured to death on his order because Aretus has preempted him.[6]

A similar – though less sadistically staged – ending awaits Maximus, Valentinian's successor, who is symbolically murdered by the Empress Eudoxa with a poisoned wreath: power and the court are tantamount to poison in Rome. Similarly to *The Prophetess*, then, *Valentinian* exposes the disintegration of the bodies natural of the Roman emperors. As for

2 The emperor in agony in the final act of *Valentinian*

Rome's body politic, it does not seem to fare much better. In this respect, *Valentinian* offers by far the most desolating, claustrophobic, and disturbing portrayal of ancient Rome in the entire canon.

VIOLENCE, CORRUPTION, AND CRUELTY: THE LOSS OF THE ROMAN VALUES

Valentinian is set, in Philip J. Finkelpearl's pithily effective phrasing, in 'a peaceful, sophisticated Rome in a state of moral decay and stricken with a widespread malaise', with the Roman Empire worryingly at risk of revolt in the provinces: as Aëtius relates to the emperor, the soldiers grieve 'To see the nations ... / Fall from their obedience' (1.3.171, 175).[7] The corruption of Rome is especially dependent on the behaviour of Valentinian, a sensualist, Neronic tyrant who has surrounded himself with a host of bawds, panders, and 'base informers' (1.3.54, 232) in order to satisfy his each and every whim and urge. Valentinian's lust and pleasures 'Exceed the moderation of a man' (1.3.60) and are not limited to women, as Maximus makes clear by alluding to the unspecified 'trick[s]' of the emperor's 'eunuchs' and 'black-eyed boys' (3.3.119–20), their especially lustrous eyes suggesting their proclivity to pleasure, which mirrors that of the emperor. No wonder that Aretus styles him as 'a beast' and 'a sensual bloody thing' (5.2.61, 62), Lucina describes him as the 'bitter bane o'th' Empire' (3.1.31–6), and the soldier Pontius claims that 'The Emperor is made of nought but mischief. / Sure, murder was his mother' (4.3.26–7).

Valentinian's lack of self-governance – understood as the inability to control the appetites through the exercise of reason – is to be viewed as an unequivocal signal of the corruption of the state. As Rebecca W. Bushnell argues, in Fletcher's plays 'the king's private life acts as both a metaphor for and microcosm of his government, when he enacts laws and edicts in attempting to satisfy his lust', so that the 'tyrants' sexuality eventually becomes a political problem'.[8] The idea that self-governance is a prerequisite to the rule of others is frequent in Fletcher's plays. For example, in *The Humorous Lieutenant*, Leontius explains to Demetrius that 'that man's unfit to govern / That cannot guide himself'; in *Valentinian*, Pontius tells Aëtius, 'Why, I can govern, sir', to which Aëtius replies 'I would thou couldst, / And first, thyself' (4.4.144–5); in *Bonduca*, Poenius tells Petillius, moments before taking his own life: 'Farewell, captain! / Be a good man and fight well, be obedient, / Command thyself, and then thy men' (4.3.151–3); in *The False One*, Scaeva reproaches Caesar for his instantaneous attraction to Cleopatra by reminding him that an emperor is 'A man that first should rule himself, then others' (2.3.180).[9]

That the central event of the play is Valentinian's rape of Lucina – 'The sacrilegious razing of this temple' (3.1.39), which echoes the rape of Lucrece by Sextus Tarquin – cannot but emphasize the depravity, the wickedness, and the brutality that now permeate imperial Rome: as Margarita tells the Duke in *Rule a Wife and Have a Wife* (1624), "Tis sacrilege to violate a wedlock'.[10] Given that Lucina's 'outstanding chastity and incorruptibility … make her a figurehead for the ideal "empire", even to those who do not respect virtue as such', the play frames the tyrant's invasion of the woman's body, as Sandra Clark suggests, in terms of a 'violation of the family as well as of the individual' and makes it 'emblematically stand for his pollution of the state'.[11] That in the age of the Empire one needs to be wary at every turn of the danger of pollution, poisoning, and infection is an idea that does emerge repeatedly in the play: as Marina Hila notices, *Valentinian* frames political vice as 'palpable and contagious, like disease. The bawds are diseased (1.2.141); the emperor is a poison to the empire (3.1.45); Pontius's disloyalty could set a bad example and spread itself like a poison through the army (2.3.43–4).'[12] As Phidias tells Aretus upon Aëtius' corpse:

> He that would live now
> Must, like the toad, feed only on corruptions
> And grow with those to greatness. Honest virtue
> And the true Roman honour, faith, and valour,
> That have been all the riches of the empire,
> Now like the fearful tokens of the plague
> Are mere forerunners of their ends that owe 'em. (4.4.281–7)

The Romans who still survive are as slimy and potentially poisonous as toads, while the ancient Roman values are now construed as symptoms of the plague, visibly marking those few who carry them as dead people walking.

The savagery and amorality slowly stifling the Roman state are similarly – though less luridly – perceptible in *The Prophetess*. Not only did Aper, 'as he bore him company, / Most privately and cunningly' kill Numerian (1.1.26–7), he even had family ties to the dead emperor, as the play makes clear in the opening scene, in which Carinus explains that 'My brother [Numerian] honoured him [i.e. Aper]: / Made him, first, captain of his guard, his next friend; / Then, to my mother (to assure him nearer) / He made him husband' (1.1.52–5). This state of things inevitably frames Aper's crime as all the more treacherous in its being not just the murder of the head of state (which would be chilling in itself to an early modern audience), but, on top of that, the killing of a relative – albeit an in-law. Indeed, while the play manifestly insists on the name Aper (meaning 'boar' in Latin) in connection with the prophecy Delphia had made to Diocles several years earlier – '*Imperator eris Romae cum Aprum grandem interfeceris*' ('You will be Rome's Emperor after you kill the big boar', *Prophetess*, 1.2.33) – as shall be discussed in Chapter 4, Aper's name seems at the same time to be deployed more covertly as a way to foreground the character's bestiality and inhumanity. And while a new emperor is appointed as soon as Numerian's death is divulged and publicly avenged, it is also true that Diocletian in fact obtains the imperial mantle as a reward for answering a proscription call and taking revenge for Numerian by killing Aper – soon after murdering Camurius in cold blood too – through what amounts to a summary execution (and not even by prevailing in man-to-man combat). By doing so, Diocles somehow comes across as a sort of bounty hunter ahead of his time, despite his own solemn claim that 'This is an act of justice, and no murder' (2.2.102) after killing Camurius.

This not only makes Carinus' claim that ''Tis virtue, and not birth, that makes us noble. / Great actions speak great minds, and such should govern, / And you are graced with both' (2.3.98–100) ring considerably hollow, insofar as Diocles' execution of Aper does not really come across as a noble feat; more disquietingly, it also signals an all-out decrease in the currency and prominence of the ideals of honour and *virtus* in Rome, hand in hand with a more generalized feeling that violence is now gaining the upper hand. The times recalled by Don Henrique in *The Spanish Curate* (1622, with Massinger) now look incredibly far away:

> Happy the Roman state, where it was lawful,
> If our own sons were vicious, to choose one
> Out of a virtuous stock, though of poor parents,
> And make him noble.[13]

Diocles has indeed been chosen as the new emperor despite his 'being the son of a tanner', that is, 'a man most miserable, / Of no rank, nor no badge of honour on him, / Bred low and poor, no eye of favour shining' (1.3.20, 1.2.17–19), but not so much because of his merits as for his deftness in unhesitatingly killing Aper. Savagery, not virtue, has been rewarded, and even though Diocletian will turn out not to be vicious at all – despite the possibilities that the historical accounts did offer in relation to his atrocious persecutions of the Christians, as will be further discussed in Chapter 4 – the political mechanisms and workings of the Roman Empire stand out as discouragingly flawed, while the ideal touchstones of Roman honour and *virtus* appear increasingly distant.

Such a distance is also evident in *Bonduca*, though in this case at a significant remove from the Roman court, which was, at any rate – as the majority of the audience would probably have known – then ruled by

Nero, aptly recalled in *The Custom of the Country* as 'Smeared o'er with blood'.[14] The depiction of the Romans in *Bonduca* has been subjected to considerable critical scrutiny. As the play unfolds, argues Andrew Hickman, the Romans turn out to be 'consistently but unobtrusively guilty of the dishonorable conduct for which Caratach reprimands his own side' in the opening scene of the play.[15] Here, Caratach firmly criticizes Bonduca's scornful treatment of 'These Roman girls' (1.1.11) – since such upbraidings cannot but render their victory worthless, as there can be no honour for the Britons in beating girls (1.1.34–8) – and counters the contrast between Roman pusillanimity and the Britons' bravery put forward by Bonduca with an account of Roman courage and the Britons' fearfulness (1.1.56–124), which 'suggests that the two sides rank equally'.[16]

Fletcher then sets up a telling contraposition between Caratach's generous feeding and release of the famished Romans captured by Bonduca, her daughters, and Nennius in Act 2, scene 3, on the one hand, and the vicious Roman strategy of starving the British fugitives Caratach and his young nephew Hengo in Act 5, scene 1, on the other. Caratach blames and sermonizes at Nennius and Bonduca's daughters at length for having dishonourably tried to take advantage of the captured Romans' hunger (2.3.42–50) and later even prevents Bonduca's daughters from deceiving the enemy through a ruse that he regards as vile and duplicitous (3.5.53–86), namely a fake love letter from Bonvica that lures the Roman officers Junius, Curius, Decius, and their soldiers into a trap. In both cases, Caratach sets the prisoners free because he wants to win honourably (2.3.43–5; 3.5.63–9), and he seems unable to stomach the idea that the other Britons are fighting, in Ronald J. Boling's phrasing, 'according to the necessary dictates of guerrilla resistance'; in other words, while Caratach punctiliously follows the rules of his idealized Rome, the Romans clearly do not.[17] In this sense, Caratach might strike one as a more extreme example of the problem that Aufidius famously identifies in *Coriolanus* – 'I would I were a Roman, for I cannot, / Being a Volsce, be that I am' (1.10.4–5) – though with a much more idealistic and blinkered notion of Roman *virtus*.

When, after the battle, it is the Britons who are starving, the Romans use their enemies' hunger to their own advantage: the enticement of food brings Hengo down from the steep rock on which they had been hiding, and the Roman Judas kills the boy with an arrow – which is particularly ironic, given that Caratach had earlier forbidden Bonduca's daughter the use of that very weapon against the Roman prisoners (3.5.81–2). General Suetonius' words of encouragement to his troops – 'We have swords and are the sons of ancient Romans, / Heirs to their endless valours: fight and conquer!' (3.2.80–1) – come across as empty and utterly inadequate either to describe or offset the actual demeanour of the Romans. As Hickman helpfully summarizes,

> Despite their protestations of honor, the Romans seek military advantage ruthlessly ... Caratach saves the Roman prisoners from harm and torture, and he shows hospitality; in contrast Junius announces that he has tortured, off-stage and relatively unnoticed, the fellow sent by Bonvica to guide the Romans (3.2.40). Junius' action smacks of policy and reveals his awareness of the harshness of war; Caratach's good manners are foolhardy. Caratach flamboyantly frees prisoners, whereas it is implied that the Romans take none alive.[18]

Consequently, while the Romans never refrain from opportunistic conduct to achieve devious victory and implicitly condone Judas' duplicitous murder of Hengo by taking 'full advantage of Caratach's vulnerability in the wake of his nephew's death', as Claire Jowitt observes, the Britons are instead militarily 'hampered by Caratach's strident principle of honor, which, although admirable, proves disadvantageous in practice', as Hickman contends. This ideal is ultimately revealed to be a delusion, notwithstanding Caratach's exhibition of a stronger Roman *virtus* than that of the Romans themselves by dint of his being more self-disciplined and self-controlled.[19]

Aside from being unappealingly opportunistic and devious, however, the Romans in *Bonduca* are even more explicitly framed as vicious in two additional ways. First, the play makes clear that the Romans have previously raped Bonduca's virgin daughters, thereby impressing on them an indelible stain and a severe psychological trauma from which they can never completely recover. In order to avoid experiencing this again should the Romans capture them alive, they rather decide to commit suicide, as shall be discussed in further detail in Chapter 4. What is more, the images the Romans use for Bonduca's daughters as damaged goods are especially violent and nasty: for instance, Petillius describes the younger daughter as 'cracked in the ring' (1.2.271), an image derived from coinage that also recurs in *The Captain* (1609–12, with Beaumont), in which Jacomo mentions to Fabrizio the possibility of marriage to a woman 'After she's cracked i'th' ring', and in *The Humorous Lieutenant*, in which King Antigonus refers to Celia as a 'cracked coin' (3.1.17).[20] As Bernard Joseph Nolan observes, 'There was a ring a short way inside the outer edge of a coin, and any crack which reached from the outer edge beyond this inner ring rendered the coin useless.'[21] Given that the ring was also a metaphor for the hymen, the image deployed by Petillius foregrounds Bonduca's daughter's perceived lack of worth in the social or marriage market, while the casualness with which Petillius resorts to such a violent image – 'cracked' evoking a break, a fracture in something that was previously intact – gives the impression that brutality such as this is the order of the day for the Roman soldiers.

Second, during Bonduca's last stand in her fort, the audience sees Suetonius order his soldiers to 'go charge the breach' (4.4.78) that the Romans have managed to open and that Nennius and the other Britons reportedly defend till the last gasp. After the battle has ended, Decius observes that "Tis won, sir, and the Britons / All put to th' sword' (4.4.154–5). His concise report significantly underplays the tragic ending of the Britons, all the more so given that Suetonius' immediately ensuing speech completely ignores Decius' information – 'Give her fair funeral. / She was truly noble, and a queen' (4.4.155–6). Nevertheless, such a merciless massacre would have been familiar to any playgoers conversant with either British or Roman history. Holinshed recounts that the massacre was perpetrated with unwonted brutality,

> For the straits, being stopped with the charets, stayed the flight of the Britons so as they could not easily escape; and the Romans were so set on revenge that they spared neither man nor woman, so that many were slain in the battle, many amongst the charets, and a great number at the wood's side (which way they made their flight) and many were taken prisoners.[22]

Tacitus similarly reports that 'the soldiers spared not from killing so much as the women, and their horses and beasts thrust through increased the heap of bodies'.[23]

As Bonduca cries out to the Romans, Rome is 'vicious' and 'Aspires the height of all impiety' (4.4.17–18); hence, it deserves none of the adoration it regularly receives. The Britons' perception of the bestial cruelty of the Romans is trenchantly encapsulated in the insults that Bonduca's daughters hurl at their prisoners before Caratach orders them to be released:

> *1 Daughter.*   Oh, how I'll trample on your hearts, ye villains,
> Ambitious salt-itched slaves, Rome's master-sins!
> The mountain rams tupped your hot mothers.
> *2 Daughter.*   Dogs,
> To whose brave founders a salt whore gave suck!
> (3.5.47–50)

Bonduca's daughters evoke the story of Rome's foundation according to which a she-wolf nursed the brothers Romulus and Remus until a herdsman found and raised them. The young women's retelling makes recourse to misogynist invective by attempting to transfer their own stained reputation as whores (because of their rape) to the Roman soldiers' mothers. The she-wolf becomes a bitch in heat ('salt whore') – as Clifford J. Ronan points out, 'the wolf ha[d] a reputation of hypersexuality' and *'lupus* meant not just "wolf" but also "prostitute"' – while the mothers of the Romans are accused of having had bestial intercourse with 'mountain rams' ('to tup' being the verb used to refer to the ram's copulation with the ewe), thus passing their own restless hankering after sexual satisfaction ('salt-itched') on to their children.[24] Such a violent attack on Rome's founders goes hand in hand with the resolution of the Persian King Cosroe's sister Cassana in *The Prophetess*: 'we'll leave to Rome / Her *native* cruelty' (4.6.14–15, my emphasis). In light of the fact that Cassana's treatment of Aurelia, Carinus' sister, in captivity is much more honourable than Aurelia's treatment of Cassana – Aurelia refusing all the Persian ambassadors' offers of ransom and telling them she would not even accept 'your King's own head, his crown upon it, / And all the low subjections of his people' (3.3.11–12) – the play also seems subtly to suggest that Persia might now be somehow a better place in which to live than Rome.

The notion that Rome had been born cruel, as it were, did have some currency in the early modern English imagination. It was connected to an anecdote recounted in Dionysius of Halicarnassus' *Roman Antiquities* and in Livy's *Roman History*, which offered an explanation for the Tarpeian Rock's having been renamed Capitoline Hill.[25] During the digging for the construction of a new temple for Jupiter, the workmen allegedly uncovered a man's severed head, still dripping blood. The Etruscan divines who were asked to provide an explanation of the omen (after the Roman ones had failed to do so) interpreted the portent to mean that Rome would become the head (*caput*) of all Italy. Therefore, the hill on which they had found the head was renamed Capitoline.[26]

Side by side with this interpretation, however, there coexisted another, to which Andrew Marvell would also famously allude in his *Horatian Ode upon Cromwell's Return from Ireland* (1650):

> So when they did design
> The Capitol's first line,
> A bleeding head, where they begun,
> Did fright the architects to run;
> And yet in that the state
> Foresaw its happy fate.[27]

Marvell resorts to a Roman precedent while commenting on Oliver Cromwell's ruthlessly effective Irish campaign of 1650. He sets up an analogy between the foundation of Rome and the foundation of the Commonwealth of England, Scotland, and Ireland as an auspicious omen for future successes on the battlefield. At the same time, however, Marvell also implicitly suggests that the foundations of Cromwell's republic rest upon the decapitated head of King Charles I, just as Rome's rested on that anonymous bleeding head, which cannot bode well for England. The finding of the severed head in Rome could therefore be construed as meaning that violence would lie forever at the foundation of Rome's glory, which would in turn be marked by the eternal recurrence of that same foundational violence.

Moreover, the history of Rome had begun with Romulus' bloody fratricide of Remus, which could also be seen as one of the ultimate causes of Rome's fall. For example, Sonnet 10 in Joachim du Bellay's *Antiquités de Rome* (Paris, 1558) – which was translated into English by Edmund Spenser as *The Ruins of Rome* in 1588 as part of his collection *Complaints* – depicts the Romans as eventually falling because they

> Amongst themselves with cruel fury striving,
> Mowed down themselves with slaughter merciless,
> Renewing in themselves that rage unkind,
> Which whilom did those earthborn brethren blind.[28]

As these lines testify, the potential to attribute to Rome an innate cruelty was readily available to the early modern mind, and Fletcher seems to have taken advantage of this possibility not only in *Bonduca* and *The Prophetess*, but also in *Valentinian* and *The False One*.

In *Valentinian*, Afranius apostrophizes 'froward Rome', 'that lov'st to breed / Sons for the killing hate of sons' (5.4.69, 70–1) in a never-ending chain of violence and blood, and Romulus is invoked as the 'father of our honour' (5.8.8), which is particularly disturbing and ominous, given that, on top of having killed his own twin brother, he had also been responsible for the rape of the Sabine women, as Lucina reminds Valentinian after having been sexually assaulted:

> The curses that I owe to enemies
> (Even those the Sabines sent, when Romulus,
> As thou hast me, ravished their noble maids),
> Made more, and heavier, light on thee. (3.2.87–90)

The founder of Rome is therefore also the ultimate origin of its evil, as implied in *The False One*, in which Septimius mentions Romulus' fratricide as part of a violent outburst aimed at criticizing the Romans' exploitative colonial attitude towards foreign populations:

> Rome, that from Romulus first took her name,
> Had her walls watered with a crimson shower
> Drained from a brother's heart. Nor was she raised
> To this prodigious height that overlooks
> Three full parts of the earth that pay her tribute
> But by enlarging of her narrow bounds
> By the sack of neighbour cities, ne'er made hers

Till they were cemented with the blood of those
That did possess 'em. (5.2.12–20)

According to Septimius, the desire to take hold of other peoples' possessions has been inscribed in the Roman people's genetic inheritance since the very foundation of the city, Romulus and Rome being linked etymologically as well as through their viciousness. Septimius also stresses the fact that Roman glory is built on gore and fratricide rather than nobility – blood being metaphorically equated to cement, the material for the actual construction of the city – and maintained through rapine and violence. In describing the walls of Rome as covered in fraternal blood, Septimius expresses an idea similarly set forth in the abovementioned *Antiquités de Rome*. Sonnet 24 blames Rome's fall on 'brothers' blood, the which at first was spilled / Upon your walls, that God might not endure / Upon the same to set foundation sure'.[29]

It is true that the turncoat Septimius, described as 'a revolted Roman villain' in the list of 'The persons represented in the play' in the Second Folio, is biased against Rome and that he is portrayed as a very despicable man. Septimius is indeed a greedy, bloodthirsty, and miserable knave, as well as probably 'the false one' of the title by his own admission (5.3.12–13). Nonetheless, his words chime with Acoreus' warning to Ptolemy that there are two main reasons why 'Rome ever raised her mighty armies: / First, for ambition; then, for wealth' (3.3.14–15) before the masque of Nilus and with his later comment to the King that 'I advised your majesty / Never to tempt a conquering guest nor add / A bait to catch a mind bent by his trade / To make the whole world his' (4.1.3–6). Septimius' words are also consonant with Achillas' report to Ptolemy that, 'since the masque, [Caesar] sent three of his captains, / Ambitious as himself, to view again / The glory of your wealth' (4.1.44–6), as well as with Caratach's description of the Roman colonial *modus operandi* in *Bonduca*:

> Those men, beside themselves, allow no neighbour;
> Those minds that, where the day is, claim inheritance,
> And, where the sun makes ripe the fruits, their harvest,
> And, where they march, but measure out more ground
> To add to Rome, and here i'th' bowels on us. (1.1.163–7)

For Caratach, Rome advances like an unstoppable juggernaut that seeks to take possession of everything it sees, touches, and treads upon. These ideas about Rome's rapacity are then confirmed by Scaeva himself in *The False One* immediately before the masque, when he prides in his memory that 'In Gaul and Germany we saw such visions / And stood not to admire 'em but possess 'em. / When they are ours, they are worth our admiration' (3.4.4–6). Hence – in light of Caratach's allegations in *Bonduca* – Pothinus' and Septimius' joined accusations in *The False One* (together with Acoreus' less heated but equally negative considerations) contribute to showing any Roman claims to foreign conquest in a bad light, all the more so judging from the play's foregrounding of Caesar's rapacious attraction to riches.

As it happens, the dazzling exhibition of 'the glory / And wealth of Egypt' (3.3.7–8) during what the captain of Ptolemy's guard Achillas labels a 'masque' (4.1.44) has such a powerful effect on Caesar that it momentarily eclipses his love for Cleopatra, which had been previously staged as sudden, passionate, and unrestrainable. Flabbergasted at the sight of the infinite Egyptian riches, Caesar proclaims himself ashamed for having embarked on a bloody civil conflict against Pompey when he could have easily taken hold of such staggering sums abroad. He cries out:

> I am ashamed I warred at home, my friends,
> When such wealth may be got abroad. What honour,
> Nay, everlasting glory had Rome purchased,
> Had she a *just cause* but to visit Egypt! (3.4.77–80, my emphasis)

Caesar's attraction to riches is depicted as so unwholesome that he has to leave the room abruptly after crying 'The wonder of this wealth so troubles me / I am not well. Goodnight' (3.4.100–1). Apart from the irony implied in the scene, there are two aspects that seem to cast a particularly negative light on the Romans' frame of mind.

First, it is possible that Fletcher and Massinger wanted to hint at the now controversial lines of Shakespeare's *Julius Caesar* – 'Know Caesar doth not wrong but with *just cause*, / Nor without cause will he be satisfied' – not as they appear in the 1623 Folio of *Mr. William Shakespeare's Comedies, Histories, & Tragedies*, but as are mockingly cited in Jonson's *Discoveries* (1641) and *The Staple of News* (1626), and as have been integrated into the text in the Oxford editions of Shakespeare's complete works since 1986.[30] As will be further discussed in Chapter 4, Fletcher and Massinger were avowedly aware that a play focusing on Caesar and Cleopatra would be expected to reckon with both *Julius Caesar* and *Antony and Cleopatra*. In this case, the two playwrights may have thought that such an allusion – oblique as it might have been – would hardly escape the minds of the most attentive playgoers, who would easily be able to identify the reference to the 'just cause' flaunted by Shakespeare's Caesar. Foregrounding the idea that all Caesar would have needed in order to plunder Egypt without restraint was to find – or, one might maliciously suggest, to invent – a 'just cause' (such as the one Shakespeare's Caesar maintains always to have on his side when 'doing wrong') would cast Fletcher and Massinger's Caesar's – and, by extension, Rome's – shamelessly predatory stance in quite a grim light.

Second, Caesar's exclamation has to be read in light of an earlier soliloquy, in which he showed no regrets for the massacres of foreign populations:

> I am dull and heavy, yet I cannot sleep.
> How happy was I in my lawful wars
> In Germany and Gaul and Britany,
> When every night with pleasure I set down
> What the day ministered! Then sleep came sweetly.
> But since I undertook this home division,
> This civil war, and passed the Rubicon,
> What have I done that speaks an ancient Roman,
> A good, great man? (2.3.29–37)

In the lines that immediately follow, Caesar goes on to vent his remorse over the carnage and destruction brought about by internecine strife but shows no regret for the destruction and pillage of foreign countries and populations: in fact, he considers them absolutely 'lawful'. This soliloquy is especially poignant, both in that, as David Farley-Hills remarks, Fletcher generally avoids 'the soul-revealing soliloquy of Shakesperean [sic] tragedy in preferring the theatrical "aside"' and insofar as Fletcher and Massinger's Caesar ends up evoking again, by way of contrast, Shakespeare's, who is denied even the shortest soliloquy or the least significant aside.[31] Moreover, combined with Caesar's words during the Egyptian masque, this monologue decisively contributes to shedding further negative light on the Romans' rapacious and ruthless expansionism. Accordingly, Caesar seems to deserve the label of 'armèd thief' (4.1.26) that Pothinus attributes to him while recounting the moment when he saw 'how falcon-like [Caesar's eye] tow'red and flew / Upon the wealthy quarry, how round it marked it' (4.1.10–11) during the masque, and his behaviour cannot but reflect bleakly on the Romans as a whole.

PROVING MALE *VIRTUS* ON THE BATTLEFIELD

Yet despite all his negative traits, *The False One*'s Caesar is dramatized as eventually able to overcome his inability to restrain himself from overindulging in the allure of sexual pleasure and riches. The completion of his process of temptation, fall, and regeneration occurs on the battlefield, where Caesar finally redeems himself and his Roman *virtus*. The full recovery of his masculinity and honour bears down on the Egyptians like a bolt from the blue. In Achillas' account of the decisive battle, Caesar's martial zeal is hailed as superior to that of Mars: Caesar has finally retrieved 'his dreadful looks' (5.4.155) and taken on quasi-supernatural features (5.4.148–53). He is once again like a god in his destructive splendour, as vividly epitomized by his swim towards Pharos:

> in one hand
> Holding a scroll he had above the waves
> And in the other grasping fast his sword
> As it had been a trident forged by Vulcan
> To calm the raging ocean, he made a way
> As if he had been Neptune. (5.4.157–62)

This anecdote is found with slight variations in Plutarch, Suetonius, and Cassius Dio.[32] They all relate that Caesar managed to swim while keeping a parchment scroll out of the water in order not to get it wet, but no one mentions the sword. The trenchant image of Caesar keeping the scroll above the waves while hitting them with his sword – likened to Neptune's trident to underscore the god-like connotations of his power – testifies to the completion of his process of regeneration, also in sharp contrast to the depiction of Caesar offered in Shakespeare's play, in which the titular character is even said to have had to be saved from drowning by Cassius (*Julius Caesar*, 1.2.102–17).

Diocletian experiences a similar fate in *The Prophetess*. After he has misguidedly pursued Aurelia's love instead of marrying Drusilla as he had promised to Delphia, the prophetess punishes Diocletian by helping the Persians kidnap Aurelia, Carinus, and Maximian. This is the moment at which Diocletian realizes that the Roman Empire has been wounded in its honour, glory, and dignity because of his 'breach of faith / To Delphia and Drusilla' (4.2.61–2) and decides to fight as bravely as possible against the 'immortal squadrons' (4.4.48) of the Persian army in order to 'redeem my friends / And with my friends mine honour; at least fall like myself, / A soldier' (4.2.43–5), finally leading the Roman army to a splendid victory. Thus, it is only on the battlefield that Diocletian appears 'In his full lustre' (4.1.7), compared as he is to the god of war himself in Niger's report of the battle:

> The Persians shrink; the passage is laid open;
> Great Diocletian, like a second Mars,
> His strong arm governed by the fierce Bellona,
> Performs more than a man. His shield, struck full
> Of Persian darts, which now are his defence
> Against the enemies' swords, still leads the way. (4.5.21–6)

The battlefield, Fletcher appears to suggest in these two plays, seems to be the very last arena left to the Romans successfully to prove their *virtus*. On the battlefield, victorious generals can even be hailed as gods. And even though, because of its ambiguous judgement on the Romans' defeat of the Britons discussed above, *Bonduca* only partly fits this pattern, Poenius' reaction to his own poor decision not to appear for the decisive encounter against the Britons further strengthens the point.

Though portrayed by Caratach to his fellow Britons in the opening scene of *Bonduca* as valiant, puissant, and honourable (1.1.98–102, 115–25), Poenius refuses to comply with Suetonius' muster to arms both because he regards the battle as foolishly dangerous, in that he knows that the Romans will be outnumbered (2.1.34–56), and – much less honourably – because he cannot stand the idea of taking orders from Suetonius, who is less experienced than him (2.1.1–20, 110–15). However, in the wake of the Roman victory, Poenius realizes his own 'foul' and 'black' error (4.3.73), which makes it impossible for him to live under the weight of shame:

> I have lost mine honour, lost my name,
> Lost all that was my light. These are true Romans,
> And I a Briton coward, a base coward!
> Guide me where nothing is but desolation,
> That I may never more behold the face
> Of man, or mankind know me. Oh, blind fortune,
> Hast thou abused me thus? (3.5.162–9)

Not only is he a Roman man who has opted out of battle; the idea of having lost such an opportunity to gain glory on the battlefield is even more intolerable because by doing so he has prevented his army from achieving distinction in war, rather than have his valour reflect on his soldiers: 'I have robbed ye of your virtues' (4.3.21), he cries out. He is so ashamed that he even throws himself on the ground after lamenting that his honour 'Is gone for ever, ever, ever' (4.3.12), the anguished repetition of the adverb meant to emphasize his dejected state. He anticipates his destiny as being

> left to scornful tales and laughters,
> To hootings at, pointing with fingers: 'That's he,
> That's the brave gentleman forsook the battle,
> The most wise Poenius, the disputing coward.' (4.3.13–16)

Unable to tolerate the idea that he will become the laughing stock of Rome and will have to renounce forever the possibility of viewing the reflection of his *virtus* as a Roman soldier in his peers' gaze because he has indulged in the false wisdom of idle disputations regarding the most expedient course of action rather than actually fighting on the battlefield, Poenius eventually commits suicide.

The fact that *Bonduca* dwells at such length on Poenius' story and protracted outburst of despair is all the more significant, insofar as the sources only make passing mention of him. Holinshed, following Tacitus very closely, only reports that

> Poenius Posthumus, master of the camp of the second legion, understanding the prosperous success of the other Roman captains, because he had defrauded his legion of the like glory and had refused to obey the commandments of the general, contrary to the use of war, slew himself.[33]

The rest is Fletcher's invention. Such a focus on the importance of victory in battle for the upholding of the Romans' identities clearly shows that military honour is an absolutely crucial ingredient of any proper Roman (male) identity in Fletcher's vision of Rome, as exemplified positively by Caesar and Diocletian, who only in war manage to rectify their previous errors, enact *virtus*, and start a new personal path in their lives, and negatively by Poenius, whose self is completely crushed, shattered, and dissolved as a result of his short-sighted refusal to fight.

The desirability of martial glory also seems to be implied by the recurrence across the canon (with a few variations) of what Estefania describes in *Rule a Wife and Have a Wife* as an 'old Roman axiom: / The more the danger, still the more the honour' (4.1.42–3).[34] This maxim is also mentioned in *The Mad Lover* when the Page tells the Fool: '*Tanto melior*, / For so much more the danger, the more honour' (1.1.275). Here, the comic context does not detract from the original meaning of the *sententia*, which comes right after a Latin tag, thus making its association with *Romanitas* immediately perceptible. The dictum later reappears in *Women Pleased* (1619–23) – 'Where the most danger is, there's the most honour' – and, in a slightly different form, in *The Island Princess*: as Pinheiro claims, 'Danger is a soldier's honour'.[35] In *The Double Marriage*, a play that – as shall be demonstrated in Chapter 3 – is exceedingly concerned with Roman values and paradigms, Villio says 'The more danger, / Still the more honour'.[36] *Bonduca* also presents a variation on the theme when Decius exclaims while preparing for battle, 'More wounds, more honour' (3.5.122), an utterance that seems to conflate the *sententia* with the importance attached to scars and the physical signs of battle on a soldier's body in the Roman military ethos famously dramatized in *Coriolanus*. As Christopher Hicklin points out, while R. W. Bond 'suggests as the source a line from Terence's *Heautontimorumenos* ... 2.3.73, "No great and memorable enterprise can be done without danger"', the 'sentiment goes back at least to Thucydides's first Periclean oration: "Remember too that for states and individuals alike the greatest dangers give rise to the greatest glory"'.[37] Embracing danger (and wounds) without hesitation thus seems to rank among the staples of Romanness according to Fletcher. As Leandro would have it in *The Spanish Curate*, 'Difficilia pulchra' (2.1.45, 'Difficult enterprises are beautiful').

Consequently, if in Fletcher's Rome testing oneself on the battlefield is so vital for the maintenance of one's (male) identity, the fact that Valentinian has completely deprived the Roman soldiers of any possibility of asserting their masculinity and enacting their *virtus* through martial exploits has to be viewed as all the more reprehensible. As Vimala C. Pasupathi aptly comments, '*Valentinian* is a soldier's tragedy' that 'seems to mourn ... the moral collapse of an entire profession'.[38] The emperor is utterly indifferent to war and military matters. As Allman points out, '[s]eduction is the only war in which that Prince excels; he is general and master strategist of his army of bawds and panders'; Lucina ironically congratulates him on his rape by telling him: 'Call in your lady bawds and gilded panders / And let them triumph too, and sing to Caesar, / "Lucina's fall'n, the chaste Lucina's conquered"' (3.1.70–2). The only way in which Valentinian might be able to lead a triumphal procession would be to rejoice publicly for having raped a chaste wife, who can be his only conquest: Valentinian is exclusively interested in sex, not war. His bawds and panders – the play makes a point of stressing – are now far more revered than soldiers, who are regarded as 'Fencers and beaten fools' (1.3.140); as Maximus laments, none 'are called / And chosen to the steering of the empire / But bawds and singing-girls' (1.3.6–8).[39] As Pontius illustrates to Aëtius, 'when the slave drinks wine, we durst be thirsty' (2.3.68). The army lies so wretchedly neglected and despised, adds Pontius, that

> trees and roots
> [Are] our best paymasters, the charity
> Of longing women that [have] bought our bodies,
> Our beds, fires, tailors, nurses. (2.3.69–72)

The now miserable soldiers have been forced to prostitute themselves to survive. They do not want money; all they ask is 'employment' and a way to live honourably (2.3.91, 92), because inaction is slowly wearing them down. As Aëtius relates to the emperor, the soldiers 'cry for enemies' and wish they could display their prowess away from Rome, where now their 'weapons / And bodies that were made for shining brass / Are both unedged and old with ease and women' (1.3.182–4). They long to 'fight like Romans' (1.3.190) against such valiant foes as the Germans, the Spaniards, the French, or the Parthians, but are now obliged to content themselves with dolefully surveying their old scars and recalling their former glory. They bewail Valentinian's effeminacy and lechery, as well as the ease and luxury of their own life in the city, which weakens them and makes them live in dishonour. They crave an emperor who might revive an aggressive expansionist policy such as those pursued by Julius Caesar or Germanicus (1.3.195–6); lamentably, however, Valentinian is miserably following in the wantonly decadent line of Tiberius, Caligula, and Nero (1.3.202–5), three of the most licentious and sanguinary tyrants in the history of the Roman Empire. As Aëtius relates to Valentinian himself, the soldiers even maintain 'that of late time, like Nero, / And with the same forgetfulness of glory, / You have got a vein of fiddling' (1.3.145–7). By subtly recalling the anecdote of Nero's merrily playing his instrument while watching Rome burn to the ground, the play heaps a further instance of reprehensible behaviour on Valentinian and ominously comments on the present and the future of Rome.

To be sure, as Charles L. Squier observes, 'the deplorable softness of peace and the neglect of the professional soldier in peacetime' is 'one of Fletcher's recurrent themes'.[40] This motif informs – with a number of variations – such plays as, for example, *A King and No King*, *The Captain*, *The Mad Lover*, *Thierry and Theodoret*, *The Loyal Subject*, and *Sir John Van Olden Barnavelt*, plays in which, as Pasupathi points out, 'Fletcher ultimately locates the figures' tragic condition in their status as ill-used potential or overused labour'.[41] Yet even though this theme is not exclusive to Fletcher's Roman plays, it does seem to acquire added relevance and poignancy when introduced in Fletcher's Roman world by virtue of the pre-eminent value the playwright openly bestows on military action and martial ethos in his Rome, which seems to be especially embodied by such generals as Caesar and Diocletian. In this sense, Valentinian also seems to be contrasted with Caesar, inasmuch as Caesar's veterans too criticize their leader's conduct in terms similar to those used by Valentinian's unemployed soldiers:

> *1 Soldier.* The pleasure Caesar sleeps in makes us miserable.
> We are forgot, our maims and dangers laughed at;
> He banquets, and we beg.
> *2 Soldier.*   He was not wont
> To let poor soldiers that have spent their fortunes,
> Their blood and limbs walk up and down like
> vagabonds. (*False One*, 3.2.159–63)

Like Valentinian, Caesar is attacked for neglecting his martial duties and his soldiers while wallowing in the pleasures that Cleopatra's arms offer him. The difference, however, is that these comments are not as protracted as those in *Valentinian* and that Caesar eventually emerges from his military neglect and recovers his own martial zeal, which Valentinian seems hardly ever to have possessed. In addition, the comments on Caesar's infatuation by Antony, Dolabella, and Scaeva at the outset of the same scene (3.2.1–50), while never forgetting the political and military implications of Caesar's neglect of the affairs of state, tend to be more humorous and ironic, and they completely lack the feeling of desperation conveyed by the words of Aëtius and Pontius in *Valentinian* – Antony even partially justifying Caesar on the grounds of Cleopatra's undeniably irresistible allure.

THE INADEQUACY OF THE POLITICAL LEADERS

Yet if Fletcher's Rome does have excellent *military* leaders galore (Suetonius in *Bonduca* and Aëtius in *Valentinian* are also winning generals), it simultaneously appears badly in need of proper *political* leaders. In dramatizing this contrast, Fletcher may have been making a general point about the English political system – though obliquely so. What might be the proper relationship between a political caste and a military one? One reason why some early modern commentators were keen on the Goths was that they were supposed to have appointed a *dux bellorum* who led in times of war and discreetly retired in times of peace, a mechanism similar to that of the *dictator* in early republican Rome, who was entrusted with the full authority of the state to deal with a military emergency but had to resign his office once he had accomplished his task, or at the expiration of six months. Shakespeare's history plays suggest that there used to be a lot of noblemen who could turn their hands to war when needed. Under the Tudors, however, that system atrophied. Indeed, the career of Robert Devereux, 2nd Earl of Essex, who ultimately proved to be unreliable as a general and whose parable ended with beheading for his attempted rebellion against the queen, might have suggested that England would now have a problem if the necessity of fighting should arise.

Writing under James, Fletcher may have grappled with an even more fraught situation, given the king's aspiration to terminate all hostilities with foreign powers and be hailed as *Rex pacificus*. James's pacifism was strikingly at odds with the bellicose image the English had of their own country: a foreign policy inspired by the motto *Beati pacifici* made the nation appear to their eye effeminate, weak, and more vulnerable to foreign attacks. As the years went by, James became less and less popular with those who wished to see a more active and aggressive exercise of England's power as a Protestant nation. Fletcher himself seems to have been unhappy with the king's passive attitude in matters of foreign policy, as can be gleamed from an extant document in his own hand, a letter to Elizabeth Stanley Hastings, Countess of Huntingdon, the wife of his patron Henry Hastings, fifth Earl of Huntingdon, whose country-based politics and 'pastoral, anticourt, Protestant [and] anti-Spanish' views Fletcher seems to have shared, as reflected in the attitude of some of his plays.[42] After disparaging knights, lords, and masques, Fletcher claims in the letter not to be interested 'whether it be true / We shall have wars with Spain' but then parenthetically comments: 'I would we might.'[43] The importance Fletcher seems to have placed on military engagement is reflected in the crucial role a martial ethos plays in his Roman world as a structuring feature of the identity of the nation and its soldiers, as well as in the potential of martial prowess to rehabilitate leaders who are not as effective politically as they are on the battlefield. This is the case with Caesar and Diocletian, as I shall discuss below. That the worst emperor Fletcher portrays is Valentinian, that is, the one who is not also a warrior, forcefully exhibits the extent to which aspects of military and political leadership were interrelated for Fletcher, and makes his treatment of the discrepancy between Roman models of those two types of leadership even more compelling.

While it is true that, as Finkelpearl observes regarding Fletcher and his collaborators' canon at large, 'We find no good kings, no virtuous courts in their work', the Roman imperial context provides Fletcher with the opportunity more consistently, more deeply, and more provocatively to delve into the general crisis of authority of an entire world.[44] Tellingly, the common people, who are an important presence in Shakespeare's Roman world, never appear in Fletcher's. Yet they do have a significant role elsewhere in his oeuvre, as for example in *Philaster* (1609–10, with Beaumont), in which, argues Judy H. Park, 'the popular uprising against the King's plans to execute Philaster ... suggests that in the world of the play the common good can be pursued by virtuous citizens regardless of inherited position', and in *Cupid's Revenge* (1606–11, with Beaumont), which, as Gordon McMullan argues, offers 'perhaps the most unnerving representation of political unrest in the early plays'.[45]

In the Roman Empire as depicted by Fletcher, however, there is no space for any significant movement coming from below. Even when modelling Diocles' speech in *The Prophetess* on Antony's funeral oration in *Julius Caesar* (as shall be discussed in Chapter 4), Fletcher has his character address a group of soldiers, not the populace, thus narrowing down the scope of the potential for political agency to emperors, generals, and soldiers. The worldview developed in Fletcher's Roman plays seems all the more grim, insofar as they do not propose any political alternatives, not even a fleeting glimpse of what scholars have labelled as a 'mixed monarchy' or 'monarchical republic', namely a system in which, in Andrew Hadfield's helpful description, 'a coterie of virtuous advisers and servants would always have the constitutional right to counsel the monarch, and so influence and control his or her actions within the limits of the law'.[46]

The only play that hints at anything like that is *The False One* with regard to the Egyptian court. However, as Edward Paleit argues, in that case the play seems at most to advocate a system keen 'on containing vices within a relatively stable, hierarchical political order assumed ... to rest on the order of nature'.[47] As a matter of fact, any potentially 'radical' arguments as the claim that 'kingship rests simply on an originary act of violence or the exercise of brute power' come from Pothinus – who sneeringly mentions 'the ignorant people' (5.2.26) only in passing – thus losing any positive value.[48] *The False One*, adds Paleit, does not advocate an alternative system of government either – not even implicitly – despite the clearly 'sympathetic response to the *Bellum Ciuile*'s treatment of the loss of republican *libertas*', as demonstrated by the fact that 'the most explicit denunciation of Caesar ... is assigned not to a Roman or even a loyal Egyptian, but the perfidious courtier P[oth]inus after his rebellion against his master's authority'.[49] By not offering any potential alternative, Fletcher manages sharply and painfully to focus on the fact that nobody seems completely fit to rule in these plays: none of the Roman political leaders are depicted as completely effective, admirable, or even able rulers, which leads to a pervasively seeping sense of disorientation in the characters and the audience. While the question is not directly touched upon in *Bonduca* – although the fact itself that the events of the play take place under the reign of Nero, as remarked above, is potentially terrifying – and whereas Valentinian is an obviously vicious tyrant, the cases of Caesar and Diocletian are, again, more nuanced but eventually seem to corroborate this impression.[50]

As mentioned above, Caesar needs to struggle at length with his own self-governing qualities before proving to be worthy of his role as the leader of Rome. Surrounded by the Egyptians and forced to suffer the scoffing of his subordinates, who mockingly ask him, 'Can you kiss away this conspiracy and set us free? / Or will the giant god of love fight for ye?' (*False One*, 4.2.171–2), Caesar heroically decides to 'run the hazard: fire the palace / And the rich magazines that neighbour it, / In which the wealth of Egypt is contained' (5.2.78–80), thereby seeking to create a diversion while he tries to open a breach to his 'conquering legions' (5.2.85). The Savonarola-like act of setting the palace afire with all its riches carries crucial symbolic value, the significance of which is further underscored by its deviation from the classical sources. Lucan vividly recounts that Caesar actually ordered incendiary projectiles to be fired on the Egyptian fleet in order to cause confusion among the enemy lines.[51] As mentioned in the previous chapter, Florus records that Caesar set the neighbouring buildings on fire too. Yet the decision to burn the palace itself is the authors' own invention, symbolizing Caesar's rejection of material riches and personal profit, and his decision to pursue honour and glory in their stead.[52]

Caesar's eventual realization of the responsibilities that result from his leading role would seem to frame him as an ultimately good ruler. That being said, one may plausibly argue, with John E. Curran, Jr, that Caesar's healing seems worryingly incomplete, in that he needs to destroy the Egyptian riches in order not to be tempted by them.[53] Moreover, his last words carry disturbingly tyrannical overtones, which may foreshadow his imminent downgrading of the Senate to a mere office rubber-stamping his decrees, as well as clearly positioning Egypt as a client state.[54] As he proudly tells Cleopatra,

> we'll for Rome, where Caesar
> Will show he can give kingdoms, for the Senate,
> Thy brother dead, shall willingly decree
> The crown of Egypt, that was his, to thee (5.4.205–8).

Here, Fletcher and Massinger perhaps hint at another sinister line from Shakespeare's Caesar – 'What is now amiss / That Caesar and *his* Senate must redress?' (*Julius Caesar*, 3.1.31–2, my emphasis) – in which Caesar seems to regard the Senate as his own property. Such a notion is indeed consistent with the words Fletcher and Massinger's Caesar pronounces before setting the palace afire, claiming that fortune would never allow the man '*Rome acknowledged / Her sovereign lord* to end ingloriously / A life admired by all' (*False One*, 5.2.74–6, my emphasis). *The False One* therefore first calls into question Caesar's skills as a ruler by showing his failure to keep his most instinctual urges, impulses, and drives at bay, and then ominously hints at a potential tyrannical twist that would have crippling repercussions for Rome and Caesar himself (as the audience would be aware of the fate awaiting him some time after his return to Rome, as dramatized by Shakespeare). Besides, Caesar needs the help of a woman, Cleopatra, in order to recover his glorious self, which in an early modern context does not necessarily reflect favourably on him.

Diocletian too ultimately succeeds thanks to a woman, Delphia, whose help proves to be even more significant than Cleopatra's to Caesar. The prophetess manoeuvres Diocletian as some kind of puppet and regularly overpowers him, at least until he comes to the decision to marry Drusilla and retire to Lombardy; before the battle against the Persians, he even asks her to be 'The pilot to the bark of my good fortunes / And once more steer my actions to the port / Of glorious honour' (4.2.90–2). The pervasiveness of Delphia's influence on Diocletian's decisions and actions makes him come across as excessively dependent on external forces and intervention – be they Delphia's or fate's. His *Weltanschauung* seems to be moulded and determined at all times by what happens just outside him; as Curran points out, he exhibits a certain 'short-sightedness and smallness of vision. Always stuck in the moment, he reacts only to immediate superficies, at times at the expense of principle, dignity, and sincerity.'[55] As a matter of fact, upon donning the imperial robes, Diocletian proves unable to resist the seductiveness of courtly ambition as embodied by Aurelia, as shall be further discussed in Chapter 4. By chasing Aurelia and neglecting Drusilla, Diocletian initially fails to keep his promise to Delphia, thus forgetting his debt of gratitude, which does not bode well as to his fitness as a ruler. By starting to counter his initiatives and enabling the Persians to kidnap Aurelia, Maximian, and Carinus, as remarked above, Delphia gradually makes Diocletian realize that he cannot ignore her contribution and eventually leads him to understand that the best course of action for him is to abandon power in order to 'find content' (4.6.91) in 'a most private grange / In Lombardy' (5.1.9–10), where in the end he 'securely tastes / The certain pleasures of a private life' (5.1.13–14).

While this prevailing of the simple life in the countryside over the artificial life of the court could be seen as a positive choice for Diocletian as an individual, it simultaneously indicates that he is unable to withstand either Delphia's sway (which significantly limits his freedom of action) or the weight of power and the corrupting influence of ambition. This remains true despite his military prowess, his capacity to keep his appetites under check unlike Caesar and Valentinian, his display of *clementia* to Cosroe, Cassana, and the Persians, and his 'conciliatory temper that exalts him above everyone else', of which the play offers ample evidence.[56] Apparently, Diocletian can only live an uncorrupted life by removing himself from Rome and making himself completely irrelevant in the political arena, which actually needs to be interpreted as disheartening news for the Romans. Furthermore, the fact that after his retirement the tension rapidly increases between the now co-emperors Carinus and Maximian, who emerge as unattractively petty in their claims and mean fights in Act 5, scene 2, cannot but make the audience wonder whether Diocletian has in fact made the best decision in the interest of the Roman Empire.

THE DISTANCE OF THE GODS

The inevitable sense of disorientation that the Roman plays in the Fletcher canon exude owing to this lack of dependable leaders – Valentinian, Caesar, and Diocletian all being flawed, though to different extents and in different ways – is compounded by what amounts to a generalized detachment of and from the gods, who no longer seem to preside over human events. True, this consideration is broadly applicable to the entire Fletcher dramatic canon, which does not emerge as much concerned with emphasizing the metaphysical or the cosmic. As Marco Mincoff points out, in Fletcher's plays, any real

> sense of mystery is lacking. He has no ghosts except in *The Triumph of Death*. He has a rather ironical apotheosis in ... *The Mad Lover*, and an omen or two in *Valentinian*. But he is on the whole honest in eschewing the outer signs of the supernatural ... He has, like Shakespeare, allusions to heaven and providence that might provide the same background sense of mystery, but somehow do not.[57]

Clifford Leech adds that 'there may be a reference to destiny or the gods, but these references are never vitally felt', while H. J. Makkink also notes that several Fletcherian characters do 'say their prayers regularly, but we find nowhere that their prayers lend them strength to bear whatever fate may send them'.[58] When a (Greek) god does appear on stage and take action in the Fletcher canon, it proves to be a vindictive and pernicious force. The action of *Cupid's Revenge* is set in motion by King Leontius' order for the suppression of the cult of the eponymous god in Lycia at the request of his daughter Hidaspes, to whom the king has promised to grant any wish on her birthday. The god's statues are therefore taken down, and his temples dismantled. As a result, Cupid spectacularly descends to earth and appears on stage, chorus-like, to vow revenge. Nothing will change his mind: 'nor shall the prayers / Nor sweet smokes on my altars hold my hand / Till I have left this a most wretched land'.[59] He will reappear a little later to manifest again his intention 'To sow a world of helpless misery / In this unhappy kingdom' (2.1.3–4). In the end, his revenge brings about the death of all three members of the royal family, together with four other people associated with them.

With the negative exception of this inexorably vengeful Cupid, the plays in the Fletcher canon would not seem to suggest that a being above has anything at all to do with their denouement, which is all the more surprising given that Fletcher was the son of a bishop and had attended such a religiously oriented institution as the grammar school of the cathedral church in Peterborough. This attitude also appears oddly at loggerheads with the devotional thrust of such a poem as 'Against Astrologers' – as Misha Teramura has renamed the poem traditionally known as 'Upon an Honest Man's Fortune' – which is explicit in expressing a strong belief in 'God's unwavering attention to humanity' and is even 'strongly redolent of early modern sermons'.[60]

Though habitual in Fletcher's dramatic output, however, such a faint presence of the gods appears especially on display when translated to a Roman context and can be hardly explained away as 'rather understandable', in Pavel Drabek's words, 'given the ideological context in which the plays came to existence, and the attention the censors paid to the plays of the King's Men'.[61] Whenever the gods are called upon in desperate situations, they provide no significant signs of any interest in human affairs. Moreover, this is true not merely for the Roman deities, but also for the others, as exhibited in the unresponsiveness of the 'powerful gods of Britain' in *Bonduca* (3.1.1). Bonduca, her daughters, and Nennius make a fifty-line appeal for the intervention of the thunder god Tiranes in order to avenge their 'Insulting wrongs and ravishments of women' (3.1.28) and defeat the Romans, but Bonduca dejectedly finds out that 'The gods are deaf and drowsy. No happy flame / Rises to raise our thoughts' (3.1.38). Smoke begins to appear only when Bonvica starts more intensely to bewail the suffering caused to her and her sister by the Romans' rape and asks for vengeance. Yet the value of this response is called into question by Caratach, who comments that 'no flame rises' and encourages the petitioners to

> Cease your fretful prayers,
> Your whinings and your tame petitions.
> The gods love courage armed with confidence
> And prayers fit to pull them down; weak tears
> And troubled hearts, the dull twins of cold spirits,
> They sit and smile at. (3.1.53–8)

Caratach then addresses the goddess of victory Andate himself by requesting justice and impartiality rather than favour, which Andate seems to approve – '*A flame arises*' (3.1.75SD) – even though her sign again rapidly 'flames out' (3.1.76), thus breeding additional uncertainties as to the meaning of the gods' response. Accordingly, Caratach can only assert that the destiny of the battle 'hangs in our resolution' (3.1.79) and that 'Our valours are our best gods' (3.1.82). Though reflecting admirably on Caratach's fortitude and presence of mind, these utterances also sharply convey a painful feeling of abandonment by the gods.

The sense of being left to one's destiny is particularly penetrating in the case of Bonduca's daughters, who have been raped by the Romans before the beginning of the play: 'can ye be gods, / And these sins smothered?' (3.1.51–2), Bonvica incredulously asks. That there is no god willing to avenge rape unites Bonduca's daughters with *Valentinian*'s Lucina, who bitterly has to realize that there is no justice in store for her. The emperor not only tells her that 'Justice shall never hear ye: I am justice' (3.1.34), he even speciously deploys the early modern doctrine of the divine right of kings to justify his crime: 'Nor can the gods be angry at this action, / For as they make me most, they mean me happiest, / Which I had never been without this pleasure' (3.1.129–31). As a result, Lucina ends up grimly denying the very existence of the gods: 'I see there is no god but power' (3.1.145).

Ironically, that the gods play no active part in Fletcher's Roman world is also brought into stark relief in Valentinian's own ranting during his deathbed torments. The gods are not listening to his prayers, nor watching the 'powerful sacrifice' (5.2.58) he asks Eudoxa to offer them; no divine intervention is coming to rescue him from his atrocious sufferings. Moments before dying he accuses the gods:

> I do despise ye all: ye have no mercy,
> And, wanting that, ye are no gods. Your parol
> Is only preached abroad to make fools fearful
> And women made of awe believe your heaven. (5.2.122–5)

In his final speech, the divinely appointed emperor, as Leech comments, 'veers between contempt for the gods' cruelty, doubt of their existence, and begging them for a reprieve'.[62] Although his words are those of a depraved villain on his deathbed, they still resonate with the larger notion that the individual is left alone on this earth, which seems to be another unifying trait of Fletcher's Roman world. As a matter of fact, the idea that the gods 'are asleep' and that 'They are dreams / Religious fools shake at' is also explored in *The False One* (5.4.113, 118–19) by Pothinus. True, after his plans are thwarted, he acknowledges the existence of the gods (5.4.171–4), but this is done rather perfunctorily, inasmuch as there is no suggestion in the play that the gods have anything to do with Caesar's victory and the Egyptians' defeat. Besides, Caesar's use of the verb 'blaspheme' (2.3.189) and of the noun 'blasphemy' (5.1.22) to refer to insults against Cleopatra contributes to demoting the role of religion in the play's world. Even more significantly, *The False One* features the priest of Isis, Acoreus, among its characters. Although the play suggests that Ptolemy would have fared much better had he heeded Acoreus' wise advice, it is also true that, when things get really bad for Egypt, Acoreus' only response is to pray to or invoke the gods (4.1.48–9, 5.1.48–51), which, however, clearly yields no results. Acoreus himself will die 'trod to death / By the pursuers' (5.4.168–9) during the final battle. Not even a priest – the only spokesperson of religion in the play – then, is able to communicate effectively with the gods, who do not seem to be willing to listen.

The scepticism about the gods is developed one step further in *The Prophetess*, in that they seem to have been utterly replaced by Delphia, who claims to be acting on their behalf and appears to be just as powerful as them. As Molly Hand sums up, Delphia

> performs rites to Hecate and Ceres ... The moon, an emblem for Hecate, hides when Delphia crosses the sky, afraid that Delphia will 'force her from her sphere', just as she forced Ceres's dragons into submission (2.3.341). Delphia raises a she-devil for the fool, Geta ... She engages the services of Ceres and Pan for a marriage masque ... (5.3.386); she calls forth the angry hand of a god armed with a thunderbolt. (5.3.388)[63]

Delphia herself tells Drusilla that she has 'now grown / Perfect in all the hidden mysteries / Of that inimitable art, which makes us / Equal even to the gods and nature's wonders' (2.1.61–4), and everyone mistakes her intervention for the gods' (2.3.51, 66–7). When Diocletian, after the Persians have kidnapped Carinus, Aurelia, and Maximian, bewails that 'the gods fight against me, and proud man, / However magnified, is but as dust / Before the raging whirlwind of their justice' (4.2.2–4), he is in fact referring to actions that have been set in motion by Delphia, not the gods. The gods seem now so distant that humans can no longer tell the difference. Delphia's admirers call her a goddess (1.3.222), and Diocletian remarks that she seems to have

> free access to all the secret counsels
> Which a full senate of the gods determine
> When they consider man. The brass-leaved book
> Of fate lies open to thee, where thou readst
> And fashionest the destinies of men
> At thy wished pleasure. (4.2.73–8)

This reads indeed as the description of some kind of divinity, and it is indisputable that Delphia does control the destiny of the play's characters and events; what is more, as Lucy Munro remarks, 'she appears to use no intermediary devils or spirits', having instead a direct contact with the divine forces she summons and controls.[64] Besides, *The Prophetess* brilliantly showcases the political consequences of Delphia's dazzling magical performance more than once: dragons, a she-devil, a spirit, and a hand with a thunderbolt all stand as demonstrations of her unmatchable puissance. The gods cannot help the Romans; Delphia can.

A DISORIENTED IMPERIAL ROME

The loss of the ancient values, the spread of corruption, and the lack of reliable leaders and dependable gods cannot but make Fletcher's Rome exhibit a sharp sense of disorientation, which ultimately appears to be the cipher of his vision of Rome. It is probably in this disorientation that the strongest unifying principle of the reimagining of Rome offered by the Fletcher canon is to be identified, rather than in the dominance of a specific source on characterization, as is the case with Shakespeare's use of Plutarch, or in the concern with the painstaking recreation of the Roman past in its antiquarian details so as to endow it with a particular sense of immediacy, as with Jonson.[65] Several main characters have to go through a disorienting path: Caesar loses control because of Cleopatra and wealth; Diocletian temporarily strays from his righteousness upon becoming emperor because he is unable to resist the allure of the court; Maximus is deranged by the emperor's heinous rape of his wife, which disintegrates all his certainties regarding politics, the family, and the self. His words 'I am no Roman, / Nor what I am do I know' (*Valentinian*, 3.3.129–30) seem thus not only to signal his own personal identity crisis but could in fact be taken as effectively encapsulating the loss of stable points of reference and the dissolution of traditional beliefs that come across so piercingly in the Roman plays of the Fletcher canon.

Maintaining such a grim outlook on Rome certainly depends in part on Fletcher's decision to focus on the age of the Empire rather than the Republic. Fletcher seems to share Shakespeare's view as illustrated by Paul A. Cantor, who argues that 'for Shakespeare, Roman as a term of distinction means primarily Republican Roman, and … with the death of the Republic, true Romanness in Shakespeare's view begins to die also'.[66] As a matter of fact, whenever a positive reference to Rome emerges in Fletcher's plays, it is to the republican period.[67] In one of the passages that the Master of the Revels, Sir George Buc, marked for deletion in the manuscript of *Sir John Van Olden Barnavelt*, the eponymous protagonist of the play draws an analogy between the Dutch present and the Roman past that would seem to exemplify the view expressed in the canon regarding the momentous institutional shift that was the transition from Republic to Empire and its wide-ranging consequences on Rome:

> Octavius, when he did affect the empire
> And strove to tread upon the neck of Rome
> And all her ancient freedoms, took that course
> That now is practised on you, for, the Catoes
> And all free spirits slain or else proscribed
> That durst have stirred against him, he then seized
> The absolute rule of all.[68]

Fletcher and Massinger resort here to the names of Octavius and Cato as paradigmatic of the well-known political values embodied by the two different forms of government, empire and republic respectively. True *Romanitas*, it would seem, cannot survive under imperial, absolutist rule.

As Maximus wonders: 'are we now no more the sons of Romans, / No more the followers of their happy fortunes, / But conquered Gauls, or quivers for the Parthians?' (*Valentinian*, 1.3.38–40). The ancient values can be manifested only in the freedom guaranteed by the republic rather than under the control of (mostly evil, as Fletcher's Roman plays suggest) princes. In the opening scene of *The False One*, the Pompeian general Labienus describes Caesar's soldiers at Pharsalus 'as if they had been / So many Caesars and like him ambitious / To tread upon the liberty of Rome' (1.1.208–10), and gives a very specific interpretation of Caesar's decision to attack the senators while forbidding his troops 'To waste their force upon the common soldier' (1.1.228):

> Full well he knows that in their blood he was
> To pass to empire and that through their bowels
> He must invade the laws of Rome and give
> A period to the liberty of the world.
> Then fell the Lepidi and the bold Corvini,
> The famed Torquati, Scipios and Marcelli –
> Names, next to Pompey's, most renowned on earth. (1.1.231–7)

This speech is closely based on a passage of Lucan's *Pharsalia*, upon which it draws for the grieved expression of the sorrow for the loss of the *libertas* that characterized 'the Roman republic, conceived of as a framework of laws and freedom overturned by Caesar's pursuit of *imperium*', as Paleit remarks.[69] In his report, Labienus very clearly identifies Caesar as the man who consciously started Rome's transition to the imperial era and put a full stop to the freedom of the western world, while at the same time destroying a host of noble and virtuous Roman *gentes*, whom Labienus duly lists in his dispiriting war bulletin. The latter actually expands on Lucan by adding the Marcelli, probably owing to Gaius Claudius Marcellus having been consul in 49 BCE when Caesar crossed the Rubicon as well as one of the strongest advocates for the Senate to take extreme measures against Caesar. The Egyptians then discuss at length what to do with Pompey, and there is a strong sense here and in Act 2, scene 1, that the head of Pompey is the correlative of the Republic.

This symbolic superimposition of the two acquires even darker implications when the head of Pompey is grotesquely seized in turn by Septimius, Achillas, and Pothinus (the most negative personalities on the Egyptian side), who all hope to be able to use it as a way to enter Caesar's graces. Although their attempt to please Caesar miserably fails, the image of the severed head of Pompey carelessly tossed around in the Egyptian court provides a trenchant image of the ultimate fate of the Roman Republic. It is also grimly ironic that in exulting at having managed to behead

Pompey, the renegade Roman Septimius employs several rhetorical devices typical of Roman oratory:

> 'Tis here! 'Tis done! Behold, you fearful viewers!
> Shake, and behold the model of the world here,
> The pride and strength! Look, look again: 'tis finished!
> That that whole armies, nay, whole nations,
> Many and mighty kings have been struck blind at
> And fled before, winged with their fears and terrors;
> That steeled war waited on and fortune courted;
> That high-plumed honour built up for her own;
> Behold that mightiness, behold that fierceness,
> Behold that child of war with all his glories
> By this poor hand made breathless! (2.1.1–11)

This is not simply Fletcher's way of dressing Septimius' 'foolish boasts in a kind of pseudoelevated style', as Eugene M. Waith argues.[70] In fact, it is a bleak debasement of Roman rhetoric. The speech opens with a *tricolon crescens* of exclamations on line 1 ('Tis here! 'Tis done! Behold, you fearful viewers!) and closes with another *tricolon crescens* of imperatives that takes up lines 9–11 (Behold that mightiness, behold that fierceness, / Behold that child of war with all his glories / By this poor hand made breathless!), further emphasized by the anaphora of 'behold'. These *tricola* frame the central section of the speech (4–8), which is also based on anaphora (That ... That ... That ...). Albeit not as rhetorically elaborate and effective as, say, Marullus' speech to the commoners in the opening scene of Shakespeare's *Julius Caesar*, Septimius' speech employs tropes and techniques characteristic of Roman rhetoric, but it does so perversely, with a view to celebrating not only the orator's baseness and villainy but, even more discouragingly, the death of Pompey, the last armed champion of the Republic, whose idealization obtains further resonance by his never entering the stage, other than as a decapitated head occupying what Margaret E. Owens describes as 'a disturbingly liminal state somewhere between subject and object status'.[71]

Hence, when the Chorus in *The Prophetess* laments that 'there wants / Room in this narrow stage' (4.1.4–5), it is perhaps not only referring to the physical inadequacy of the theatrical space for the representation of Diocletian 'In his full lustre' (4.1.7), but also – by playing on the familiar room/Rome early modern pun – to the fact that Rome itself, understood as an unreachable model and as the supreme treasury of liberty and *virtus*, is now lacking. The conspiracy itself as depicted in *The Prophetess* no longer carries any shade of nobleness as that in *Julius Caesar* did, at least in principle: Aper makes absolutely no reference to the common good and is only motivated to slay Numerian by individual ambition, personal enmity, and private gain. As Sempronius bewails in *Valentinian*, 'O Brutus, / We want thy honesty again' (5.4.18–19). And when Antony acknowledged the power of Caesar's fortune in Shakespeare's *Antony and Cleopatra*, the implication was that Caesar would use his luck to become the sole ruler of Rome and the world; in *Valentinian*, the sentence 'The very dice obey him' (*Antony and Cleopatra*, 2.3.33) is instead grimly literalized in the emperor's using his luck at gambling to get the wedding ring from Maximus with a view to raping Lucina by rolling actual dice (*Valentinian*, 2.1.27), which tellingly portrays the degradation of authority in Rome.

FLETCHER AS A PHILOSOPHER OF HISTORY: THE ROMAN PLAYS AS *TRAUERSPIELE*

Fletcher's dramatic portrayal of a Rome in dissolution provides fresh insights into his *Weltanschauung* by making him emerge as a far deeper thinker than usually recognized, endowed with a much sharper awareness of the wider mechanisms, processes, and trends influencing history, politics, and human life than previously acknowledged. As it happens, Fletcher's vision of human life as it becomes manifest across the Roman plays makes them appear eerily akin to the seventeenth-century German *Trauerspiel* as famously described by Walter Benjamin in *Ursprung des deutschen Trauerspiels* (1928). Although Benjamin deliberately never offers a formal definition of the *Trauerspiel* – a label that he applies to a group of seventeenth-century German plays barely known outside the German-speaking world – he sees it as different from *Tragödie* and argues that

> The very name of trauerspiel [sic] already indicates that its content wakens mourning in the viewer. But that does not at all mean that this content could be better expressed in the categories of psychology than could the content of tragedy; it might sooner mean that these plays could enable a description of mourning far more readily than could the condition of sorrow. For they are not so much plays that make one mournful as plays through which mourning finds satisfaction: plays for the mournful.[72]

Just like the *Trauerspiel*, Fletcher's Roman plays enact a painfully disenchanted apprehension of a bleak present that is mixed with a sorrowful sense of being immersed in a permanent state of historical crisis. Just like the *Trauerspiel*, Fletcher's Roman plays stage the disintegration of postclassical humankind and replace the traditional role of the tragic hero with a plurality of more or less dismayed individuals, who are not really tragic but are made consonant with the play of mourning. Just like the *Trauerspiel*, Fletcher's Roman plays are marked by a pronounced stress on secularization and immanence: they can be inscribed neither in any sacral or religious perspective nor in a profane one upheld by strong and meaningful ideals or tensions for which to fight, as evidenced by the almost complete absence of the gods. Just like the *Trauerspiel*, Fletcher's Roman plays appear to be entirely rooted in history, feeding themselves on that immanence that defines their vision of life as the inexorable revolving of the wheel of fortune, as an empty alternation of the potentates on the world's stage. Just like the *Trauerspiel*, Fletcher's Roman plays treat historical time as a mere and mechanic flow devoid of any development or novelty, purposely captured in its moments of corruption and decadence, and largely portrayed as an eternal return of the same, as a destiny with no visible escape nor any indication of the existence of an *eschaton* or *telos* able to transcend it. This aspect is partly shared by some of Fletcher's tragicomedies, which depict, according to Herbert Blau, 'a history without progression', characterized by 'a restlessness that goes nowhere historically'.[73] Fletcher even seems to move one step further than the *Trauerspiel* in his pessimistic depiction of history in the Roman plays: whereas the *Trauerspiel* implicitly praises martyrs and their impassivity as a form of endurance in the face of the futility of human affairs that is situated halfway between neo-stoicism and Christianity, Fletcher often seems to criticize the general tenets of stoicism, especially as they are embodied in the passivity enshrined in the condition of Roman women, as will become more evident in the next chapter.

When Fletcher's Roman plays are viewed in connection with the defining traits of the *Trauerspiel*, the disorientation that characterizes them starts to make more sense, becomes more compelling, and comes to the fore as much wider-ranging in its implications as to Fletcher's broader conception of history and reality. The result is a significant shift in our perception of a playwright whose penetrating and disenchanted outlook on the more profound workings of politics, religion, and history makes him emerge as a more serious thinker than traditionally assumed, not only adept at using the classical past to make topical comments on Jacobean domestic and foreign policy, but also capable of a higher, more abstract level of historical and political thinking.

As remarked above, in Fletcher's Rome the role of the gods in human life is heavily downplayed in favour of a portrayal of human affairs as no longer guided by an inscrutable but benevolent providence. Human accomplishments, sufferings, desires, and frustrations seem to acquire more importance than any potential intervention by divinity. Humanity has been left alone on earth. Fletcher seems to be interested in religion only insofar as belief or disbelief in the gods creates a certain response in the human mind: the Roman plays appear to be especially concerned with the depiction of the potentially devastating effects of the failure of traditional beliefs on individuals and with the human effort to come to terms with the awareness that a sense of protection from above and stability below has irrevocably disappeared. It is now human will – Fletcher's Roman plays seem forcefully to assert – that primarily determines human destinies.

Like the *Trauerspiel*, this group of plays would therefore seem to be characterized by a similar approach to the depiction of historical reality as the one that Ivo Kamps has identified in *Sir John Van Olden Barnavelt*, a play in which Fletcher and Massinger 'speak out strongly against deification and privatization and in favor of the recognition that power rises from below – from history – and does not descend from above, from a divine source'.[74] In this sense, Fletcher would appear to exhibit an instinctive awareness and to conduct an innovative – though, because of its very intuitiveness, not so articulate – exploration of what Kamps describes as 'the fundamentally *im*personal forces … that determine history and the lives of individuals in ways ultimately beyond the control of even the most powerful princes'.[75] This finds at least partial actualization in Valentinian's speech bewailing Lucina's death. Unable to accept the fact that there exist situations over which he has no control whatsoever, he cries out:

> She cannot die, she must not die. Are those
> I plant my love upon but common livers,
> Their hours as others', told 'em? Can they be ashes?
> Why do ye flatter a belief into me
> That I am all that is, the world's my creature,
> The trees bring forth their fruits when I say 'Summer',
> The wind, that knows no limit but his wildness,
> At my command moves not a leaf, the sea
> With his proud mountain waters envying heaven,
> When I say 'Still', run into crystal mirrors?
> Can I do this, and she die? Why, ye bubbles
> That with my least breath break, no more remembered,
> Ye moths that fly about my flame and perish,
> Ye golden cankerworms that eat my honours,
> Living no longer than my spring of favour,
> Why do ye make me God that can do nothing?
> Is she not dead? (4.1.17–33)

Lucina's death forces the emperor to realize that he is no god, thereby diminishing Valentinian's image of himself and making him face the ugly truth that, for all his absolute power, he is rooted in the never-ending struggle of history just like everybody else: the current of history moves in a much more powerful sweep than he does. 'Is she not dead?' (4.1.82), he will frantically ask again fifty lines later, while ignoring whatever 'may concern the empire' (4.1.81). As Curran points out, 'Obsessing over Lucina's death hermetically seals him in the world of his own mind; he doubts his power and his identity ... Not accidentally, it is at this moment that he gets taken in by Maximus's plot ... isolation from the real world conduces to the supreme policy error.'[76] Valentinian's burning frustration, a feeling utterly unknown to such a spoiled emperor as he is, is soon converted into an unrestrainable fit of rage addressed to all his flatterers, panders, and bawds.

Maximus' ensuing revenge, accession, and death further prove the correctness of Lucina's view that 'there is no god but power' (3.1.145), that is, the notion that, in Hila's formulation, 'it is political structures and historical processes rather than individual agents that contain the seeds of political change'.[77] *Valentinian* exhibits no providential pattern in its depiction of Roman history; in fact, it rather seems to exhibit a bleakly cyclical one: an evil tyrant is killed for his vicious actions; his successor experiences the very same fate; any future emperor is expected to do the same. The play ends uncertainly after Eudoxa's revenge, and there seems to be no man sent from the gods nor providence to set things right. And while the workings of providence might be still regarded as possible in the tragicomedies to which Fletcher contributed – for example, *Philaster* – they no longer are in his Roman plays, which accordingly seem to eschew the typical Elizabethan history-play pattern as famously described by Alvin Kernan:

> a weak or saintly king makes political mistakes and is overthrown by rebellious and arrogant subjects; the kingdom becomes a wasteland and society a chaos in which every man's hand is set against his fellow; after a period of great suffering, reaction against the forces of evil occurs, and a strong and good king restores order.[78]

As Kamps points out with reference to other history plays by Fletcher, even though

> The order-chaos-order formula is still discernible in *Henry VIII* and *Barnavelt* ... its resolution is no longer due to the seizing of power by a single individual ... and as a whole the drama withholds any evidence that God guides the hand of certain noble individuals, and crushes their heretical or rebellious opponents.[79]

Hence, the Roman plays in the Fletcher canon would seem to go a step further in generally portraying what is at best a temporary – though blatantly precarious – restoration of order at the end, which is presented as almost invariably in danger of being undermined. *The False One* ends well for Caesar and Rome, but the happy ending is tainted by the awareness that in a matter of a few years Caesar will be murdered by a conspiracy of republican senators, which will eventually bring the transition from Republic to Empire to completion. *The Prophetess* concludes with Delphia's thwarting Maximian's attempt to kill Diocletian, thus foregrounding an atmosphere of unrest in Rome that cannot bode well for the future of the Empire. *Bonduca* closes on the Roman victory over the Britons and Caratach's submission, but the play has given ample evidence of the divisions, rivalries, and jealousies that endanger the unity of the Roman army, which renders it difficult for the audience to trust in the integrity of Roman civilization in the near future, conveying instead an impression of instability and ever-impending strife for the Empire. In *Valentinian*, rebellion and tyrannicide are carried out at the expense of personal devastation, and the play denies full closure by ending with no emperor on the throne and the fate of the Empire hanging in the balance as the barbarians (as many in the audience would know) ominously press on Rome's borders after Aëtius' demise.

CONCLUSION

In considering the Roman past as it related to the early seventeenth century not only at the more focused level of potential similarities between past and present events, trends, and behaviours, but, more importantly, tackling bigger-picture questions concerning the disorder and opacity of history, Fletcher seems to have looked at ancient Rome not just as a playmaker but also in the role of the philosopher of history. Fletcher's Roman plays refrain from enacting any unitary, predetermined, and transcendent vision of human experience. They avoid any attempts to rearrange the disharmony of reality by imposing on it any fictitious order, intent as they prove to be on reproducing the actual fragmentation, movement, and unceasing contradictoriness of history and life. In this way, Fletcher seems to have been able to channel in his Roman world the disturbing awareness of being caught between an irretrievable past and an unsteady present with no guarantee as to a stable future that people may have felt during the Jacobean era, a time in which ideas about the state, individuals, and society were being shaped by a painfully growing scepticism and a momentous transformation of values.

It is perhaps not coincidental that all the Roman plays in the Fletcher canon were probably written after both Prince Henry Frederick's death in 1612 and Princess Elizabeth's marriage to Frederick V, the elector palatine of the Rhine, in 1613, when disillusionment with Stuart policy started to grow further and was felt more and more burningly by increasing numbers of the English population, and when the question of whether

England could and would fight against the Catholic European powers became a real one. The uncertainty of the immediate political and historical contexts that infiltrated Fletcher's artistic creation may also account for the fact that in his Roman plays no convincing alternative world vision is ever provided. And although this cannot but remain at the level of speculation, it might be plausible to argue that the precariousness that marks these plays' endings might even signal some sort of prescience on Fletcher's part concerning the future of England, a country that would be plunged into internecine strife in a matter of little more than twenty years. Fletcher was unable, in the 1610s and 1620s, to prophesy the specific issues of the 1630s that would ultimately lead to the outbreak of civil war in England; moreover, the political events of the Jacobean era cannot unequivocally be seen as having a direct relationship to what happened in 1642. Yet Fletcher might have envisioned what could happen to a country steered by an inadequate leader, thus oddly predicting the shape of things to come in England in the 1640s. On a personal level, the disorientation that is manifested in such plays as *Valentinian* and *Bonduca* might have at least partly resulted from the recent termination of Fletcher's partnership with Beaumont, a loss from which he was perhaps still reeling.

Fletcher's depiction of history strikes me as unusual in the early modern era, his pessimism making his plays in some respects similar to Walter Ralegh's *History of the World*, a work that can be considered rather eccentric in the Tudor and early Stuart historiographical landscape. Even though Ralegh regarded the Old Testament as 'the unimpeachable source' and still viewed all events as preordained by God, his *History*, as Daniel R. Woolf argues, exudes 'sceptic[ism] toward the past. Though it shares a common vocabulary with other histories, there is a dark element in the *History* which sets it apart from most contemporary works. Ralegh could not resist cutting legends down to size.'[80] What is more, as Woolf adds, Ralegh's *History* exhibits

> no discernible *telos* to the chaos of historical events ... not even the providential goal of man's salvation ... This aimlessness is best illustrated by the *History*'s total lack of closure: it does not so much conclude as simply stop, in a famous apostrophe to death ... which, for Ralegh, signified not the soul's reunion with the godhead but a 'long and darke night' ... which entailed the annihilation of individual consciousness.[81]

Ralegh wrote the *History* during his imprisonment in the Tower, so it is not surprising that his disillusionment and bitterness regarding the circumstances of his own life would shape his depiction. In addition, Ralegh penned the *History* under the patronage of Prince Henry. By the time it was published in 1614, however, Henry was dead. This momentous event seems to have had an impact on both Ralegh's and Fletcher's perception and depiction of history on page and stage respectively, so much so that, in *Bonduca*, Fletcher had Caratach pronounce a touchingly memorable elegy for the death of the young boy Hengo, the imagery of which is particularly resonant with that which was repeatedly deployed after the tragic demise of Henry, of whom Hengo – with his youthful masculinity and unadulterated yearning to fight for British victory – seems to be the play's correlative:

> Farewell the hopes of Britain!
> Thou royal graft, farewell for ever! – Time and Death,
> Ye have done your worst. Fortune, now see, now proudly
> Pluck off thy veil and view thy triumph: look,
> Look what thou hast brought this land to. – O fair flower,
> How lovely yet thy ruins show, how sweetly
> Even death embraces thee! The peace of heaven,
> The fellowship of all great souls, be with thee! (5.3.160–7)[82]

More than just a lament for the death of Hengo, these words appear to have been meant as a most afflicted musing over the present and future of England after the death of a 'royal graft' who did embody, for many, 'the hopes of Britain'. The prevailing sentiment in the passage is one of grief for what could have been and never was. Fletcher seems to have conceptualized Hengo's passing in the play as the moment at which for Britain the foremost hope for a bright future vanished into thin air, thus plunging people into an uneasy state of unbearable uncertainty.

In what follows, we shall see that, on top of staging the trajectory of Roman history with a sense of disorientation and pessimism, Fletcher's Roman plays also voice a deep scepticism over Roman models and *exempla*, which is consistent with his irreverent approach to classical sources and his grim depiction of a savage, unsettled imperial Rome. In general terms, the impression is that Fletcher does not really believe in anything that might be labelled 'the myth of Rome'; in fact, he seems actively intent on debunking any such thing and, more generally, on questioning the entire idea of Rome as a model to follow. The two ensuing chapters will therefore seek to show the extent to which the Roman plays in the Fletcher canon are permeated by the notion that Roman paradigms and assumptions are often no longer adequate as examples, and that models consequently need to be sought elsewhere.

NOTES

1 Christopher Marlowe, *Doctor Faustus: A- and B- texts (1604, 1616)*, ed. David Bevington and Eric Rasmussen (Manchester: Manchester University Press, 1993), B.3.Chorus.18.

2 William Shakespeare, *Julius Caesar*, ed. David Daniell (Walton-on-Thames: Nelson for Arden Shakespeare, 1998), 1.2.243–9, my emphasis. All references to the play are to this edition. Subsequent references will be incorporated parenthetically into the text.
3 William Shakespeare, *Coriolanus*, ed. Peter Holland (London: Bloomsbury Arden Shakespeare, 2013), 1.1.54–6, 2.1.230, 3.3.119–20, 4.6.99; William Shakespeare, *Antony and Cleopatra*, ed. David Bevington (Cambridge, Cambridge University Press, updated edn, 2005), 5.2.210–12. All references to the plays are to these editions. Subsequent references will be incorporated parenthetically into the text.
4 On the doctrine of the king's two bodies, see Ernest H. Kantorowicz, *The King's Two Bodies: A Study in Mediaeval Political Theology*, ed. William Chester Jordan (Princeton, NJ: Princeton University Press, 1997).
5 Aspasia Velissariou, 'Female Fetishised Deaths in Jacobean Tragedy', *Gender Studies* 12 (2013), 194–212 (208).
6 Allman, *Jacobean Revenge Tragedy*, 149.
7 Finkelpearl, *Court and Country Politics*, 213.
8 Rebecca W. Bushnell, *Tragedies of Tyrants: Political Thought and Theater in the English Renaissance* (Ithaca, NY: Cornell University Press, 1990), 163, 159.
9 John Fletcher, *The Humorous Lieutenant*, ed. Cyrus Hoy, in Bowers (gen. ed.), *Dramatic Works*, 5.303–409, 2.2.10–11.
10 John Fletcher, *Rule a Wife and Have a Wife*, ed. George Walton Williams, in Bowers (gen. ed.), *Dramatic Works*, 6.501–77, 5.5.87–89. All references to the play are to this edition. Subsequent references will be incorporated parenthetically into the text.
11 Clark, *Plays of Beaumont and Fletcher*, 107.
12 Hila, '"Justice shall never heare ye, I am justice"', 751.
13 John Fletcher and Philip Massinger, *The Spanish Curate*, ed. Robert Kean Turner, in Bowers (gen. ed.), *Dramatic Works*, 10.301–95, 1.3.27–30. All references to the play are to this edition. Subsequent references will be incorporated parenthetically into the text.
14 John Fletcher and Philip Massinger, *The Custom of the Country*, ed. Cyrus Hoy, in Bowers (gen. ed.), *Dramatic Works*, 8.642–739, 2.4.15. All references to the play are to this edition. Subsequent references will be incorporated parenthetically into the text.
15 Andrew Hickman, '*Bonduca*'s Two Ignoble Armies and *The Two Noble Kinsmen*', *Medieval and Renaissance Drama in England* 4 (1989), 143–71 (155).
16 Hickman, '*Bonduca*'s Two Ignoble Armies', 155.
17 Ronald J. Boling, 'Fletcher's Satire of Caratach in *Bonduca*', *Comparative Drama* 33 (1999), 390–406 (399).
18 Hickman, '*Bonduca*'s Two Ignoble Armies', 157.
19 Jowitt, 'Colonialism, Politics, and Romanization in John Fletcher's *Bonduca*', 487; Hickman, '*Bonduca*'s Two Ignoble Armies', 157.
20 John Fletcher and Francis Beaumont, *The Captain*, ed. L. A. Beaurline, in Bowers (gen. ed.), *Dramatic Works*, 1.550–650, 2.1.79. All references to the play are to this edition. Subsequent references will be incorporated parenthetically into the text.
21 Nolan, 'A Critical Edition of John Fletcher's *Bonduca*', 109.
22 Raphael Holinshed, *The First and Second Volumes of Chronicles* (London, 1587), 2.45.
23 Tacitus, *The Annals of Cornelius Tacitus. The Description of Germany*, trans. Richard Greenway (London, 1598), 212.

24 Ronan, 'Antike Roman', 137.
25 Dionysius of Halicarnassus, *Roman Antiquities*, trans. Earnest Cary (London: Heinemann, 1939), 4.59.1–61.4; Livy, *History of Rome*, trans. Rev. Canon Roberts, 2 vols (New York: Dutton, 1912), 1.55.5–7.
26 Varro, *On the Latin Language*, vol. 1, trans. Roland G. Kent (London: Heinemann, 1938), 5.41.
27 Andrew Marvell, *The Poems of Andrew Marvell*, ed. Nigel Smith (Harlow: Pearson, 2007), 276–7, ll. 67–72.
28 Edmund Spenser, *Complaints: Containing Sundry Small Poems of the World's Vanity* (London, 1588), R3r, translating Joachim du Bellay, *Le premier livre des antiquitez de Rome: contenant une générale description de sa grandeur et comme une déploration de sa ruine* (Paris, 1558), 4r: 'D'une horrible fureur l'un contre l'autre armez / Se moissonnarent tous par un soudain orage, / Renouvelant entre eulx la fraternelle rage, / Qui aveugla iadis les fiers soldatz semez.'
29 Spenser, *Complaints*, S2v, translating du Bellay, *Le premier livre des antiquitez de Rome*, 7v: 'Ne permettant des Dieux le iuste iugement, / Voz murs ensanglantez parla main fraternelle / Se pouvoir asseurer d'un ferme fondement.'
30 William Shakespeare, *Julius Caesar*, ed. John Jowett, in *The Oxford Shakespeare: The Complete Works*, ed. Stanley Wells and Gary Taylor (Oxford: Oxford University Press, 2nd edn, 1986), 627–54, 3.1.47–8, my emphasis; William Shakespeare, *Julius Caesar*, ed. Sarah Neville, in *The New Oxford Shakespeare: The Complete Works: Modern Critical Edition*, ed. Gary Taylor, John Jowett, Terri Bourus, and Gabriel Egan (Oxford: Oxford University Press, 2016), 1607–75; Ben Jonson, *The Staple of News*, ed. Joseph Loewenstein, in *The Cambridge Edition of the Works of Ben Jonson*, ed. David Bevington, Martin Butler, and Ian Donaldson, 7 vols (Cambridge: Cambridge University Press, 2012), 6.15–157, Induction.30; Ben Jonson, *Discoveries*, ed. Lorna Hutson, in Bevington, Butler, and Donaldson (gen. eds), *Cambridge Jonson*, 7.495–596, 480–1. For a more detailed discussion of Fletcher and Massinger's use of this phrase, see Domenico Lovascio, 'Julius Caesar's "just cause" in John Fletcher and Philip Massinger's *The False One*', *Notes and Queries* 62 (2015), 245–7.
31 David Farley-Hills, *A Critical Study of the Professional Drama, 1600–25* (Basingstoke: Macmillan, 1988), 173.
32 Plutarch, 'The Life of Julius Caesar', in *Lives*, 787A; Suetonius, *The History of Twelve Caesars Emperors of Rome, Written in Latin by C. Suetonius Tranquillus and Newly Translated into English, with a Marginal Gloss and Other Brief Annotations Thereupon*, trans. Philemon Holland (London, 1606), 26; Suetonius, 'The Life of Julius Caesar', in *The Lives of the Twelve Caesars*, trans. J. C. Rolfe (London: Heinemann, 1913), 3–119, 54.1; Cassius Dio, *Roman History*, trans. Earnest Cary and Herbert Baldwin Foster, 9 vols (London: Heinemann, 1914–27), vol. 4, 42.40.4–5.
33 Holinshed, *Chronicles*, 2.65.
34 See also Archer Taylor, 'Proverbs in the Plays of Beaumont and Fletcher', *Southern Folklore Quarterly* 24 (1960), 77–100 (80); Morris P. Tilley, *A Dictionary of the Proverbs in England in the Sixteenth and Seventeenth Centuries* (Ann Arbor, MI: University of Michigan Press, 1950), D35.
35 John Fletcher, *Women Pleased*, ed. Hans Walter Gabler, in Bowers (gen. ed.), *Dramatic Works*, 5.448–529, 3.2.66; John Fletcher, *The Island Princess*, ed. Clare McManus (London: Methuen for Arden Shakespeare, 2012), 1.1.101. All references to the plays are to these editions. Subsequent references will be incorporated parenthetically into the text.

36 John Fletcher and Philip Massinger, *The Double Marriage*, ed. Cyrus Hoy, in Bowers (gen. ed.), *Dramatic Works*, 9.95–220, 3.2.130–1. All references to the play are to this edition. Subsequent references will be incorporated parenthetically into the text.
37 Christopher Hicklin, 'A Critical Modern-Spelling Edition of John Fletcher's *Rule a Wife and Have a Wife*', unpublished PhD thesis, University of Toronto, 2010, 308 nn.42–3; Thucydides, *The Peloponnesian War*, trans. Martin Hammond (Oxford: Oxford University Press, 2009), 1.144.
38 Vimala C. Pasupathi, 'Shakespeare, Fletcher and "the gain o'th' martialist"', in *Shakespeare and Fletcher*, ed. Clare McManus and Lucy Munro, *Shakespeare* 7 (2011), special issue, 297–309 (301).
39 Allman, *Jacobean Revenge Tragedy*, 49.
40 Charles L. Squier, *John Fletcher* (Boston, MA: Twayne, 1986).
41 Pasupathi, 'Shakespeare, Fletcher and "the gain o'th' martialist"', 300. On soldiers in Fletcher, see also Mincoff, 'Fletcher's Early Tragedies', 76–80; Vimala C. Pasupathi, 'The King's Privates: Sex and the Soldier's Place in John Fletcher's *The Humorous Lieutenant* (ca. 1618)', *Research Opportunities in Medieval and Renaissance Drama* 47 (2008), 25–50.
42 Finkelpearl, *Court and Country Politics*, 48.
43 *Historical Manuscripts Commission Report on the Manuscripts of the late Reginald Raudon Hastings, Esq.*, ed. Francis Bickley (London: HM Stationery Office, 1930), 2.58–9. See also Samuel A. Tannenbaum, 'A Hitherto Unpublished John Fletcher Autograph', *Journal of English and Germanic Philology* 28 (1929), 35–40.
44 Finkelpearl, *Court and Country Politics*, 80.
45 Judy H. Park, 'The Tragicomic Moment: Republicanism in Beaumont and Fletcher's *Philaster*', *Comparative Drama* 49 (2015), 23–47 (37); McMullan, *Politics of Unease*, 94.
46 Hadfield, *Shakespeare and Republicanism*, 17. See also Patrick Collinson, 'The Monarchical Republic of Queen Elizabeth I', *Bulletin of the John Rylands Library* 69 (1987), 394–424; Patrick Collinson, '*De Republica Anglorum*: Or, History with the Politics Put Back', in *Elizabethan Essays* (London: Hambledon, 1994), 1–29.
47 Paleit, *War, Liberty, and Caesar*, 145.
48 Paleit, *War, Liberty, and Caesar*, 145.
49 Paleit, *War, Liberty, and Caesar*, 146–7.
50 Frénée-Hutchins, *Boudica's Odyssey in Early Modern England*, 164, identifies in *Bonduca* a displaced discussion of rule whereby Suetonius is a 'mirror image of James', but I tend to see more of James in Caratach than in Suetonius, as suggested by Crawford, 'Fletcher's *The Tragedie of Bonduca* and the Anxieties of the Masculine Government of James I', 374.
51 Lucan, *Pharsalia*, 10.491–2.
52 Curran, 'Fletcher, Massinger, and Roman Imperial Character', 326–7.
53 Curran, 'Fletcher, Massinger, and Roman Imperial Character', 327.
54 Kewes, 'Julius Caesar in Jacobean England', 178.
55 Curran, 'Fletcher, Massinger and Roman Imperial Character', 332.
56 Curran, 'Fletcher, Massinger and Roman Imperial Character', 329.
57 Farley-Hills, *A Critical Study of the Professional Drama*, 180; Leech, *The John Fletcher Plays*, 110; Mincoff, 'Shakespeare, Fletcher and Baroque Tragedy', 4–5.
58 Leech, *The John Fletcher Plays*, 110; H. J. Makkink, *Philip Massinger and John Fletcher: A Comparison* (Rotterdam: Nijgh & Van Ditmar, 1927), 133.
59 Francis Beaumont and John Fletcher, *Cupid's Revenge*, ed. Fredson Bowers, in Bowers (gen. ed.), *Dramatic Works*, 2.315–448, 1.3.18–20. All references to the

FLETCHER'S ROMAN PLAYS AS *TRAUERSPIELE* 103

play are to this edition. Subsequent references will be incorporated parenthetically into the text.
60 Misha Teramura, 'Archival Reflection: The Fortunes of Fletcher's "Against Astrologers"', *Modern Philology* 118 (2020), 130–57 (151, 152).
61 Drabek, *Fletcherian Dramatic Achievement*, 24.
62 Leech, *The John Fletcher Plays*, 130.
63 Molly Hand, '"You take no labour": Women Workers of Magic in Early Modern England', in *Working Subjects in Early Modern English Drama*, ed. Michelle Dowd and Natasha Korda (Aldershot: Ashgate, 2011), 161–76 (170–1).
64 Lucy Munro, *Shakespeare in the Theatre: The King's Men* (London: Bloomsbury Arden Shakespeare, 2020), 131.
65 Yet Mincoff, 'Fletcher's Early Tragedies', 83–4, argues that 'The background to these Roman plays is drawn not without a certain care ... [Fletcher's] characters are not ... Elizabethans parading under Roman names ... and Fletcher even gives a hint of local color. The examples cited by the characters are from Roman history. Much of the imagery, especially the references to temples, Vestals and classical mythology, though in the Renaissance tradition, seems to have been introduced with a purpose, and it is never, except in the bawdry of the comic scenes in *Bonduca*, markedly un-Roman. A[ët]ius' body is to be burnt on a pyre (he hopes to dwell in Elysium), and in *Bonduca* there are references to the forks as a punishment.' It therefore seems excessive to describe the plays based on history in the Fletcher canon as 'pseudohistorischen', as does Ulrich, *Die pseudohistorischen Dramen*, IX.
66 Paul A. Cantor, *Shakespeare's Rome: Republic and Empire* (Ithaca, NY: Cornell University Press, 1976), 27.
67 See, for instance, John Fletcher, Philip Massinger, and Nathan Field, *The Queen of Corinth*, ed. Robert Kean Turner, in Bowers (gen. ed.), *Dramatic Works*, 8.10–93, 5.4.134–6; *A Very Woman*, 5.4.32–7; *The Knight of Malta*, 1.3.152–4. All references to *The Queen of Corinth* are to this edition. Subsequent references will be incorporated parenthetically into the text.
68 John Fletcher and Philip Massinger, *The Tragedy of Sir John Van Olden Barnavelt*, ed. Fredson Bowers, in Bowers (gen. ed.), *Dramatic Works*, 8.503–89, 4.5.190–196. All references to the play are to this edition. Subsequent references will be incorporated parenthetically into the text.
69 Paleit, *War, Liberty, and Caesar*, 147.
70 Eugene M. Waith, 'The Death of Pompey: English Style, French Style', in *Shakespeare and Dramatic Tradition*, ed. William R. Elton and William B. Long (Newark, DE: University of Delaware Press, 1989), 276–85 (281).
71 Owens, *Stages of Dismemberment*, 20.
72 Walter Benjamin, *Origin of German Tragic Drama*, trans. Howard Eiland (Cambridge, MA: Harvard University Press, 2019), 115.
73 Herbert Blau, 'The Absolved Riddle: Sovereign Pleasure and the Baroque Subject in the Tragicomedies of John Fletcher', *New Literary History* 17 (1986), 539–54 (549). For an excellent recent application of Benjamin to Shakespeare, see Hugh Grady, *Shakespeare and Impure Aesthetics* (Cambridge: Cambridge University Press, 2009), 133–239.
74 Kamps, *Historiography and Ideology*, 158.
75 Kamps, *Historiography and Ideology*, 93.
76 Curran, 'Fletcher, Massinger, and Roman Imperial Character', 344.
77 Hila, '"Justice shall never heare ye, I am justice"', 757.
78 Alvin B. Kernan, 'From Ritual to History: The English History Plays', in *The Revels History of Drama in English: Vol. 3: 1576–1613*, ed. J. Leeds Barroll, Richard

Hosley, Alvin B. Kernan, and Alexander Leggatt (London: Methuen, 1975), 262–99 (264).
79 Kamps, *Historiography and Ideology*, 166.
80 Woolf, *Idea of History*, 49.
81 Woolf, *Idea of History*, 50–1.
82 The first to have identified the analogy seems to have been Appleton, *Beaumont and Fletcher*, 55–6.

CHAPTER 3
'HAD LUCRECE E'ER BEEN THOUGHT OF BUT FOR TARQUIN?' THE INADEQUACY OF ROMAN FEMALE *EXEMPLA*

Depictions of 'masculine' women who stand out for their heroism, dominance, and agency are so numerous in the Fletcher canon that Philip J. Finkelpearl argues that 'in the world of Fletcher's plays there seem to be more female "male spirits" than male ones'.[1] For Gordon McMullan, Fletcher's penchant for populating his plays with 'assertive and dominant women' results from a desire to explore 'brief alternative realms' that may offer 'glimpses of possible new worlds which are much more appealing than the pragmatics that indicate how impossible they are'.[2] In all probability, these portrayals of 'masculine' female characters were decisively shaped by Fletcher's first-hand experience of that 'feminocentric country environment' in which he seems to have participated at Ashby de la Zouch, Leicestershire, the seat of his literary patrons, Henry Hastings, fifth Earl of Huntingdon, and his wife Elizabeth Stanley Hastings, whom the Earl himself praised for her 'judicious conceit and masculine understanding'.[3]

Prima facie, a Roman context might seem potentially fertile ground for delineating female characters specially endowed with 'masculine' virtues, given the abundance of examples that the historical records offered of powerful women who contributed to shaping Roman history by dint of their political influence. Yet this turns out to have been only partially the case, in that as much as the Roman (as opposed to the *non*-Roman) women in the Fletcher canon are indeed able to display qualities such as constancy and fortitude, very rarely do they emerge as assertive or dominant.[4] To be sure, this is partly due to the strong patriarchal stance encoded in the society of ancient Rome (possibly even stronger than that encoded in early modern English society), which posed an inescapable limit to Fletcher's and his collaborators' creative freedom. More importantly, however, the playwrights seem to have wished to emphasize in several ways the limitations of Roman models, so that their portrayals of Roman women end up radiating a tangible sense of scepticism and disenchantment about the trans-temporal viability of the female values and paradigms that the classical world had bequeathed to the early modern era.[5]

The four Roman plays in the Fletcher canon feature a total of seven Roman women. In purely numerical terms, then, the Roman female characters in Fletcher's oeuvre equal those in Shakespeare's, which is the most immediately comparable body of early modern English Roman plays (Lavinia in *Titus Andronicus*; Portia and Calpurnia in *Julius Caesar*; Octavia in *Antony and Cleopatra*; Volumnia, Virgilia, and Valeria in *Coriolanus*). Yet Shakespeare's Roman women are not only more evenly distributed across the different tragedies; they also generally seem to have more relevance – at least plot-wise – in the plays in which they appear than their Fletcherian counterparts: four of these have (very) minor roles (Ardelia, Phorba, Claudia, and Marcellina in *Valentinian*); two may be described as supporting characters with a limited influence on the plot (with Eudoxa's role in *Valentinian* being more consequential than Aurelia's in *The Prophetess*); and the only one who can be considered a protagonist (Lucina in *Valentinian*) dies halfway through the play in which she appears. Hence, there are six Roman women in *Valentinian*, one in *The Prophetess*, and none in either *Bonduca* or *The False One*.

Strikingly, each of these latter two plays features a well-known non-Roman queen as a main character (Bonduca and Cleopatra respectively), while Delphia, the eponymous prophetess of the 1622 play, is a Celtic Druidess, whose character Fletcher and Massinger developed from meagre historical information.[6] As this chapter seeks to demonstrate, the generally marginal roles of the Roman women in the Fletcher canon are thrown into even sharper relief by the conspicuous pre-eminence accorded to *non*-Roman women in three out of the four Roman plays. This is, incidentally, not dissimilar to what famously occurs in Shakespeare's *Antony and Cleopatra* with the contrast between the passive Octavia and the flamboyant Cleopatra, although in Fletcher's case the polarity is not confined to a single play but develops across his entire Roman corpus. This contrast emerges as a trenchant exemplification of Fletcher's scepticism about the currency and validity of Roman paradigms and seems to foster the impression that he found the women of ancient Rome hardly adequate for the development of his ideal 'masculine' female characters.

Scepticism concerning the value system encoded by Roman female models also seeps from the allusions and appeals to Roman paragons that recur so frequently across the canon, their largest share pointing to *exempla* drawn from the history of the Roman Republic and especially to Lucrece and Portia. These allusions would cumulatively seem to suggest that, for Fletcher, Roman female *exempla* are no longer sacrosanct; inscribed as they are in the early modern discourses of misogyny, patriarchy, and politics, any occurrence of their application to the present ought at least to be seen with cautious distrust. It is above all the passivity embodied in these Roman models that seems to arouse Fletcher's sceptical attitude, as especially exemplified in *The Double Marriage*'s Juliana, who is explicitly modelled on Shakespeare's Portia, whose virtues she manages to outdo. As this chapter argues, this approach chimes with the canon's general tendency either to shun or implicitly criticize the tenets of stoicism. In line with Fletcher's stance regarding classical texts, these female *exempla* are shown as not viable as guides solely by virtue of their antiquity.

THE ROMAN WOMEN

The four minor Roman female characters of Fletcher's Roman world, all in *Valentinian*, can be divided into two pairs: the emperor's bawds, Ardelia and Phorba, and Lucina's waiting women, Claudia and Marcellina. These characters are all Fletcher's invention, as neither of the two main sources for the play, Book III of Martin Fumée's French translation of Procopius' *The History of the Wars* and the 'Histoire d'Eudoxe, Valentinian, et Ursace' in Honoré D'Urfé's *L'Astrée*, mentions either bawds or handmaids. Cramming the play with as many as two bawds and four freedmen acting as panders (Balbus, Proculus, Chilax, and Lycinius), all invented by Fletcher and added to the eunuch Lycias (who replaces Heracle l'Eunuque of *L'Astrée*), decisively contributes to setting up the bleakly oppressive atmosphere that pervades Valentinian's court. The same holds true for the sophisticated rhetorical strategies that the bawds employ to manipulate language in order to persuade Lucina to sleep with the emperor, which fully expose, as Marina Hila points out, 'the inversion of values and moral relativism for which Valentinian is responsible'.[7] Pontius will later lament that 'to live here and study to be true / Is all one to be traitors' (4.3.30–1). The speciousness of the bawds' rhetoric is evident, for example, in their claims that 'The honour of a woman is her praises, / The way to get these, to be seen and sought to' (1.2.11–12), and that 'Virtue is either lame or not at all, / And love a sacrilege and not a saint, / When it bars up the way to men's petitions' (1.2.23–5). Nothing seems to be absolute for Ardelia and Phorba, whose words ooze an astonishing cynicism. 'Honour' is not an intrinsic value but merely the superficial reflection of external 'praises', which must be obtained by showing oneself in public and actively seeking suitors, while 'virtue' is but a hindrance to being courted and enjoyed by men. Lucina calls the bawds 'devils' (1.2.41), and it would be hard to counter her view that 'There is no wonder men defame our sex / And lay the vices of all ages on us, / When such as you shall bear the names of women' (1.2.45–7).

In order to make their moral degradation even more explicit, Fletcher presents the bawds' actions in such a way as to make them appear much craftier and more experienced than the apparently incompetent panders, much as occurs in *The Humorous Lieutenant*.[8] There, after the disappointing attempts of the panders Charinthus, Timon, and Menippus, it is only through the intervention of the bawd Leucippe that King Antigonus manages to track down Celia – with whom his son Demetrius is in love – and lure her to court in order to test her character and chastity (though he is then overcome by the desire actually to seduce her). Leucippe is probably one of Fletcher's most memorable comic characters, depicted as she is at work in her office, methodically administering a huge and efficient business set up to satisfy the appetites of the king and his court as promptly as possible, with two assistants and a card file in which all the information on the beauties of the land is arranged alphabetically. Reverting to *Valentinian*, Ardelia and Phorba are eventually murdered by 'the women of the town' (5.2.158), as a messenger reports soon after Valentinian's death.

Far less negative characters than the bawds, the maids Claudia and Marcellina have, however, an even more limited and less relevant role in the play. Their frivolous witticisms and ultimate acceptance of Valentinian's panders' amorous offers when they get to court – 'they have had some sport too, / But are more thankful for it' (3.1.133–4), Valentinian scornfully informs Lucina after raping her – mainly serve as foil to Lucina's constancy and fortitude.

The only Roman woman in *The Prophetess*, Aurelia, whose actions in the play have no authority in the sources, is also depicted in a negative light, albeit for different reasons. In Act 3, scene 3, haughty in her treatment of the Persian ambassadors and the Persian princess Cassana, who is her prisoner, Aurelia is even dispossessed of her agency and becomes a mere puppet at the mercy of Delphia, whose spells make Aurelia ludicrously lust after Maximian in order to take her far from Diocletian, who prefers her to Delphia's niece Drusilla (3.3.1–4, 18–26, 37–109). Towards the end of the play, in order to support her now husband Maximian, who feels as if he is 'walk[ing] / With heavy burdens on a sea of glass' because he is afraid that Diocletian might one day reclaim the imperial seat that he has ceded to him and because he fears the opposition of his co-emperor Carinus, she offers him a cynically Machiavellian perspective according to which

> Nearness of blood,
> Respect of piety and thankfulness,
> And all the holy dreams of virtuous fools
> Must vanish into nothing when ambition,
> The maker of great minds and nurse of honour,
> Puts in for empire. (5.2.48–53)

Even though Maximian and Aurelia actually owe their freedom to Diocletian and his army, who rescued them after the Persians had taken them hostage,

Aurelia contemptuously labels Diocletian as 'simple', because 'he was the master / ... of a jewel, / Whose worth and use he knew not', while at the same time coldly referring to her brother Carinus as 'a stranger, / And so to be removed' (5.2.54–7, 59–60). This unscrupulousness grants her Maximian's excited praise:

> Thou more than woman,
> Thou masculine greatness, to whose soaring spirit
> To touch the stars seems but an easy flight.
> Oh, how I glory in thee! Those great women
> Antiquity is proud of, thou but named,
> Shall be no more remembered; but persevere,
> And thou shalt shine among those lesser lights
> To all posterity like another Phoebe
> And so adored as she is. (5.2.59–67)

As Maximian's words make clear, Aurelia does conquer the laurel of 'masculine' woman, but for all the wrong reasons, so that the idea of her future superseding 'Those great women / Antiquity is proud of' is particularly disturbing. Her self-interest and ambition are further underscored by her spurring – Lady Macbeth-like – the hesitant Maximian to action when they finally reach Diocletian's country house with the army in order to kill him: 'Be speedy in your work (you will be stopped else), / And then you are an emperor' (5.4.57–8). Only after Delphia's irresistible demonstration of power does Aurelia agree to 'enjoy the riches of [Diocletian's] goodness' (5.4.147).

Aurelia embodies the courtly temptations and ambition that threaten to make Diocletian stray from honouring his initial pact with Delphia, in a country-versus-court dynamic that is at the heart of several of the plays in which Fletcher was involved. The fact that Aurelia serves a function for Maximian that is the opposite, as we shall see, of that served by Cleopatra and Delphia for Caesar and Diocletian respectively makes her treatment in the play sharply ironical and reflects badly on the possibility of agency for Roman women.

The two remaining Roman female characters, Lucina and Eudoxa, deserve a lengthier discussion. Lucina's is a fairly large role – Thomas Whitfield Baldwin puts it at 307 lines, which makes it the fourth largest in the play and similar in size to those of Cleopatra in *The False One* (316) and Delphia in *The Prophetess* (340) – and she is probably the Roman character in the canon who has attracted the highest amount of critical scrutiny, together with *The False One*'s Julius Caesar.[9] As has been often argued, Lucina is delineated in *Valentinian* as a touchstone of chastity, constancy, and integrity, her story being explicitly modelled on that of Lucrece, possibly the most celebrated *exemplum* of female virtue in Roman history, and her name, as remarked in Chapter 1, being an epithet of Diana, the goddess of chastity.[10] As Chilax explains to the other panders, Balbus, Lycinius, and Proculus, in the opening scene of the play:

> if there can be virtue, if that name
> Be anything but name and empty title,
> If it be so as fools have been pleased to feign it,
> A power that can preserve us after ashes
> And make the names of men out-reckon ages,
> This woman has a god of virtue in her. (1.1.68–73)

Lucina resists all the panders' and bawds' temptations, does not surrender even to the emperor's own insistence, and is eventually raped. Then, aware of the indelible stain that she and her family would have to carry if she continued to live, she resolves to commit suicide with the blessing of her husband Maximus.

Lucina's behaviour is that of an impeccably chaste Roman matron, yet the play also seems to make a point of emphasizing that what she embodies is an exemplary form of *passive* heroism. From the outset of the play, as Marina Hila points out, 'Lucina's body is introduced to us as a political site over which she has no control. Valentinian's bawds believe that the redemption of the Empire will take place through her; A[ët]ius suggests that she should postpone suicide in order to reclaim the emperor to virtue.'[11] Lucina's passivity is further compounded by the fact that, even though everyone is talking about her from the very first line of the tragedy, she is not referred to by name until 1.2.97, that is, not until 210 lines into the play, as if she were a nameless entity rather than a human being. That Lucina is perceived as a piece of property just like horses, orchards, and houses is also evidenced in the fact that 'Maximus plays the ring, a love token and symbol of her chastity, at dice, and loses it to the emperor'.[12] Later on, Lucina herself resentfully brands Valentinian a 'Glorious thief' for stealing her chastity (3.1.57).

Moreover, not only does Lucina's rhetorical power prove to be limited in failing first to persuade Valentinian not to rape her and to make him feel ashamed or guilty afterwards, Fletcher also crucially departs from *L'Astrée* – in which Isidore makes her husband vow to avenge her on Valentinian after the rape and remains alive long enough to rejoice at the sight of the emperor's gory corpse – in having Lucina die of grief, shame, guilt, and fear as soon as she enters her house after taking her last leave of her husband. Overwhelmed by the unbearable tangle of intense emotions, which she is shown as unable to control, she dies an offstage death 'marked by silence and the lack of agency', as Marie H. Loughlin remarks.[13]

Pace Suzanne Gossett, who argues that '[t]he very silence reveals that the method of death is insignificant', the manner of Lucina's death seems in fact to take on especial consequence, insofar as she 'is prevented, even in a Roman context, from actually striking the blow herself', as Nancy Cotton Pearse notes.[14] Not only is her will irrelevant before, during, and after the rape; even her death, planned in the form of that supreme act of self-will, suicide, turns out to be unassertive. In this sense, Lucina seems to fall short of Lucrece's example, additionally because there is no overthrow of absolute monarchy and establishment of a republican state in store for Rome at the close of the play.

Lucina thus presents a contrast with other early Jacobean characters placed in similar positions. In Thomas Heywood's *The Rape of Lucrece* (1607–08), faithful to the historical account, Lucrece relates to her husband Collatine what happened to her, makes him swear that he will avenge her rape, and commits suicide; similarly, in Thomas Middleton's *Second Maiden's Tragedy* (1611), the Lady kills herself rather than being seized by force and raped by the Tyrant. In both cases, the woman forcefully asserts her will and takes her own life. The contrast with *Valentinian* might have been especially striking in the case of Middleton's play, given that it is not unlikely that the boy actor Richard Robinson, who played the Lady in 1611, would also have been cast as Lucina.

Lucina's passivity partially contrasts with the agency that Fletcher bestowed on Valentinian's wife Eudoxa, who seems to outdo Lucina in managing to complement such 'female' qualities as chastity and faithfulness with the 'male' traits of assertiveness and rational planning. As Gwynne Kennedy observes, Eudoxa 'places herself beyond erotic desire and remains an exemplary faithful widow', thus refusing to submit herself to Maximus; at the same time, however, as Eileen Allman argues, Eudoxa is not 'confined to family, nor her virtue to chastity. Although she wishes for death, she does not commit suicide over her husband's murder; neither does she run Gertrude-like into the arms of another man.'[15] Finally, Eudoxa takes action and responsibility and upstages Maximus, thus proving to be, in fact, 'more manly than the revenger'.[16] Fletcher's desire to make Eudoxa more 'masculine' is substantiated by a couple of deviations from the sources. First, as Marco Mincoff points out, 'the manner in which she is forced to marry her husband's murderer is passed over, whereas for D'Urfé it is of cardinal importance'.[17] Second, while in the sources Eudoxa enlists the help of the Vandal King Genseric to take revenge on Maximus, *Valentinian* does not follow this narrative, with Eudoxa taking matters into her own hands instead.

And yet, notwithstanding Fletcher's apparent effort to enlarge Eudoxa's 'manly' role, at the same time the impact of her actions is somehow curtailed by other dramatic choices. Not only does she appear on stage in just three scenes in Act 5, and never alone; more importantly, even though her capacity to take action clearly challenges the maleness-authority nexus that lies at the foundations of Roman society, the play nevertheless does not culminate with gynaecocracy, and Rome's power inevitably remains in the hands of men: Eudoxa's revenge, despite punishing Maximus, does not set in motion any real political revolution.[18] Hence, the play minimizes the consequences of her revenge and her influence in intervening in the traditionally 'masculine' spheres of power and politics, thus 'successfully dissuad[ing] its audience from considering her as a political actor or revenger like the other male characters whose actions raise questions about political loyalty', as Kennedy points out.[19] In other words, as active and assertive as a Roman woman can be for Fletcher, only temporarily and only to a limited extent can she take on the male voice and inhabit male space.

Revealingly, *Valentinian* never extols Eudoxa in relation to any ancient Roman *exemplum*. This makes her stand out in a play that, as Hila points out, is profoundly informed by 'a cyclical view of history based on the premise that political roles and beliefs determine individual behaviour, rather than vice versa ... Lucina plays Lucrece; Valentinian retraces the footsteps of Nero and Caligula; Maximus follows the example set by Valentinian' rather than the one set by Lucrece's husband Collatine.[20] As a matter of fact, the Eudoxa narrative in the play actually resembles a non-Roman story that was popular in early modern England, that of Sinorix and Camma. Camma is happily married to the tetrarch Sinatus. His rival Sinorix, however, lusts after her. As Camma resists Sinorix's amorous offers, he murders Sinatus in order to woo and marry her, but she poisons both him and herself on their wedding day. 'For this deed', Pearse remarks, 'she was frequently extolled as an exemplum of wifely loyalty'; indeed, at the end of *Valentinian* the soldiers honour Eudoxa as a 'saint' (5.8.116), much as Camma was also honoured.[21] Eudoxa is not alone in being hailed as a saint in *Valentinian*; Lucina is viewed as even superior to a 'saint' (1.1.54) before she is raped. In fact, these associations might be seen as reinforcing the idea of passivity associated with these Roman women by subtly hinting, in a not uncommon instance of early modern slippage back-and-forth between ancient and Renaissance Rome, at the Catholic saints, traditionally viewed as powerful symbols of passive resistance and heroism in their determination to oppose the Roman persecutions without resorting to violence, but by refusing to comply with authority, even if this meant suffering martyrdom. At any rate, what emerges rather clearly from a scrutiny of the female Roman characters in

Valentinian is that Fletcher appears to have found the women of ancient Rome hardly adequate for the development of his ideal 'masculine' female characters, so much so that when he decided to endow Roman women with a certain degree of agency he ended up either resorting to a non-Roman model (Camma for Eudoxa) or casting their actions in a negative light (Ardelia, Phorba, and Aurelia).

THE NON-ROMAN WOMEN

Such inadequacy becomes even more apparent when the Roman women are compared with the three non-Roman women who have important roles in Fletcher's Roman plays, all of whom prove to be more 'masculine' than their Roman counterparts. In *The False One*, Cleopatra is such an actively decisive force in determining Caesar's path of temptation, fall, and regeneration that she finally manages to rise to the role of Caesar's deuteragonist.[22] During the siege of the palace towards the end of the play, Cleopatra emerges as able to 'stand unmoved', 'And with a masculine constancy deride / Fortune's worst malice' (5.4.15, 18–19), displaying dignity, courage, and nobility in the face of potential death and rising as a positive example that infuses courage in her sister.[23] As depicted in Figure 3, she does not even shed tears at the view of her brother Ptolemy's mangled corpse, because only 'common women do so' (5.4.137). More importantly, it is Cleopatra who prompts Caesar to regain his masculinity after being feminized by lust and luxury in the first part of the play, thereby making his victory against the Egyptian rebels possible; moreover, not only does she showcase, unlike Eudoxa, her ability to play a significant role in the political arena in ultimately obtaining what she wanted all along, that is, 'The crown of Egypt' (5.4.208), she also demonstrates, unlike Lucina, full control over her own body, in that she deliberately sleeps with Caesar for political gain: 'Though I purchase / His grace with loss of my virginity, / It skills not if it bring home majesty' (1.2.104–6).

As to Delphia, she is not only the eponymous character in *The Prophetess*, but its veritable puppeteer. Her importance is also mirrored in the line-count of the play. As Lucy Munro points out, 'Delphia's 340 lines give her the third largest role in *The Prophetess*; moreover, while the largest role in *The Prophetess*, Diocles, has 501 lines, the second largest, Maximinian (343 lines), is almost identical in size to Delphia'.[24] Delphia's agency and dominance are repeatedly foregrounded throughout the play: she determines Diocletian's rise to emperor and then makes him realize that being such is not so desirable after all; she seeks revenge on behalf of Drusilla rather than for herself; and she protects Diocletian's choice of a humble

3   The Egyptians defeated by the Romans at the end of *The False One*

life by using her magic to thwart Maximian and Aurelia's final assault (5.4.103–20). And even though, as McMullan observes, 'until the final act ... Delphia is at best a figure of moral ambivalence', she ultimately imparts positive moral teachings by exposing ambition, vice, and betrayal, while simultaneously making Diocletian come to appreciate such values as loyalty, gratitude, and mercy; Diocletian, as Molly Hand remarks, then 'passes them along to Maximinian, and so forth, in a great chain of reform and redemption'.[25] Such a capacity for redeeming powerful Roman generals puts Delphia on a par with *The False One*'s Cleopatra, thereby creating (as remarked above) a stark contrast with Aurelia's negative influence on Maximian; even more significantly, such a high degree of dominance and agency seems to be dependent on a characterization that, as Hand notes, evidently 'incorporate[s] essential characteristics of the male magician figure', thus making Delphia come off as a '[d]escendant of Prospero and Faustus'.[26] Hence, there is indeed at least one 'masculine' woman who manages to determine the political trajectory of the male-dominated Roman political world in the Fletcher canon, but she is a foreign sorceress.

Although Bonduca is unlike either Cleopatra or Delphia in being eventually unsuccessful in political and military terms (which partly gets her close to Eudoxa) as well as in being overshadowed by her cousin Caratach in dramatic terms, she indisputably exhibits over four out of five acts of the play (unlike Eudoxa, who only appears in the final act of *Valentinian*) those 'masculine' traits of agency and assertiveness that are hardly identifiable in the Roman women of the Fletcher canon. Even though Fletcher does not take advantage of the possibility of dramatizing the queen's vigorous speech to her troops that he would have found in Holinshed, the play has Bonduca (whom the list of 'The persons represented in the play' in the Second Folio labels 'a brave virago') mention her former victories against the Roman army – 'Twice we have beat 'em' (1.1.12) – and even though she finally succumbs, there is no doubt that her bellicosity did pose a significant threat to the world of heroic male values and that she was admirable and worthy of the male warriors' respect: 'She was truly noble and a queen' (4.4.156), comments Suetonius after her death. Bonduca's agency finds another (barbaric) outlet beyond the battlefield in her instructing her daughters to torture their Roman prisoners – 'Come, hang 'em presently ... Torment 'em, wenches' (2.3.1, 16) – and a final instantiation in her suicide during the Romans' siege of the Britons' fort (4.4.134–53), through which Bonduca avoids the humiliation of capture and triumph and also appropriates a typical Roman fashion, which is all the more significant when viewed against *Valentinian*'s Lucina's failure to take her own life.

Cleopatra, Delphia, and Bonduca evidently display superior dynamism, initiative, assertiveness, vitality, and complexity as compared to the Roman women of the canon, who never really manage to establish separate identities of their own, dependent as they are on patriarchal values and male gazes, their roles being limited to those of wives, widows, or prostitutes. More than examples of chastity, virtue, or corruption, these non-Roman women wield actual power and accomplish actions that have significant bearing upon reality. And even though they are either ultimately defeated by male power (Bonduca) or cooperate with it for positive ends (Delphia and Cleopatra, as opposed to Aurelia), each vies for pre-eminence with her male co-protagonist (Caratach, Diocletian, and Caesar). The agency of the foreign Cleopatra, Delphia, and Bonduca in the Roman plays ends up further highlighting the lack thereof in the Roman women, thus fostering the impression that there might be, as it were, something amiss in being a Roman woman in the Fletcher canon.

THE ROMAN FEMALE *EXEMPLA*

Scepticism as to the value system encoded by Roman female models is also apparent in the allusions and appeals to Roman paragons that recur so frequently across the canon, their largest share pointing to *exempla* drawn from the history of the Roman Republic and especially to Lucrece.[27] Whereas some of these allusions, as Pearse remarks, are deployed by Fletcher to compare his heroines (the majority of whom are 'wives ... or troth-plight wives') 'explicitly and implicitly to classical archetypes' as a way to 'glorify these heroines' or, adds McMullan, even 'to authorize their activities', in several places it is possible to discern what Jocelyn Catty describes as 'an equally strong tendency to undermine [those same *exempla*] through subversive rewriting', which actually conveys a palpable sense of unease as to their currency and validity.[28]

Significantly, it is the Lucrece narrative that is turned topsy-turvy most often; in particular, the rewritings tend to focus on the issue of Lucrece's consent to sex with Sextus Tarquin, with her resistance being construed as either a sign of coyness or a ruse to increase male desire, in line with early modern assumptions concerning insatiable female sexual voracity. In *The Triumph of Death* (1613–19), the villain Lavall, burning with desire for the chaste Gabriella, declares that he will ravish her 'like lusty Tarquin / Turned into flames with Lucrece's coy denials'; rather than an act of violence against Lucrece, Tarquin's rape is refashioned as actually being encouraged by her coyness, in a tendentious exploitation of the all-too-familiar no-means-yes topos.[29] Turning to the results of the attack rather than the feigned modesty that allegedly prompted it, the old bawd

Cassandra tries (unsuccessfully) to convince the beautiful and chaste Evanthe, the queen's waiting woman, to sleep with King Frederick in *A Wife for Month* (1624):

> Had Lucrece e'er been thought of but for Tarquin?
> She was before a simple unknown woman.
> When she was ravished, she was a reverend saint.
> And do you think she yielded not a little
> And had a kind of will to have been re-ravished?[30]

In this version, then, Lucrece liked intercourse with Tarquin so much that she wanted to have another go: Cassandra overturns the story to the point of transforming that great archetype of chastity into an incentive to lust, and constructing rape not just as a claim to renown and honour, but as a path to sanctity.

Bonduca's elder daughter proposes a very similar reading of Lucrece and her suicide. During their last stand against the Romans besieging their stronghold, she cries out to the assailants:

> Show me a Roman lady in all your stories
> Dare do this for her honour: they are cowards
> Eat coals like compelled cats. Your great saint Lucrece
> Died not for honour: Tarquin tupped her well,
> And mad she could not hold him bled. (4.4.115–19)

Lucrece is again referred to as a saint, but her sanctity is immediately called into question – together with the honourable pretensions of her gesture – by her allegedly unrestrainable desire to keep Tarquin for herself after their encounter, a reading that identifies in her a desperately addictive enjoyment of his sexual prowess: once more, the emblem of chastity becomes, in Andrew Bretz's phrasing, 'a leaky vessel of desire'.[31]

These depictions of Lucrece are not so unlike the one Oriana ironically provides in *The Wild-Goose Chase* (1620–21) when De Gard recommends more discretion about her love for Mirabel to protect herself from the people's opinion. Fiercely ranting against the people, Oriana claims that, if they drink enough,

> they'll swear Lucretia
> Died not for want of power to resist Tarquin,
> But want of pleasure that he stayed no longer;
> And Portia (that was famous for her piety
> To her loved lord), they'll face ye out, died o' th' pox.[32]

Exploiting once again the image of an insatiable Lucrece dying from insufficient sexual gratification and adding to the mix the vision of an unfaithful, syphilitic Portia, Oriana's reply both foregrounds, as McMullan observes, 'the implicit violence of popular male attitudes to women' and suggests the instability of these *exempla* together with the dangers of applying them across different historical periods.[33] In an early modern context, not even the *exemplum* of Lucrece can stop the 'people' from formulating judgements on women that project on to history their own expectations as a way more readily to inscribe them in the patriarchal order: if all women are insatiable strumpets, then even Lucrece and Portia must have been horny harlots, and history is in need of rewriting.

Ironically, when Lucrece's chastity is taken as a paragon in *Cupid's Revenge*, it is used as a term of comparison speciously to praise the lascivious Bacha; as Leucippus, who has already slept with her, tells his father Leontius,

> she is, by heaven,
> Of the most strict and blameless chastity
> That ever woman was. Good gods forgive me:
> Had Tarquin met with her, she had been killed
> With a slave by her ere she had agreed. (2.2.156–60)

In this case, the Lucrece *exemplum* is deprived of any ethical valence and becomes a mere instrument for sophistry. Although, as Ian Donaldson notes, the vision of Lucrece as a lustful woman was certainly not unique, these allusions would cumulatively seem to suggest that, for Fletcher, Roman female *exempla* are no longer untouchable; incorporated as they are in the early modern discourses of misogyny, patriarchy, and politics, any instances of their application to the present should at least be viewed with suspicion.[34] To be sure, as Catty points out, all these rewritings 'are made through the voice of a particular character'; nevertheless, they do seem to contribute to destabilizing and undermining the validity and meaning of the value system encoded in the traditional images of exemplary Roman women.[35]

OUT-PORTIA-ING PORTIA: JULIANA IN *THE DOUBLE MARRIAGE*

Among the allusions to Lucrece just surveyed, one also references Portia, known to early moderns as an *exemplum* of wifely loyalty to Marcus Junius Brutus, the leader of the conspiracy that killed Julius Caesar. Portia is especially relevant to the present discussion, in that she serves as a paragon for Juliana in *The Double Marriage*, which is set in Naples. Although other female characters in the plays of Fletcher may be viewed as re-enacting, to various degrees, Roman models in non-Roman contexts – such as Merione in *The Queen of Corinth* and Sophia in *Rollo* – Juliana is a more interesting character to consider, inasmuch as she is possibly the non-Roman character in the entire canon who is most explicitly, closely, and programmatically modelled against the background of a Roman *exemplum*.[36] To be more precise, however, Fletcher and Massinger do not just refer to the historical *exemplum*; they also have in mind Shakespeare's appropriation of that *exemplum*. As shall be discussed in further detail in the ensuing chapter, Fletcher often seems to put Shakespeare's Roman plays on the same level as the accounts of the classical historians, to the point of interweaving Shakespeare's dramatic retellings of Roman history with the actual historical accounts in order to infuse his characters with a heightened awareness of themselves and of their historical context, as well as spurring reflections in the audience on the validity of Roman *exempla*. That the model of Juliana in *The Double Marriage* is Shakespeare's Portia is clear from the first scene of the play, which re-enacts the well-known orchard conversation between Brutus and Portia in *Julius Caesar*, with Juliana even mentioning Brutus by name to extol the patriotic endeavour to purge one's country of a tyrant (1.1.140). Daniel Morley McKeithan has duly noted the similarities between the two scenes, but it is the differences that chiefly seem to matter in this case.[37]

Although early moderns often extolled Portia as a model of constancy and fortitude, Shakespeare's character is in fact not so steadfast and strong. As Julia Griffin points out, Shakespeare 'shows her in a state of panic while Brutus is en route to the Senate (2.4); in this scene – almost ignored by critics, and often cut in performance – she appeals for constancy and laments "how weak a thing / The heart of woman is!"'[38] Later, in a speech that appears to have no parallel in any other tellings of Portia's story, Brutus relates to Cassius how she died:

> Impatient of my absence,
> And grief that young Octavius with Mark Antony
> Have made themselves so strong – for with her death
> That tidings came – with this she fell distract,
> And, her attendants absent, swallowed fire. (*Julius Caesar*, 4.3.152–6)

Rather than exhibiting 'manly' constancy, Griffin remarks, Portia 'dies ... out of sickness and panic ... Portia, in this account, is "distract" – the word used for the desperate Titus Andronicus, Ophelia and King Lear: crazy'.[39] It is this version of Portia that Fletcher and Massinger especially want the audience to keep in mind at the outset of *The Double Marriage*; as a matter of fact, as Pearse observes, 'The suggestions of *Julius Caesar* in [the first] scene are so many that it [*sic*] will arouse in the audience a strong expectation that Juliana will behave like Shakespeare's Portia and, through nervousness and curiosity, teeter on the edge of revealing her husband's plans.'[40]

In fact, the play defies any expectations the audience might have formed. Unlike Portia, who feels the necessity to ask Brutus, 'Think you I am no stronger than my sex, / Being so father'd, and so husbanded?' (*Julius Caesar*, 2.1.295–6), Juliana does not need the authority of any male figures to vouch for her strength. Unlike Portia, Juliana does not have to hurt herself in order to convince her husband Virolet to share his plans; he does so because he is extremely impressed with the extent to which she exceeds the integrity of her sex – 'Oh, more than woman, / And more to be beloved!' (*Double Marriage*, 1.1.150–1) – as it emerges from her willingness even to renounce him if it is for the general good. As he exclaims after she leaves the stage just before the conspirators' entry, 'Such a masculine spirit, / With more than woman's virtues, were a dower / To weigh down a king's fortune' (1.1.181–3). Unlike Portia, who laments 'How hard it is for women to keep counsel' (*Julius Caesar*, 2.4.9), Juliana proves not to be 'leaky' at all. Virolet wonders 'can I find out / A cabinet to lock a secret in / Of equal trust to thee?' (*Double Marriage*, 1.1.151–3); she even resists torture and refrains from revealing her husband's secret to the tyrant of Naples Ferrand; and, as Cyrus Hoy points out, 'Like Dorothea in [Thomas Dekker and Massinger's] *The Virgin Martyr*, she tires the executioners, and the patience with which she bears her sufferings reduces her tormentors to a state of impotent frustration, as the stoic endurance of the tortured senators does Caesar in *The Roman Actor*.'[41] On the rack, Juliana endures a much more intense physical pain than that produced by a self-inflicted wound in the thigh and is even deprived of her ability to bear children in the process.

Unlike Portia, as Ira Clark observes, 'Juliana actively plots with Virolet' and forcefully encourages him to action: 'Oh, may it [i.e., your sword] / Pierce deep into this tyrant's heart, and then, / When you return bathed in his guilty blood, / I'll wash you clean with fountains of true joy' (1.1.171–4).[42] Unlike Portia, Juliana is able to suppress 'Weak women's fear' (5.2.43) in order to take action and stab the man she thinks is her husband's enemy, Ronvere. Finally, unlike Portia, Juliana does not commit suicide in her husband's absence, and is in fact as constant as to refuse to kiss Virolet even after he is free from his obligations to Martia, the daughter of the pirate Sesse (4.3.157–212). As Pearse remarks, 'the scene is incredibly ingenious in presenting the only possible temptation to the chastity of such an exemplary lady as Juliana', which suggests that 'Fletcher evidently intended to show that a woman who could display extraordinary fortitude under torture would be as extraordinarily chaste', with a view to 'creating an exemplum of womanly behavior that exceeds the precedents of ancient [hi]story', in that Juliana even 'patiently gives up her husband to her rival'.[43]

And yet it seems impossible to ignore the fact that Juliana, as Ira Clark points out, ultimately sacrifices herself 'for the honor of public masculine pride', thereby exhibiting 'the epitome of a norm of conventional feminine excellence'.[44] In other words, the play seems to suggest that, as Sandra Clark argues, 'manliness in a woman is admirable' when 'it overgoes what is naturally womanly' only as long as 'it supports rather than challenges male prerogatives, and a male-centred concept of virtue', and 'is therefore non-threatening to the accepted hierarchy of male–female relations'.[45] This conclusion is further borne out by the much more unpalatable version of the 'masculine' woman that the play offers in its depiction of Martia. As Munro persuasively argues,

> Emerging from the homosocial male world of the pirate ship, Martia is seen initially by the audience as a 'martial maid' and an '*Amazon*', fighting as bravely as any of the men. A sudden infatuation with her father's enemy, however, leads her to reject Sesse, and she increasingly turns to stereotypically 'female' crimes, working to achieve her revenge through sexual manipulation. While Sesse's piratical energies are eventually harnessed in service of a movement from tyranny to liberation, Martia actually forms an alliance with the tyrant. In redeeming Sesse as a liberator, *The Double Marriage* locates concerns about the disruptive energies of piracy in the ambiguous figure of a woman who is simultaneously masculine and hyper-feminine ... while Sesse's actions enable the political tragicomedy of the tyrant's death, Martia's lead to sexual tragedy.[46]

In becoming the cause of the divorce between Juliana and Virolet, adds Munro, Martia 'disrupts conventional bonds of marriage', ultimately leading to Virolet's father's decision 'to disinherit him and instate Juliana as his heir'.[47] Such a depiction of Martia as a dangerously destructive virago plays on early modern anxieties about women or men who do not conform to conventional gender roles, thus even more strongly affirming the *Double Marriage*'s negative stance regarding *excessively* masculine women.

Such a consideration also helps to explain the treatment of the title character in *Bonduca* as opposed to that of Cleopatra and Delphia. While Cleopatra and Delphia collaborate with men in power, Bonduca arrogates a military role that is the prerogative of the masculine world and fails effectively to cooperate with male authority: 'who bid you / Meddle in men's affairs?' (3.5.133–4), Caratach asks when the decisive battle against the Roman army takes a turn for the worse. As *Antony and Cleopatra* illustrates perfectly, to the early modern mind things are bound to go awry when women are actively involved in martial matters. Their presence is undesirable, if not unacceptable. As Bobadilla tells Clara in *Love's Cure, or The Martial Maid* (1611–17, with Massinger), 'Remember, mistress: nature hath given you a sheath only, to signify women are to put up men's weapons, not to draw them.'[48] In the plays of Fletcher, as Sandra Clark further clarifies, 'women who are too powerful, such as the Queens Bacha, Bonduca, and Brunhalt, are readily co-opted into the stereotype of the monstrous woman, and either tamed or eliminated'.[49]

Even though brought to its utmost perfection and lifted out from a more restrictive Roman context, the Roman paradigm in *The Double Marriage* still displays significant limitations: Juliana out-Portias Portia and in so doing explodes the passive Roman paradigmatic ideals of constancy, fortitude, loyalty, and chastity, which plainly emerge as truly admirable and functional only when they are combined with stoicism in order to meet the suffocating demands of a strongly patriarchal society. Impeccable as they are, Juliana's virtues are fundamentally passive and are accordingly praised as a form of saintly martyrdom – 'what new martyr heaven has begot / To fill the times with truth' (3.3.125–6) – which cannot but stress her passivity: willing even to sacrifice her biological femininity, Juliana becomes barren as a consequence of her tortures. Furthermore, her only 'real' action turns out to be disastrously mistaken: she kills the man she believes is her husband's worst enemy, Ronvere, but he is actually Virolet himself disguised. Besides, Juliana's death brings her somehow closer to *Valentinian*'s Lucina, insofar as she dies of an overwhelming emotion after having been restrained from committing suicide by her husband's command (5.2.93–105): male authority even prevents Juliana from deciding the manner and time of her own death.

The inadequacy of Roman female models is further underscored by the fact that Juliana sacrifices everything for a man, Virolet, who emerges as utterly undeserving of such a wife, being, in Pearse's words, 'one of those Fletcherian heroes who are fated and impotent in all their attempts at positive action'.[50] His very name seems to imply that his virility is at least up for discussion. In Renaissance French, *virolet* can mean 'young man' or even 'penis'; but, if 'vir-' is taken in its Latin etymology as meaning 'man' and '-let' is taken as a diminutive suffix, the implication would be that Vir-o-let is 'a little man'; moreover, when used with adult persons, the '-let' diminutive tends to be belittling, to connote paltriness and convey disdain.[51] And even if one sees Virolet as 'a well-meaning man torn apart whenever called upon to decide something', as John E. Curran, Jr, does, one still needs to acknowledge that he is 'weak … in comparison to Juliana', which seems exactly to be the point in this case.[52]

MISTRUSTING STOICISM

Such a dispirited depiction of passive female models calls to mind by association Dinant's retort to Cleremont's attempt to dissuade him from his thirst for revenge after his girlfriend Lamira has just married another man in the opening scene of *The Little French Lawyer* (1619–23, with Massinger):

> Why would you have me
> Sit down with a disgrace and thank the doer?
> We are not stoics, and that passive courage
> Is only now commendable in lackeys,
> Peasants and tradesmen, not in men of rank
> And quality as I am.[53]

Though in this instance applied to 'men', such a perspective on the inadequacy of passive endurance chimes with the judgement that the plays in the Fletcher canon seem to pass on the lack of agency of Roman female characters and the passive heroism of female *exempla*. In more general terms, it also appears to be consonant with a widespread sense of scepticism as to the lessons bequeathed by stoic philosophy that seemingly exudes from the plays in which Fletcher was involved, as anticipated at the end of the previous chapter. This provides the depiction of Rome in the canon with a very peculiar bent, given that, as Curran acknowledges, in early modern English drama Romans are generally 'imagined as: alive to their own history and their identity as Romans; attuned to their own political traditions and processes; and at least ostensibly dedicated to the directives of Stoicism'.[54] While the first two traits identified by Curran also belong to Fletcher's Romans, the third one unusually seems to be all but absent.

Stoic philosophy exerted an enormous influence on the early modern English imagination. Simply put, the ultimate goal of a stoic was to become so sage as to grow completely immune to misfortune and to regard virtue as the only necessary prerequisite for happiness. Stoicism encouraged the development of self-control and fortitude in the face of adversity as a means of overcoming destructive emotions. Mastering the passions was conceived of as indispensable in order to avoid subjecting oneself to the vagaries of fortune – something that Fletcher's characters hardly ever seem to do, given the countless high-flown outbursts of emotion that frequently threaten to interfere with their self-control and even to overwhelm their reason.

In the stoics' view, being enraged with a more powerful person was pointless, insofar as such fruitless anger would trouble one's mind and might even have destructive physical consequences as a result of potential retaliation by said person. This stance, when taken to extreme under the combined influence of so-called 'black' Tacitism – a branch of Tacitean thought advocating a passive response to such tyrannical excesses as those depicted in Tacitus' histories – would translate in an early modern context into an attitude of utter indifference to external affairs and of completely passive endurance of wrongs, especially in the political arena, as famously exemplified in Jonson's *Sejanus* by Lepidus' claim that he manages to survive under Emperor Tiberius by virtue of 'the plain and passive fortitude, / To suffer, and be silent; never stretch / These arms against the torrent; live at home, / With my own thoughts, and innocence about me, / Not tempting the wolves' jaws'.[55] Lepidus' description of his own conduct under the tyrant is similar to what Martino says about Don John in *A Very Woman*. Commenting on Don John's (excessively) temperate reaction to his realizing that the woman he loves, Almira, will in fact marry Martino himself, the latter tells Don John: 'nothing can move you, / But, like a stoic, with a constancy / Words nor affronts can shake, you still go on / And smile when men abuse you' (1.1.269–72). Eventually, however, incensed beyond restraint by Martino's repeated insolent jabs, Don John loses patience, and a fight ensues. Martino's words thus seem both to provide a working definition of what stoicism probably stands for in the Fletcher canon and to summarize the plays' general distrust as to its effectiveness: if provoked beyond a certain limit, even a stoic is bound to lose his temperance.

No wonder, then, that *Valentinian* appears to discredit Aëtius' loyalist, stoically passive position. Aëtius represents the ideal of unquestioning obedience to the sovereign: as he tells his friend, 'We are but subjects, Maximus. Obedience / To what is done and grief for what is ill done / Is all we can call ours' (1.3.17–19) because 'majesty is made to be obeyed, / And not inquired into' (1.3.27–8). His staunch defence of divine-right monarchy is a perfectly logical and acceptable position, and the play makes it clear that his viewpoint is meant to be put to the test in the most extreme situation possible, in light of the emperor's manifest and irredeemable evil. However, I concur with Finkelpearl's view that *Valentinian* takes pains to depict Aëtius 'as a narrow fanatic' whose obedience is so immoderate 'that he kills himself when all potential executioners are too frightened to do the deed' – his ultimate suicide ironically turning out to be, as Loughlin points out, 'the final act of absolute obedience to his sovereign'.[56] The play also calls Aëtius' suicide into question because, as Curran argues,

> it is clearly on him, A[ë]tius, the famous defender of the West against the ravages of Attila, that Rome depends; the very presence onstage of

A[ë]tius disproves his theorizing by alerting us to the barbarian menace that hangs implicitly but ominously over the play. Though the play ends with a Rome struggling to put itself back together, we cannot suspend our knowledge that Valentinian's murder of A[ë]tius ensures Rome's fall.[57]

All in all, *Valentinian* seems to suggest rather uncontroversially that patient suffering and silent obedience are not ideal – or even viable – options, especially given the extent to which the play dwells on the emperor's boundless depravity and viciousness.

Revenge is not presented as an ideal solution either, insofar as Maximus duplicates his predecessor's faults as soon as he ascends the throne, and Rome is eventually left in a shambles and without a male leader. Yet the play does at least appear to imply that action is nonetheless more commendable than *in*action, which is effectively encapsulated in Aëtius' assertion that 'We are but shadows: motions others give us, / And though our pities may become the times, / Justly our powers cannot' (1.3.73–5). As a matter of fact, revenge is not *technically* punished in the course of the play. Maximus falls because he decides to overreach himself by chasing the imperial laurel and then reveals to Eudoxa that he was behind Valentinian's death. If Maximus had stopped at revenge, he would not have been chastised. Eudoxa too avenges herself on Maximus for her husband's death but is hailed as 'righteous', 'a saint', and 'our protector' (5.8.111, 116, 117) rather than punished; in fact, it seems implicit that she will have at least some role in choosing Rome's next leader. In other words, as Finkelpearl has it, the play appears to suggest that 'The way of the unresisting saint is impressive but inhumane; the way of personal vengeance is egotistical and cruel, but somehow necessary if life is to continue.'[58] No positive judgement whatsoever seems to be passed on stoic suffering.

In this sense, it does not seem coincidental either that the plays in the Fletcher canon manifest a certain eccentricity as compared to those of other contemporary playmakers in their conspicuous dearth of engagement with Seneca's works. Out of the forty-nine extant plays in which Fletcher indisputably had a hand, only four exhibit verbal echoes of Seneca, all in sections usually attributed to Massinger: *Rollo* draws upon *Phoenissae*, *The Spanish Curate* upon *Hercules furens*, *The False One* upon *Phaedra*, and *A Very Woman* upon *De beneficiis*. Furthermore, in none of these cases do the plays resort to Seneca for anything related to the tenets of stoicism. *Rollo* translates large chunks of the oration with which Jocasta tries to reconcile her sons Eteocles and Polynices to construct the remarkable speech through which Sophia manages to convince her sons Rollo and Otho to terminate hostilities between one another (albeit only temporarily). *The Spanish Curate* borrows a mere three lines in a speech uttered by Don Jamie about the value of acting quickly as opposed to hesitating when faced with the necessity of accomplishing momentous deeds. *The False One*'s Cleopatra, faced with Pothinus' insolence moments before the end of the play, wonders 'Can there be gods and hear this, and no thunder / Ram thee into the earth?' (5.4.112–13), thus echoing in a shortened form Hyppolitus' famous invocation to Jove: '*Magne regnator deum, / tam lentus audis scelera? tam lentus vides? / et quando saeva fulmen emittes manu, / si nunc serenum est?*' *A Very Woman* paraphrases Seneca's thoughts on the necessity to return gratitude for any benefits received in a speech delivered by the Captain, who, Don John remarks, has read in 'the school / Of gratitude', which is a reference to *De beneficiis*, Seneca's best-known philosophical writing in early modern England together with *De constantia*.[59]

Even more interestingly, two of the plays in the canon each mention one of the major exponents of stoicism, namely Epictetus and Seneca himself. In *The Captain*, Angelo bewails the fact that he is unable to keep at bay his attraction for Lelia and claims: 'I have read Epictetus twice over against the desire of these outward things, and still her face runs in my mind' (4.4.11–13). The stoic advice of Epictetus to be indifferent to external events and factors in order to find happiness within oneself is here presented as totally ineffective. As it happens, a new translation of Epictetus' *Enchiridion* had been published in London in 1610 as *Epictetus His Manual, and Cebes His Table, out of the Greek Original*, translated by John Healey – and *The Captain* was written between 1609 and 1612, more probably at the end of this timespan. Rather than a casual mention of the stoic philosopher, then, the allusion may have been specifically to the recently published book.

In the first chapter of the *Manual*, Epictetus explains that

> In the order of the world's existence, there are some things naturally subjected unto our command and some that exceed it. Of the first sort ... all actions whose performance is peculiarly resident in ourselves; of the latter sort ... all things whose perfections depend not on ourselves, but *ab externo*.[60]

Chapter 3 of the *Manual* offers a 'general *memento*: if thou repute those things that are naturally servile to be really free and confound thy proper goods with mixture of those external ones, thou shalt never want woe but be driven by sorrow and perturbation', so that it is advisable to 'hold all those external goods, as they are, truly aliens from thy state'.[61] The ideas Epictetus puts forward at the beginning of the *Manual* are the same that underpin Angelo's words and predicament in his unrequited desire for Lelia. Such a passing mention of Epictetus is perhaps not sufficient to include his work among the sources of *The Captain*. Yet if the allusion is indeed to Healey's 1610 translation, this would offer further evidence of Fletcher and his collaborators' habit of drawing upon recently published volumes for the composition of their plays.[62]

As for the direct mention of Seneca, it is to be found in *The Loyal Subject*. When the Duke and Boroski visit Archas's house and find he is preserving part of the treasury of the old Duke, they notice 'a little trunk' (2.6.78). The Duke has the attendants open it to reveal that it only contains 'a poor gown' and 'a piece of Seneca' (2.6.84, 85). To the Duke's mocking disbelief, Archas proclaims that what he has in the trunk is 'more worth than all your gold' (2.6.86) and that the (unspecified) book of Seneca's writings is an 'unvalued treasure' (2.6.94). Yet given Archas's predicament and intense sufferings in the play – he even has to undergo torture – the impression one gets is that Seneca has not proved to be a particularly effective guide for him.

All in all, the notion of noble suffering does not appear to have excited particular admiration in Fletcher's eyes.[63] What seems to be evident, though, is the fact that his engagement with ancient Rome ended up affecting his production even beyond those plays specifically set in ancient Rome, which makes his reading and reworking of the classics even more significant, remarkable, and momentous.

CONCLUSION

Going back to women, Munro provides an important *caveat* concerning the frequent recurrence of strong, 'masculine' female characters in the plays of the Fletcher canon. While discussing *The Tamer Tamed*, she remarks that

> Fletcher is sympathetic to the plight of women caught within patriarchal structures, but he is not a twenty-first century feminist, and it is unrealistic to expect him to be able to imagine a realistic alternative to these structures ... A temporary inversion of gender roles is possible, and may have beneficial long-term results, but it can only be temporary.[64]

The impression that one gains from the Roman plays in the canon is that the Roman women are hardly ever allowed even that short glimpse of a temporary, radical inversion of roles, caught up as they are, for all their exemplarity, in an excessively passive fulfilment of their fixed roles as mothers, wives, widows, saints, or whores. In Roman society as dramatized by Fletcher, the hierarchy of gender roles is never as destabilized as elsewhere in the canon, and the audience hardly ever witnesses the 'theatrical triumph of witty women over misogynist men' that Kathleen McLuskie sees as typical of many plays in which Fletcher had a hand; when this occurs, what the audience sees is at best the success of such non-Roman characters as Delphia and Cleopatra.[65] Female power lies or comes from outside Rome in a sort of inverted penetration; if Roman masculinity is in crisis in Fletcher's Roman world (as the 'feminized' or unconfident depictions of Valentinian and, to a lesser extent, Caesar would seem to suggest), so is femininity, and the 'masculine' qualities that would make Roman women assertive and dominant rather than mere paragons of constancy, self-sacrifice, and chastity are transferred on to non-Roman women as a way to put this situation into even sharper focus: the women who at least collaborate decisively with powerful Roman men, namely Delphia and Cleopatra, are patently not Roman. The only Roman woman who does, Aurelia, cynically pursues selfish goals.

Even the rhetorical skills of these Roman women are presented as either limited or ineffectual. There is no Volumnia in Fletcher's Roman world. Apart from Lucina, the case of *Rollo*'s Sophia is also particularly significant. Despite only achieving a temporary truce and ultimately having to acknowledge her own inability to operate in the realm of politics, her plea for reconciliation between her two sons, Rollo and Otho, is an admirably powerful and moving specimen of rhetoric, which translates (as mentioned above) passages from Seneca. Tellingly, as we have seen, when writing *Rollo*, Fletcher and his collaborators chose to change the setting from imperial Rome to medieval France, so that even such an instance of powerful oratory as Sophia's becomes that of a non-Roman woman, which might have been one of the reasons why the playwrights decided to subject the source material to such a radical change.

The plays considered here therefore contrast markedly with the comedies and (most of the) tragicomedies of the Fletcher canon, which often manifest 'the immense theatrical potential of women's conflicted, combative relationships with men'.[66] In fact, the Roman plays seem painfully to expose the limitations of Roman female *exempla*, which are exhibited as undependable and impracticable even in their most perfect realization outside a Roman context, that is, Juliana in *The Double Marriage*. The excessive passivity enshrined in these virtuous Roman female models seems to be presented with more than an ounce of scepticism. This kind of virtue is too uncompromising and exaggeratedly pristine for Fletcher not to treat it with suspicion and disapproval. The sacrifice that is required of the individual (and, often, their immediate family) is so excessive and so barely credible that the impression one gets is that Fletcher might have even found something disturbing in it.

Just as with Fletcher's choice of sources, which tended to privilege continental Renaissance publications over the classics and suggests little sense on his part of having found any solemnity or inherent superiority in classical texts, these female *exempla*, the plays would seem to suggest, cannot be followed or adopted solely by virtue of their antiquity; in fact, it is their very antiquity that keeps them firmly stuck in the past, thereby making them somewhat unpalatable and, above all, hardly viable as guides for the present and the future.

In 'A Short Discourse of the English Stage' (1664), Richard Flecknoe commented that

> Beaumont and Fletcher were excellent in their kind, but they often erred against decorum, seldom representing a valiant man without somewhat of the braggadocio, nor an honourable woman without somewhat of Dol Common in her, to say nothing of their irreverent representing kings' persons on the stage, who should never be represented but with reverence.[67]

Though it might not seem the case at a first glance, Flecknoe's notorious criticism of Beaumont and Fletcher's way of presenting masculinity, femininity, and politics on stage appears in some odd way to capture the tendencies that I have been describing in these pages. Flecknoe conceptualizes Beaumont and Fletcher's practice as something that violates 'decorum', and while such a notion might sound old-fashioned and of little interest to twenty-first-century ears, it is revealing because it implies a classical frame of reference. As Roger Ascham preached in *The Schoolmaster* (1570),

> whosoever hath been diligent to read advisedly over Terence, Seneca, Virgil, Horace, or else Aristophanes, Sophocles, Homer, and Pindar, and shall diligently mark the difference they use in propriety of words, in form of sentence, in handling of their matter, he shall easily perceive what is fit and decorum in everyone, to the true use of perfect imitation.[68]

Flecknoe's reservation about Beaumont and Fletcher's stage characterization seems therefore to have an ampler scope, as it implicitly – and correctly – identifies Fletcher's larger tendency to abstain from an adherence to classical forms, models, and paradigms, which he rather questions and modifies by contaminating them with non-classical elements. In several instances, as the next chapter shall seek to demonstrate, Fletcher seems to regard Shakespeare as a better mentor than the classics.

NOTES

1 Finkelpearl, *Court and Country Politics*, 241.
2 McMullan, *Politics of Unease*, 76.
3 McMullan, *Politics of Unease*, 194, 62.

4 On the depiction of Roman women in early modern English drama, see Lovascio (ed.), *Roman Women in Shakespeare and His Contemporaries*.
5 On women's condition in ancient Rome, see, among others, Susan Dixon, *The Roman Mother* (London: Routledge, 1988); John K. Evans, *War, Women and Children in Ancient Rome* (London: Routledge, 1991); Richard A. Bauman, *Women and Politics in Ancient Rome* (London: Routledge, 1992); Eva Cantarella, *Passato prossimo. Donne romane da Tacita a Sulpicia* (Milan: Feltrinelli, 1996); Augusto Fraschetti (ed.), *Roman Women*, trans. Linda Lappin (Chicago: University of Chicago Press, 2001); Bonnie MacLachlan (ed.), *Women in Ancient Rome: A Sourcebook* (London: Bloomsbury, 2013).
6 The name of Delphia's niece (a character invented for the play) is Drusilla. As Roman history features many famous Drusillas, one might be led to think that she is a Roman; yet nowhere does the play suggest that she is. In fact, the name Drusilla apparently has Celtic origins, which is possibly the reason behind the choice made by Fletcher and Massinger, who may have inferred the Gaulish origin of the name from Suetonius, *History of Twelve Caesars*, 89; Suetonius, 'The Life of Tiberius', 3.2, in *The Lives of the Twelve Caesars*, trans. J. C. Rolfe (London: Heinemann, 1913), 297.
7 Hila, '"Justice shall never heare ye, I am justice"', 752.
8 Pearse, *Fletcher's Chastity Plays*, 223–4.
9 Thomas Whitfield Baldwin, *The Organization and Personnel of the Shakespearean Company* (Princeton, NJ: Princeton University Press, 1927), casting-charts between pages 198 and 199.
10 As Pearse, *Fletcher's Chastity Plays*, 151, points out, 'Fletcher uses three variations of the Lucrece story. *Valentinian* follows the traditional pattern, in which the heroine dies after having been raped; *The Queen of Corinth*, a collaboration with Field and Massinger, given an anomalous inversion of this pattern; and *The Maid in the Mill*, a collaboration with Rowley, uses the modified Lucrece pattern, in which the heroine avoids rape by her own efforts.'
11 Hila, '"Justice shall never heare ye, I am justice"', 750.
12 Hila, '"Justice shall never heare ye, I am justice"', 750.
13 Loughlin, *Hymeneutics*, 164.
14 Suzanne Gossett, '"Best men are molded out of faults": Marrying the Rapist in Jacobean Drama', *English Literary Renaissance* 14 (1984), 305–27 (308); Pearse, *Fletcher's Chastity Plays*, 155.
15 Gwynne Kennedy, 'Gender and the Pleasures of Revenge', in *Feminism and Early Modern Texts: Essays for Phyllis Rackin*, ed. Rebecca Ann Bach and Gwynne Kennedy (Selinsgrove, PA: Susquehanna University Press, 2010), 152–71 (158); Allman, *Jacobean Revenge Tragedy*, 125.
16 Allman, *Jacobean Revenge Tragedy*, 127.
17 Mincoff, 'Fletcher's Early Tragedies', 72.
18 Allman, *Jacobean Revenge Tragedy*, 129.
19 Kennedy, 'Gender and the Pleasures of Revenge', 159.
20 Hila, '"Justice shall never heare ye, I am justice"', 749.
21 Pearse, *Fletcher's Chastity Plays*, 156.
22 For a fuller discussion, see Lovascio, 'She-Tragedy: Lust, Luxury and Empire in John Fletcher and Philip Massinger's *The False One*', 166–83.
23 Other women displaying 'masculine constancy' in the canon are the Queen in *The Queen of Corinth*, 5.4.129, and Zenocia in *The Custom of the Country*, 2.2.51. As this phrase always occurs in plays to which Massinger contributed, it is possible to concur with Cyrus Hoy, 'Massinger as Collaborator: The Plays with Fletcher

and Others', in *Philip Massinger: A Critical Reassessment*, ed. Douglas Howard (Cambridge: Cambridge University Press, 1985), 51–82, in viewing this as 'Massinger's highest tribute to the kind of fortitude great ladies are capable of displaying in adversity' (67).
24 Munro, *Shakespeare in the Theatre*, 140.
25 McMullan, *Politics of Unease*, 184; Hand, '"You take no labour"', 174.
26 Hand, '"You take no labour"', 170. See also Munro, *Shakespeare in the Theatre*, 140–3.
27 Pearse, *Fletcher's Chastity Plays*, 151–90.
28 Pearse, *Fletcher's Chastity Plays*, 228; McMullan, *Politics of Unease*, 166 (but see also 167–72); Jocelyn Catty, *Writing Rape, Writing Women in Early Modern England: Unbridled Speech* (Basingstoke: Palgrave Macmillan, 1999), 94, 98.
29 John Fletcher and Nathan Field, *Four Plays, or Moral Representations, in One*, ed. Cyrus Hoy, in Bowers (gen. ed.), *Dramatic Works*, 8.223–344, 6.92–3.
30 John Fletcher, *A Wife for a Month*, ed. Robert Kean Turner, in Bowers (gen. ed.), *Dramatic Works*, 6.355–482, 4.3.40–4.
31 Andrew Bretz, '"Are you my sweet heart?" *Bonduca* and the Failure of Chivalric Masculinity', *Research on Medieval and Renaissance Drama* 54 (2015), 59–72 (67–8). On women as 'leaky vessels' in the early modern social imagination, see Gail Kern Paster, *The Body Embarrassed: Drama and the Disciplines of Shame in Early Modern England* (Ithaca, NY: Cornell University Press, 1993), 23–63.
32 John Fletcher, *The Wild-Goose Chase*, ed. Sophie Tomlinson, in *Three Seventeenth-Century Plays on Women and Performance*, ed. Hero Chalmers, Julie Sanders, and Sophie Tomlinson (Manchester: Manchester University Press, 2006), 61–176, 1.2.116–20.
33 McMullan, *Politics of Unease*, 168.
34 Ian Donaldson, *The Rapes of Lucretia: A Myth and Its Transformations* (Oxford: Clarendon Press, 1982), 36–7.
35 Catty, *Writing Rape, Writing Women*, 99.
36 On Merione, see Pearse, *Fletcher's Chastity Plays*, 156–63; Gossett, '"Best men are molded out of faults"', 316–7; Loughlin, *Hymeneutics*, 104–7, 121–38; Curran, 'Declamation and Character in the Fletcher-Massinger Plays', 103–5. On Sophia, see Clark, *Plays of Beaumont and Fletcher*, 114–16; Curran, 'Fletcher, Massinger, and Roman Imperial Character', 334–5.
37 Daniel Morley McKeithan, *The Debt to Shakespeare in the Beaumont-and-Fletcher Plays* (Austin, TX: privately printed, 1938), 167–9.
38 Julia Griffin, 'Cato's Daughter, Brutus's Wife: Portia from Antiquity to the English Renaissance Stage', in *The Uses of Rome in English Renaissance Drama*, ed. Domenico Lovascio and Lisa Hopkins, *Textus: English Studies in Italy* 29.2 (2016), thematic issue, 21–40 (36); Shakespeare, *Julius Caesar*, 2.4.40–1.
39 Griffin, 'Cato's Daughter, Brutus's Wife', 36–7.
40 Pearse, *Fletcher's Chastity Plays*, 172.
41 Hoy, 'Massinger as Collaborator', 65.
42 Clark, *Moral Art*, 192.
43 Pearse, *Fletcher's Chastity Plays*, 173–5.
44 Clark, *Moral Art*, 194.
45 Clark, *Plays of Beaumont and Fletcher*, 74, 76.
46 Lucy Munro, 'Virolet and Martia the Pirate's Daughter: Gender and Genre in Fletcher and Massinger's *The Double Marriage*', in *Pirates? The Politics of Plunder, 1550–1650*, ed. Claire Jowitt (Basingstoke: Palgrave Macmillan, 2007), 118–34 (120).
47 Munro, 'Virolet and Martia the Pirate's Daughter', 126–7.

48 John Fletcher and Philip Massinger, *Love's Cure, or The Martial Maid*, ed. José A. Pérez Díez (Manchester: Manchester University Press, 2022), 2.2.91–3.
49 Clark, *Plays of Beaumont and Fletcher*, 156.
50 Pearse, *Fletcher's Chastity Plays*, 173.
51 François Rabelais, *Œuvres*, ed. Francois-Henri-Stanislas de L'Aulnaye, 3 vols (Paris: Louis Janet, 1823), 3.486.
52 Curran, 'Declamation and Character in the Fletcher-Massinger Plays', 99–100.
53 John Fletcher and Philip Massinger, *The Little French Lawyer*, ed. Robert Kean Turner, in Bowers (gen. ed.), *Dramatic Works*, 9.337–426, 1.1.6–11. All references to the play are to this edition. Subsequent references will be incorporated parenthetically into the text.
54 John E. Curran, Jr, 'Roman Tragedy: The Case of Jonson's *Sejanus*', in *The Genres of Renaissance Tragedy*, ed. Daniel Cadman, Andrew Duxfield, and Lisa Hopkins (Manchester: Manchester University Press, 2019), 100–14 (102).
55 Ben Jonson, *Sejanus His Fall*, ed. Tom Cain, in Bevington, Butler, and Donaldson (gen. eds), *Cambridge Jonson*, 2.212–391, 4.294–8. For a distinction between so-called 'red' and 'black' versions of Tacitism, see Giuseppe Toffanin, *Machiavelli e Tacitismo* (Padua: Draghi, 1921); Peter Burke, 'Tacitism', in *Tacitus*, ed. T. A. Dorey (London: Routledge and Kegan Paul, 1969), 149–71 (162–7).
56 Finkelpearl, *Court and Country Politics*, 214; Loughlin, *Hymeneutics*, 169.
57 Curran, 'Fletcher, Massinger, and Roman Imperial Character', 342.
58 Finkelpearl, *Court and Country Politics*, 218–19.
59 John Fletcher, Philip Massinger, and Anonymous, *Rollo, Duke of Normandy, or the Bloody Brother*, ed. George Walton Williams, in Bowers (gen. ed.), *Dramatic Works*, 10.166–245, 1.1.239–43, 284–301, 303–4, 309–13, 316–24, 332–8, 362–6, 370–1; *Spanish Curate*, 5.1.149–51; *A Very Woman*, 2.1.35–9, 41–2. All references to *Rollo* are to this edition. Subsequent references will be incorporated parenthetically into the text.
60 *Epictetus His Manual, and Cebes His Table, out of the Greek Original*, trans. John Healey (London, 1610), fols B1r–v.
61 *Epictetus His Manual*, fol. B2r.
62 Wiggins, *Catalogue*, 6:216, #1665, lists the allusion as a mention of Epictetus' *Discourses*. Yet the *Discourses* were not available in English translation until 1758, while the *Manual* (or *Enchiridion*) had been already translated in 1567 (from French) by James Sandford before Healey's 1610 translation (from Greek) appeared. On balance, then, it appears more likely that the reference is to the *Manual* rather than the *Discourses*.
63 As a matter of fact, there seem to be only two clear praises of stoic endurance in the entire canon. One appears in *The Honest Man's Fortune*, when Charlotte asks Montague: 'What more speaks / Greatness of man than valiant patience, / That shrinks not under his fate's strongest strokes?' (Nathan Field, John Fletcher, Philip Massinger, and Robert Daborne, *The Honest Man's Fortune*, ed. Cyrus Hoy, in Bowers [gen. ed.], *Dramatic Works*, 10.16–111, 4.1.171–3). This is, however, a play predominantly written by Field, and in the relevant section there seems to be no trace of Fletcher. The other instance is in *A Very Woman*, when the Doctor tells Martino that 'Who fights / With passions and o'ercomes 'em is endued / With the best virtue, passive fortitude' (4.2.153–5). Yet his words need not be taken at face value and cannot be taken as unqualifiedly sincere, insofar as the play makes it clear that the Doctor would say and do anything to cure Martino from his 'melancholy' (4.2.2).

64 Munro, 'Introduction', xv.
65 McLuskie, *Renaissance Dramatists*, 214.
66 Hero Chalmers, Julie Sanders, and Sophie Tomlinson, 'Introduction', in *Three Seventeenth-Century Plays on Women and Performance* (Manchester: Manchester University Press, 2006), 1–60 (15).
67 Richard Flecknoe, 'A Short Discourse of the English Stage', in *Love's Kingdom* (London, 1664), fols G6r-v.
68 Roger Ascham, *The Schoolmaster* (London, 1570), fol. Rir.

CHAPTER 4

'TO DO THUS / I LEARNED OF THEE':
SHAKESPEARE'S EXEMPLARY
ROMAN PLAYS

It is a truth universally acknowledged that many of the plays in the Fletcher canon stand in more or less explicit conversation with those of Shakespeare. As a matter of fact, a few of them are *defined* against Shakespeare's, as is the case, for example, of *The Tamer Tamed*, the success of which must have at least partly depended on the audience's knowledge of *The Taming of the Shrew*. If Clifford Leech generally argued that '[t]here is not ... a single play in the Beaumont and Fletcher Folios which does not display Shakespearian echoes', David L. Frost tried to be more precise by contending that '[n]o less than thirty-five ... plays in the "Beaumont and Fletcher" Folio show some knowledge of Shakespeare'.[1] More recently, Gordon McMullan has remarked that Fletcher's plays established 'a clear, if elliptical, relationship with the plays of Shakespeare right from the start'; Clare McManus has observed that Fletcher's career can be viewed as largely marked 'by his virtuosic, if irreverent, responses to Shakespeare's canon'; and Misha Teramura has described Shakespeare's oeuvre as Fletcher's 'endless mine', which the latter would never cease to subject to 'his own protean acts of homage, appropriation and parody'.[2]

As this chapter sets out to demonstrate, this diachronic collaboration emerges as especially important in the Roman plays of the Fletcher canon, insofar as Shakespeare's Roman world – unlike Jonson's, despite the warm appreciation expressed by Fletcher in his commendatory verses to the quarto edition of *Catiline* in 1611, that is, a little before he started dramatizing the Roman past himself – apparently became for Fletcher and Massinger an integral part of the treasury of Roman stories, contexts, characters, incidents, and attitudes upon which they could draw in crafting a Roman play for the London commercial stage. The events dramatized in Shakespeare's Roman plays also seem to be eerily impressed in the memories of Fletcher's characters, as a close scrutiny of *Valentinian*, *Bonduca*, *The False One*, and *The Prophetess* aptly demonstrates. As anticipated in the discussion of *The Double Marriage*'s Juliana in the previous chapter, the Roman plays in the Fletcher canon frequently depict the events and personalities of Roman history as filtered through Shakespeare's lens.

True, reminiscences of Shakespeare's Roman plays often surface in other plays of the Fletcher canon as well. It is possible to identify allusions to *Antony and Cleopatra* in *The Woman Hater*, *The Maid's Tragedy*, *The Wild-Goose Chase*, and *The Island Princess* (1619–21); to *Coriolanus* in *A King and No King*; and to *Julius Caesar* in *Philaster*, *The Maid's Tragedy*, *The Captain*, *The Chances* (1616–25), *Sir John Van Olden Barnavelt*, *The Little French Lawyer*, *The Double Marriage*, *The Lovers' Progress* (1619–24, rev. Massinger 1634), and possibly *Henry VIII*.[3] As significant as these echoes are, however, in this chapter I will focus exclusively on Fletcher's reuse of building materials from Shakespeare's Rome for the construction of his own. While this exploration will concentrate at greater length on Fletcher's reworking of multiple elements from Shakespeare's Plutarchan plays in *The Prophetess* – which has been ignored by previous scholarship but in fact proves to be especially revelatory of Fletcher's approach – it seems expedient first to survey the Roman Shakespearean intertext in *Valentinian*, *Bonduca*, and *The False One*, which, by contrast, has attracted some scholarly commentary.

As this chapter argues, Fletcher often puts Shakespeare's Roman plays on the same level as the accounts of the classical historians, to the point of interweaving Shakespeare's dramatic retellings of Roman history with the actual historical accounts in order to infuse his characters with a heightened awareness of themselves and their historical context, as well as spurring reflections in the audience regarding the validity of Roman *exempla*. Fletcher's dynamic interaction with Shakespeare's Rome is, on one level, a further indicator of what Suzanne Gossett describes as 'the tight-knit, interactive early Jacobean theatrical milieu', in which, Andrew Gurr remarks, '[o]verlaps and long-lasting tenures ensured they were all thoroughly familiar with the existing repertoire'.[4] Accordingly, as William W. E. Slights illustrates, 'an echoed line or speech created a shared theatrical in-joke of the kind that continues to be a huge part of today's cinematic collaborations of writers and knowledgeable audiences. Similarly ... the company itself was a collective, and its texts were repeatedly rewritten for fresh performances.'[5]

As shall become apparent in the ensuing pages, the implications of Fletcher's conversation with Shakespeare's Rome become much wider-ranging when this interaction is viewed in the broader context of the repertory of his theatrical company. As Lucy Munro points out, 'After Shakespeare's retirement, his plays continued to be central to the court and commercial repertoire, and to the ongoing identity and practices of the King's Men.'[6] An attention to the repertory context in which these plays were first performed and restaged proves to be particularly productive in exploring the Fletcherian characters' memory of Shakespeare, especially in terms of the possibility that different roles that are connected textually with each other may have been played by the same actor. As Marvin Carlson argues, the 'recycled body of an actor' in a performance 'will almost inevitably in a new role evoke the ghost or ghosts of previous roles', and Fletcher may have consciously exploited this mechanism in his theatrical practice.[7]

While Fletcher's conversation with Shakespeare's Roman plays spans his entire career, it intensifies in the 1619–23 period, which seems to exhibit a near obsession with *Julius Caesar* and *Antony and Cleopatra*. It is perhaps not coincidental that that period would begin precisely in 1619, when plans for the publication of Shakespeare's First Folio are likely to have been set in motion. The chapter ends by wondering whether Fletcher might have had a role – however small – in the preparation of the Folio.

VALENTINIAN

Valentinian's most obvious point of contact with Shakespeare's vision of Rome would seem to be the fact that the play revolves around the rape of Lucina, her story being modelled on that of Lucrece (as discussed in Chapter 3), which was also the subject of Shakespeare's 1594 narrative poem. Fletcher's play makes the connection between the two women explicit in the report of Balbus, one of the panders sent by Valentinian to persuade Lucina to become his mistress:

> I ask her,
> After my many offers, walking with her,
> And her as many down denials: how
> If the Emperor, grown mad with love, should force her?
> She pointed to a Lucrece that hung by,
> And with an angry look that from her eyes
> Shot vestal fire against me, she departed. (1.1.88–94)

This description of Lucina's reaction must have been extremely powerful on stage, given that Lucrece was a familiar and important figure to women in particular. What Lucina points to is either a painting of Lucrece or a needlework image of her, which she might have sewn herself: Lucrece was a very common subject for early modern women's handiwork (for example, Bess of Hardwick had a Lucrece hanging and even called her youngest daughter Lucrece).[8] Hence, many female audience members might feel like Lucina, in that they too could point 'to a Lucrece that hung by'. After the rape, Lucina curses Valentinian with these words: 'The sins of Tarquin be remembered in thee' (3.1.91).

Lucina's pointing to the image of Lucrece is also reminiscent of Lucrece's own gazing in Shakespeare's poem at 'a piece / Of skilful painting' that shows the fall of Troy as a way to assuage her grief after being ravished.[9] Lucrece scans several harrowing images of grieving Trojans before singling out that of 'despairing HECUBA' (1447), widely considered a symbol of female grief in the early modern imagination. Lucrece recognizes in Hecuba a woman from antiquity on whom she can fashion herself and against whose *exemplum* she can judge herself, similarly to what Lucina does with the image of Lucrece. Although Fletcher in *Valentinian* seems more concerned with the story of Lucrece as handed down by Livy than any early modern retellings, such a reminiscence seems to suggest that even in this case the Shakespearean precedent was to him inescapable.

Valentinian is also in conversation with *Julius Caesar*. Marco Mincoff observes that the quarrel scene between Maximus and Aëtius (3.3.71–168) owes 'a great deal to the quarrel in *Julius Caesar*, but they employ the situation very differently, and while with Shakespeare we are aware above all of a contrast of personalities', in *Valentinian* 'it is much more with the fluctuations of the emotional barometer that we are concerned'.[10] The differences, however, are more, and deeper. First, the dialogue between Maximus and Aëtius is not really a quarrel. Neither of them gets really angry or offends the other openly – Maximus rather insults himself: 'I am a coward, / A cuckold and a coward: that's two causes / Why everyone should beat me' (3.3.82–5) – and their discussion never really escalates. Second, they both resort to asides in order to conceal information from each other, which exhibits fault lines in their friendship, while the bond between Brutus and Cassius is never really in doubt in *Julius Caesar* despite the tensions between them. Third, neither Maximus nor Aëtius patronizes the other as Brutus does with Cassius at the outset of the scene. Fourth, while the cause of the 'quarrel' between Cassius and Brutus is in the past, Aëtius and Maximus have conflicting views regarding Maximus' future course of action against the emperor. Brutus and Cassius had led together the conspiracy that killed Caesar, whereas Aëtius will take part in no plot against the emperor: in fact, he tries to curb Maximus' fury, and their conversation ends with Aëtius plainly telling Maximus that he will kill him if he strikes 'this fatal blow' (3.3.160) against Valentinian. Finally, even though both Maximus and Brutus are distressed by the recent deaths of their wives, Maximus completely lacks Brutus' self-control and is depicted as a man falling apart, which helpfully corroborates the argument advanced in the previous chapter regarding Fletcher's sceptical position regarding stoicism and the control of emotions. As this comparison makes clear, Fletcher's reworking of the Shakespearean material is in this case rather radical, putting as it does a well-known theatrical situation to fresh purposes.

Valentinian echoes *Julius Caesar* at least twice more, as recorded by H. J. Makkink.[11] One of these echoes – namely Maximus' words 'He that shall live / Ten ages hence, but to rehearse this story' (*Valentinian*, 4.4.348–9), which seem to be redolent of Cassius' far more famous 'How many ages hence / Shall this our lofty scene be acted over / In states unborn and accents yet unknown' (*Julius Caesar*, 3.1.111–13) – appears to reveal that Fletcher was conferring on his characters the metatheatrical awareness typical of characters in the Roman plays of the period (e.g., *The Roman Actor*). The second resemblance, that between Maximus' 'There's no way else to do it: he must die' (*Valentinian*, 3.3.1) and Brutus' 'It must be by his death' (*Julius Caesar*, 2.1.10) – which Makkink notes but does not discuss – deserves closer analysis. In both passages, a Roman senator is musing about the projected murder of a friend (Aëtius in Maximus' case, Caesar in Brutus'), and both monologues open with the proclaiming of a decision already taken uttered through a sequence of monosyllabic words. While soliloquizing, Maximus spells out his bond of friendship with the future victim more explicitly than Brutus and, again, with crisp monosyllabic utterances: 'This friend must die' (*Valentinian*, 3.3.2) and 'A friend is more than all the world' (3.3.35). Like Brutus, who has decided to act because something *might* happen – 'And since the quarrel / Will bear no colour for the thing he is, / Fashion it thus' (*Julius Caesar*, 2.1.28–30) – Maximus has resolved to get rid of Aëtius 'for if I offer / To take my way without him, like a sea / He bears his high command twixt me and vengeance, / And in my road sinks me' (*Valentinian*, 3.3.9–12). Admittedly, Maximus cannot be absolutely sure that Aëtius will kill him if he kills the emperor, yet the play uncontroversially suggests that, given Aëtius' unwavering loyalty to the emperor despite his tyrannical behaviour, this is the most likely outcome for Maximus should he not dispose of Aëtius before avenging himself on Valentinian. Hence, Maximus' prediction is grounded in a more objective and reliable assessment of reality than that of Brutus.

What is more, Maximus never tries to rationalize his decision by fooling himself into thinking that it stems from a selfless preoccupation with the general good, fully aware as he is of the personal motivations that are leading him to take such a bloody course of action. Maximus understands and describes much more lucidly than Brutus ever manages to do both his concern with his own reputation – 'Shall not men's tongues / Dispute it afterward, and say I gave / … / The only virtue of the world to slander?' (3.3.42–3, 46) – and the emotional burden he must carry in making such a resolution: 'I am so troubled, / And such a deal of conscience presses me' (3.3.69–70). In other words, Maximus' inner conflict is framed more openly in terms of personal friendship versus reputation rather than love, Aëtius being an obstacle to Maximus' rehabilitation of his own honour through the killing of his wife's rapist. Moreover, in describing his decision as 'A hard choice and a *fatal*' (3.3.5, emphasis mine), Maximus appears to be endowed with a deeper awareness than Brutus – who cannot seem to envision any possible negative repercussions of his projected deed – as concerns the potentially destructive consequences of his imminent course of action: ''tis my killing: / Aëtius is my root, and wither him, / Like a decaying branch I fall to nothing' (3.3.19–21).

Maximus' superior clarity of vision is largely due to the fact that Valentinian is a vicious tyrant who has raped his wife rather than an ambiguous leader like Shakespeare's Caesar. Yet I am also under the impression that the Shakespearean precedent lurking in the background all the while bestows some sort of prescience on Fletcher's character. In some odd way, it is as though Maximus were familiar with Brutus' story as portrayed by Shakespeare, and thus fashions himself and makes his decisions by taking *that* story into account as an *exemplum*. This process seems akin to that at work in Shakespeare's *Troilus and Cressida* (1601–03), in which characters are positioned throughout in relation to their classical antecedents, with the result, as David Bevington points out, 'that the characters in the play seem to anticipate their own destinies. Troilus, Cressida and Pandarus, in particular, appear to understand that history will hold them up as exemplars, even as stereotypes.'[12] The characters in *Troilus and Cressida*, adds Bevington, 'do not know what we know all too well, that nothing can save them from playing out the roles that history and legend have determined for them'.[13] In the case of the Fletcherian characters, the antecedents are not their own classical or historical versions, but other Shakespearean characters in similar contexts or situations, and they do not determine their fates *tout court*. Yet the similarity is unmistakable and positions Shakespeare as a classic in Fletcher's perspective.

As will be borne out by the ensuing discussion, Shakespeare's Roman plays seem to have become an inventory of potential situations capable of providing the characters of Fletcher's Roman plays with an additional self-awareness, which helps them to achieve a better grasp of themselves and the world around them. This memory effect would have had even more impact on audiences if, hypothetically, the actors playing Maximus and Aëtius in *Valentinian* were the same as those who played Brutus and Cassius in contemporary revivals of *Julius Caesar*. We know that the play 'Caesars Tragedye' was performed at court at Christmas in 1612–13 and that it is likely to have been Shakespeare's *Julius Caesar*, but there is no evidence that *Valentinian* and *Julius Caesar* were ever staged in the same season.

BONDUCA

With regard to *Bonduca*, its most obvious Shakespearean analogue would seem to be *Cymbeline* – which has also been discussed in scholarship for its relationship to *Philaster*.[14] Both *Bonduca* and *Cymbeline* use Holinshed as a source, and William W. Appleton points out that, 'if in *Cymbeline* Shakespeare gives us a drama of a legendary English king, in *Bonduca* Fletcher ... give[s] us that of a legendary English queen', with 'Bonduca ha[ving] scarcely more importance than Cymbeline'.[15] Leech's painstaking work on the affinities between the two plays deserves extended consideration. As he argues, '[t]he most obvious resemblance is in the presentation of a conflict between Rome and Britain, and in the strange reconciliation between the opponents at the end of each play.'[16] The reconciliation in each play is described as 'strange' because in Shakespeare the Britons promise they will pay the contested tribute to Rome despite their victory, while *Bonduca* ends with Caratach's yielding to the Romans' courtesies and his consensual departure for Rome with them. Leech also identifies 'some incidental likenesses', namely the presence in both plays of 'studies in remorse' regarding, on the one hand, the fate of Posthumus, who is ultimately forgiven for his distrust of Innogen and her attempted murder, and, on the other, that of Poenius, who kills himself upon realizing the magnitude of his error in refraining from bringing his soldiers to the field with Suetonius, and whose *cognomen*, incidentally, was Posthumus.[17] Also, adds Leech, 'when Petillius persuades P[o]enius to kill himself, although Suetonius has sent him with a message of friendship and encouragement, he behaves somewhat in the fashion of Iachimo bringing false news to Posthumus concerning I[nn]ogen'.[18]

The plays also share, in Leech's view, 'some revulsion from the idea of sexual union', which is concretized in *Cymbeline* in the relationship between Posthumus and Innogen, and in *Bonduca* in the potentially destructive consequences of Julius' irrational attraction for Bonduca's younger daughter Bonvica, who leads him into an ambush through a fake love letter, and in Petillius' falling in love with Bonduca's elder daughter after her suicide, which introduces disturbing overtones of necrophiliac longing in the play's depiction of love.[19] As Leech comments, '[i]n both instances, love is simply a sickness to be laughed at or ... to be feared, and its departure is to be rejoiced in as a return to health and safety'.[20] The memory of the Romans' rape of Bonduca's daughters, as examined in Chapter 2, cannot but further contribute to the disgust for sexual union that informs the play. Besides, both plays feature the saddening death of a promising young boy, Fidele and Hengo respectively. The similarities identified by Leech between *Bonduca* and *Cymbeline* are significant and incontestable, but there seem to be crucial echoes from other Shakespearean plays as well.

As Alison Calder remarks, the eroticization of man-to-man combat in *Bonduca* was possibly inspired by *Coriolanus*, and, as Andrew Bretz suggests, *Bonduca* can be likened to *Julius Caesar*, in that, just as 'Caesar's death removes the character from the play yet his presence lives on in the force he has over the actions of the other characters, Bonduca exists as a kind of imaginative presence in the final act'.[21] I would also add that there seems to be another faint echo of *Julius Caesar* in Bonduca's comment in the opening scene about the Romans' 'Making the world but one Rome, and one Caesar' (*Bonduca*, 1.1.6), which recalls Cassius' sarcastic remark that 'Now is it Rome indeed, and room enough, / When there is in it but only one man' (*Julius Caesar*, 1.2.155–6) – both playing on the familiar early modern Rome/room pun and the idea of a single man taking up all the available space.

That being said, *Bonduca* appears in many respects more frankly reminiscent of *Antony and Cleopatra*. This might at least partly be a result of the fact that *Antony and Cleopatra* might have been revived *c.* 1613, around the time of the probable composition of *Bonduca*. Even though firm evidence of performances of *Antony and Cleopatra* in the seventeenth century has not survived (the first documented production being David Garrick's at Drury Lane in 1759), Pompey's line, 'In me 'tis villainy, / In thee't had been good service' (*Antony and Cleopatra*, 2.7.75–6) is quoted in the anonymous pamphlet *A Horrible, Cruel, and Bloody Murder* (1614).[22] Given that *Antony and Cleopatra* was not printed until 1623, this may well point to a theatrical revival, which could have left a lasting impression on Fletcher, as borne out by the analogies between his plays and Shakespeare's. As Paul D. Green usefully sums up,

> In theme and structure, as well as in patterns of plot and character, there are some striking similarities between the two tragedies. As in *Bonduca*, *Antony and Cleopatra* shifts its focus back and forth between the warring camps, and the opposition between Octavius Caesar's Rome and Cleopatra's Egypt embodies the same kind of male–female polarity as that between S[u]etonius's Rome and Bonduca's Britain. Both Bonduca and Cleopatra demonstrate inadequacies as military leaders, and both flee from battle. Like Cleopatra, Bonduca kills herself to avoid falling into Roman hands; moreover, both queens are eulogized by the victorious Roman generals.[23]

In addition, I would point out that the plays also seem to be pointedly contrasted insofar as, while in Egypt the Romans surfeit, in Britain they starve, and related memories of *Antony and Cleopatra* seem more openly to emerge in Petillius' sneering retort to the soldiers' complaining about the dearth of victuals:

> Ye rogues, my company eat turf and talk not.
> Timber they can digest, and fight upon't;
> Old mats and mud with spoons, rare meats; your shoes, slaves.
> Dare ye cry out for hunger, and those extant?
> Suck your sword-hilts, ye slaves; if ye be valiant,
> Honour will make 'em marchpane. (1.2.105–10)

Petillius' advice to the army to eat the indigestible seems redolent of Octavius' visceral description of Antony's disgusting diet at the time of the battle of Modena in *Antony and Cleopatra*:

> thou didst drink
> The stale of horses and the gilded puddle
> Which beasts would cough at. Thy palate then did deign
> The roughest berry on the rudest hedge.
> Yea, like the stag when snow the pasture sheets,
> The barks of trees thou browsèd. On the Alps
> It is reported thou didst eat strange flesh,
> Which some did die to look on. (1.4.64–9)

In both cases, *Romanitas* is associated with hardship and endurance in extreme conditions, even when this entails eating wood, mud, and unusual kinds of meat.

As interesting as all these analogies and contrasts are, however, the most conspicuous similarity between the two plays is perhaps that between the final suicides of Bonduca and her daughters on the one hand and of Cleopatra on the other, all the more so given that, as Kelly Neil observes, 'Fletcher's creation of Bonduca's lengthy and detailed suicide scene is his original contribution to the narrative', and that '[t]he escape of Bonduca and her daughters, their refuge in the fort after the battle, and the daughters' suicides do not seem to have any particular precedents in history', as Pavel Drabek points out.[24]

Indeed, the similarities are many. Even though Cleopatra kills herself in the privacy of her monument, in the company only of Iras and Charmian, whereas Bonduca and her daughters kill themselves publicly in front of the Roman leaders and soldiers, in both cases suicide becomes, in Ronald J. Boling's phrasing, 'a deliberate if desperate political act'.[25] In addition, both queens seem to situate their power resolutely in their bodies, so that their ultimate defiance lies in preserving them from Roman control, an association predicated on the common early modern idea of 'the female body as emblem of new lands waiting to be domesticated', as Samantha

Frénée-Hutchins remarks.[26] Given that both queens are powerful, non-Roman, and 'other' female characters, their suicides can also be viewed as rebellious acts of native resistance to colonial invasion, a refusal to submit their own and their countries' integrities to another nation's influence, as foreign rule and cultural miscegenation loom large.

Bonduca's and Cleopatra's deaths also have in common another crucial element, namely the use of poison. Bonduca's choice of poison as a means of taking her own life need not be read negatively as a shameful sign of fear, weakness, or excessive femininity, as Green suggests. His argument is based on the words spoken by Petillius, who describes suicide by poison as 'the death of rats and women, / Lovers and lazy boys' (4.3.139–40) and comments that 'Mithridates was an arrant ass / To die by poison' (4.3.144–5).[27] Not only are these words not necessarily trustworthy because of the identity of the character who utters them and the situations in which they are uttered – that is, Petillius' attempt to convince Poenius to commit suicide – as Andrew Hickman contends; more importantly, as Sarah E. Johnson convincingly argues, 'poison permits Bonduca to die last, only after ensuring her daughters are beyond Roman reach. Since Roman reach means rape and probably death anyway, the order of the women's deaths indicates Bonduca's determination to protect her daughters in the only way left to her, as terrible as it is.'[28] Bonduca's choice of poison therefore does not result from fear; it is rather a demonstration of motherly love and care.

Bonduca first rails against her retreating army, who abandon 'her hapless children / To Roman rape again and fury' (3.5.150–1); then, in order to stop the hesitations of Bonvica in the face of impending death, Bonduca accuses her of longing 'to prostitute thy youth and beauty / To common slaves for bread' (4.4.37–8). This is probably why, as Calder suggests, Bonduca later calls her a 'whore' (4.4.86), meaning that, if she keeps on living, her only option will be prostitution.[29] Moreover, it is only after her elder sister comforts her by describing an afterlife 'Where eternal / Our youths are, and our beauties, where no wars come, / Nor lustful slaves to ravish us', that Bonvica cries out, 'That steels me: / A long farewell to this world' (4.4.110–13), and stabs herself to death. Hence, Calder argues, it appears clear that 'it is ... the rape she is escaping, not her mother's disapproval'.[30] That the ineluctable destiny for the British women in case of capture would be – once more – rape seems indisputable, despite Suetonius' promise of 'Mercy to all that yield' (4.4.49). As Boling points out, 'Fletcher has previously depicted S[u]etonius often behaving magnanimously, generating a hope ... that his clement offer is trustworthy. Yet the Roman rapists shown in 2.3 and 3.5 are impenitent mockers', so that one is left under the impression that the Romans *cannot* ultimately be trusted.³¹ Using poison is therefore of the utmost importance because, Johnson suggests, 'As Shakespeare's Anthony [sic] memorably demonstrates, suicide by sword is far from certain; with no one left to assist Bonduca in a swift death, poison guarantees that the Romans will not be able to detain her from following her daughters.'³² In addition, Bonduca appears to view her suicide in similar terms as those Michael Neill identifies in Cleopatra's, that is, 'an occasion for resolute self-determination'.³³ Hence, Bonduca probably eschews recourse to suicide by the sword because her self-definition in the moments before her death cannot be based on a method that is traditionally – and heavily – associated with Roman masculine identity formation.

Johnson's passing observation about Antony is extremely relevant to the present discussion: much like Maximus with *Julius Caesar*, it is as though Bonduca had read or seen *Antony and Cleopatra* and were now acting accordingly – and she was possibly, in 1614, played by the same boy actor who played Shakespeare's Cleopatra, who in some sense remembers that death and recalls it for playgoers. Bonduca needs certain death, and thus she resorts to the effectiveness of poison, just like Cleopatra, and not to the unreliable metal, like Antony. Bonduca also seems to have learned from Cleopatra that suicide is the only queenly way to escape humiliation in a Roman triumph, which the Roman leaders in both plays wish to make eternally memorable through the presence of the enemy queen alive: Suetonius laments that 'There's nothing done / Till she be seized; without her, nothing won' (4.1.70–1), thereby expressing an idea akin to Caesar's 'her life in Rome / Would be eternal in our triumph' (*Antony and Cleopatra*, 5.1.62–6). As Bonduca's elder daughter tells the Romans, 'No, ye fools, / Poor Fortune's fools, we were not born for triumphs, / To follow your gay sports and fill your slaves / With hoots and acclamations' (*Bonduca*, 4.4.58–61). Similarly, Cleopatra tells Antony that 'Not th'imperious show / Of the full-fortuned Caesar ever shall be brooched with me' (*Antony and Cleopatra*, 4.15.24–6), labels Caesar as 'Fortune's knave' (5.2.3), and grimly illustrates to Iras the destiny they would have to face in Rome in terms of what Bridget Escolme poignantly describes as 'a grotesque carnival that engulfs the Cleopatra myth with the coarse reality of stinking breath':³⁴

> Mechanic slaves
> With greasy aprons, rules, and hammers shall
> Uplift us to the view. In their thick breaths,
> Rank of gross diet, shall we be enclouded
> And forced to drink their vapour.
> [...]

> Saucy lictors
> Will catch at us like strumpets, and scald rhymers
> Ballad us out o'tune. The quick comedians
> Extemporally will stage us and present
> Our Alexandrian revels; Antony
> Shall be brought drunken forth, and I shall see
> Some squeaking Cleopatra boy my greatness
> I'th' posture of a whore. (5.2.208–12, 213–20)

Bonduca therefore appears to be replicating the *exemplum* of Shakespeare's Cleopatra, who cannot tolerate the idea of being put on display in Rome in ways she would not be able to control and is therefore determined that her last moments should be stage-managed on her own terms. As Neil remarks, unlike Caratach, who is motivated by the possibility of being 'memorialized as a subject of Roman speech and song' – though, ironically, without realizing that he will be '"sung" not as a Roman citizen but as a Roman prisoner' – the Icenian queen 'fiercely defends her ability to shape her identity and prevent others from shaping it for her', thus consistently resisting 'the Romans' efforts to manage her identity' and that of her daughters.[35]

Finally, Bonduca seems to follow the example of Shakespeare's Cleopatra by making her suicide appear as a solemn ceremony. Cleopatra decides to commit suicide dressed 'like a queen', with her 'best attires', her 'crown and all' (*Antony and Cleopatra*, 5.2.226, 227, 231), which later prompts Caesar's comment: 'Bravest at the last, / She levelled at our purposes and, being royal, / Took her own way' (5.2.329–32). As depicted in Figure 4, Bonduca too appears 'in all her glory' (*Bonduca*, 4.4.6), towering above the Romans both visually and figuratively as she 'lifts "*a great cup*"' (4.4.85SD), the size of which lends a ritualistic and ceremonious quality to the scene'.[36] Bonduca's defiance in death is then praised by Suetonius, who comments that 'She was truly noble, and a queen' (4.4.156).

In sum, the Icenian queen appears to remember well the resoluteness of Shakespeare's Cleopatra in deciding to commit suicide by poison and decides to follow in her steps in order to immortalize herself in an ultimate act of defiance against Roman conquest. She also remembers Antony's suicide by the sword but avoids that course of action: she needs to be sure that her daughters will die before her and will not be captured and raped by the Romans. Hence, *Bonduca* exhibits a similar pattern to that observed in *Valentinian*, in that examples from Shakespeare's Roman plays seem to direct the choices and decisions of a Fletcherian character.

4 The Icenian queen and her daughters defy the Romans' siege in *Bonduca*

THE FALSE ONE

Besides being closely linked with *Julius Caesar*, as discussed in Chapter 2, *The False One* is also strongly connected with *Antony and Cleopatra*. The Prologue – which, as Baldwin Maxwell points out, is 'certain [to have been] originally penned for the first production'[37] – expresses the keen awareness that a new play focusing on Caesar and Cleopatra in 1619–23 would inevitably be expected to reckon with Shakespeare's Roman plays:

> New titles warrant not a play for new,
> The subject being old, and 'tis as true
> Fresh and neat matter may with ease be framed
> Out of their stories that have oft been named
> With glory on the stage. What borrows he
> From him that wrote old Priam's tragedy
> That writes his love to Hecuba? Sure, to tell
> Of Caesar's amorous heats and how he fell
> In the Capitol can never be the same
> To the judicious, nor will such blame
> Those that penned this for barrenness when they find
> Young Cleopatra here and her great mind
> Expressed to the height, with us a maid and free,
> And how he rated her virginity.
> We treat not of what boldness she did die
> Nor of her fatal love to Antony.
> What we present and offer to your view,
> Upon their faiths, the stage yet never knew.
> Let reason then first to your wills give laws
> And after judge of them and of their cause. (Prol.1–20)

In advertising *The False One* as a sort of prequel to Shakespeare's *Julius Caesar* and *Antony and Cleopatra*, the Prologue primarily tries to foreground the novelty and originality of Fletcher and Massinger's play so as to distinguish their theatrical offering from Shakespeare's and thus avoid their being taxed with 'barrenness': *The False One* stages Caesar in love with a young, virginal Cleopatra, something 'the stage yet never knew'.[38] Arguing that it is possible to compose a variation on the same theme devised by another writer without coming across as plagiarists, Fletcher and Massinger rhetorically ask: 'What borrows he / From him that wrote old Priam's tragedy / That writes his love to Hecuba?' This question is particularly interesting because it implicitly puts Shakespeare on a par with Homer and Virgil (the main sources of the story of Priam, which was then abundantly drawn upon by successive writers), thus making explicit Fletcher and Massinger's view that Shakespeare is now to all intents and purposes a classic in his own right.

Fletcher and Massinger play with the dynamic of difference/similarity not only in making Cleopatra a virgin but in another change that is not directly addressed in the Prologue: a whitening of Shakespeare's Cleopatra. Joyce Green MacDonald is probably correct in arguing that *The False One* 'skirts the questions of ... racial difference', but Fletcher and Massinger nonetheless include some pointed references to Cleopatra's skin colour.[39] Achillas refers to 'the fair Cleopatra' and then explains that this is 'An attribute not frequent in this climate' (1.1.26–7). Unless the playwrights wanted an Egyptian to imply that female beauty was altogether infrequent in Egypt – which sounds very unlikely – we probably need to interpret Achillas' words as employing an opposition between 'fair' and 'black' that is far from unusual in early modern texts. Scholars have come to different views on the complex relationship between fairness, beauty, and whiteness, which informs the equally complex relationship between *Antony and Cleopatra* and *The False One*. Kim F. Hall points out that '"black" in Renaissance discourses is opposed not to "white" but to "beauty" or "fairness"'; Ania Loomba remarks that 'blackness was ... powerfully equated with ugliness and fairness with beauty'; Eva Johanna Holmberg observes that 'In early modern England black skin was the opposite of "fair", white or beautiful.'[40] The most fraught aspect of this discussion is to what extent it may be possible to conflate the notions of whiteness and fairness (and, hence, beauty).

Farah Karim-Cooper argues that 'the terms "fair" and "white" are not always to be taken as interchangeable', inasmuch as '[p]aleness or whiteness is one thing as complexions go; however, fairness is quite another. It conveys a lustre that is comparable to silver ... to be "fair" is to be white and glistening, and to be thus is to be beautiful.'[41] Such a glistening effect, adds Karim-Cooper, could also be obtained through cosmetics. In this respect, Elizabeth Cary's *The Tragedy of Mariam* (1602–09) comes across as a particularly fruitful text to consider. As Ramona Wray argues, 'women are distinguished by, and registered through, a language of physical attractiveness' throughout the play, and physical comparison between them is one of the play's *Leitmotive*.[42] Interestingly, particular emphasis is placed 'on Mariam and Cleopatra as rival players', with the Egyptian queen functioning 'as a foil, one that draws attention to Mariam's manifestation of higher attributes'.[43] Cary's Cleopatra is significantly racialized as black, while 'Mariam is invariably described in terms of lightness and whiteness'.[44] In a play in which beauty is largely conflated with fairness/whiteness, it is therefore especially relevant to realize that, as Kimberly Woosley Poitevin points out, 'the ability of a "black" woman to paint herself fair and the possibility that a naturally "fair" woman may be accused of painting suggest that race and female "virtue" are not essential characteristics but rather performed behaviors'.[45] *The False One*, however, never suggests that Cleopatra's fairness might be artificial – an accusation that is instead levelled, for example, at Quisara in *The Island Princess*.[46]

At all events, Fletcher and Massinger have Achillas make clear a few lines into the play that this Cleopatra does not have 'a tawny front' (*Antony and Cleopatra*, 1.1.6) and is not 'with Phoebus' amorous pinches black' (1.5.29) in order to distinguish their Cleopatra from Shakespeare's. Later on, Apollodorus also mentions 'her fair hand' (*False One*, 1.2.10), and Cleopatra herself comments on her first kiss with Caesar by telling him 'You make me blush, sir, / And in that blush interpret me' (2.3.207–8), which again implies that she is not black, given that in the early modern era European writers frequently argued that black people were unable to blush.[47] Finally, Cleopatra disparagingly explains to Apollodorus that 'Caesar is amorous / And taken more with the title of a queen / Than feature or proportion' (1.2.91–3), so much so that he even 'loved Eunoë, / A moor' (1.2.93–4), which again confirms that this Cleopatra is not black as well as manifestly racializing the play's idea of female beauty.[48]

Fletcher and Massinger's treatment of Cleopatra's age, sexual experience, and race thus marks their independence from their Shakespearean exemplar even as their character simultaneously gains depth from her relationship with Shakespeare's. This interactive approach is also evident on the level of plot, as the Prologue points out. The account of the playwrights' decision not to depict 'how [Caesar] fell / In the Capitol' or 'of what boldness [Cleopatra] did die, / Nor of her fatal love to Antony' clearly spells out their simultaneous desire to build an explicit connection between their play and Shakespeare's. While forewarning playgoers regarding 'what they will not see', the Prologue acknowledges – as Hatchuel argues – that such famous episodes as Caesar's assassination or Cleopatra's suicide 'have already been shown and dramatized in other works', thereby establishing 'a kind of "continuity in dissociation" between the events in *The False One* and those in *Julius Caesar* and *Antony and Cleopatra*'.[49]

This continuity is upheld by many verbal echoes and by the play's alluding to Shakespeare's Cleopatra's famously changing moods, which Scaeva effectively foregrounds in one of his descriptions of the queen: 'She will be sick, well, sullen, / Merry, coy, overjoyed and seem to die, / All in one half hour, to make an ass of him' (3.2.36–8).[50] In order for their play to fit in a sort of partially shared universe with Shakespeare's plays, Fletcher and Massinger have Scaeva offer a condensation of Cleopatra's volatility as staged in *Antony and Cleopatra*; in addition, they provide in Act 2, scene 3, a full dramatization of the mattress episode reported by Plutarch, thereby developing the passing allusion to it in *Antony and Cleopatra*:

> *Pompey.* ... I have heard Apollodorus carried –
> *Enobarbus.* No more of that. He did so.
> *Pompey.* What, I pray you?
> *Enobarbus.* A certain queen to Caesar in a mattress. (2.6.70–2)

Fletcher and Massinger make this a pivotal scene in the economy of *The False One*, the moment at which Caesar is enthralled by Cleopatra and which determines his successive path of temptation, fall, and regeneration, which enables him to come out victorious at the end of the play. Here, a slight divergence from Plutarch's account is crucial in establishing Cleopatra's agency from the beginning, while at the same time undermining her respectability. Plutarch narrates that Caesar had secretly sent for Cleopatra to come to him; in the play, which in this respect partly follows Lucan, it is on her own initiative that she orders her servant Apollodorus to bring her to the unknowing Caesar in what the stage direction labels as a '*packet*' (2.3.61SD).[51] As soon as she springs out of it, Caesar starts describing her in courtly Petrarchan fashion (2.3.102–5). The folly and inappropriateness of such a language, which sounds 'mangily, / Poorly and scurvily' in a Roman general's mouth, is immediately censured by the disgusted Scaeva, who does not hesitate to make fun of Caesar's dreamlike amorous rantings, all the more ridiculous by reason of his age (2.3.105–11): Caesar was 52 (and Cleopatra only 21) at the time and therefore already in 'old age' by Renaissance standards.[52] While Caesar is convinced that Cleopatra is 'a thing divine' (2.3.98), Scaeva keeps labelling her as an 'apparition' (79), a 'spirit' (80), a 'tempting devil' (82), a 'damned woman' (90), 'sent to dispossess you of your honour, / A sponge, a sponge to wipe away your victories' (86–7). Scaeva's reiterated interruptions of the couple's dialogue bestows distinctively comic overtones on the scene, which is largely taken up by 'an antiphon of coarse, soldierly observations from Scaeva and enraptured comments from Caesar', as Eugene M. Waith observes.[53]

Cleopatra appeals to Caesar's generosity as much as to his masculinity, just as a damsel in distress would conventionally address a noble – and nearly divine, given her choice of words ('sacred', 'holy altar') – knight in a medieval romance (2.3.143–55): she begs him to help 'one distressed that flies unto thy justice, / One that lays sacred hold on thy protection / As on a holy altar to preserve me' (2.3.136–8). Complying with the conventions of courtly romance, Caesar explains that a request made by 'A suitor of your sort and blessèd sweetness / That hath adventured thus to see great Caesar / Must never be denied' (2.3.160–4) and promises that he will make her the Queen of Egypt again (2.3.165–9). In an aside the ultimate source of which is Lucan but which also seems influenced by the portrayal of Caesar as a slave to love offered in Petrarch's *Triumphs*, Cleopatra instantly rejoices at the success of her plan: 'He is my conquest now, and so I'll work him / The conqueror of the world will I lead captive' (2.3.170–1).[54] Fletcher and Massinger's decision to bring this spectacular episode on stage displays their desire to establish a connection with Shakespeare while at the same time setting their work in programmatic contrast with the majoritarian theatrical tradition by opposing a dazzling birth-like debut for Cleopatra to her far more frequently staged glorious death.

Reflecting on the play's conclusion, Hatchuel notes that, by 'end[ing] after Caesar has overcome all obstacles and escaped death', *The False One* 'comes to compete with Shakespeare's *Julius Caesar*, in which everything leads to, and then departs from, Caesar's demise. Cleopatra's enemies, P[oth]inus and Achillas, plot to rid themselves of Caesar and attack the royal palace, but Julius remains unscathed.'[55] Similarly to what we have witnessed for Maximus in *Valentinian* and for the eponymous queen in *Bonduca*, Caesar's ability to thwart a plot against his own life would seem to show that he has learned the lesson taught by Shakespeare's *Julius Caesar*, which conversely revolves around the fall of an (almost) completely clueless Caesar in the Senate at the hands of his (alleged) friends.

An analogous pattern can be observed in *The False One*'s Caesar's successful break from his overindulgence with Cleopatra and ultimate recovery of his role as military and political leader: in never even thinking of asking Cleopatra to join him on the battlefield, in managing 'These strong Egyptian fetters [to] break' (*Antony and Cleopatra*, 1.1.112), and in defeating the enemy, this Caesar seems oddly to have learned from the mistakes of Shakespeare's Antony, which he is careful to avoid. He thereby finds a comfortable middle ground between the passionate heat of love and the cool rationality required of politics.

Even though historically Antony and Cleopatra's love story followed Caesar and Cleopatra's, Fletcher and Massinger's Caesar takes Shakespeare's Antony as an example by opposition, in the same way as Bonduca does when deciding by what instrument to commit suicide. This weird theatrical temporality might have been exacerbated in *The False One* if *Antony and Cleopatra* and Fletcher and Massinger's play were performed alongside each other in the King's Men's repertory, especially at the moment of the first performance of *The False One*, thus achieving an effect similar to that of having the same boy actor play the roles of both Bonduca and Cleopatra around the time of *Bonduca*'s first performance. Unfortunately, there is no evidence that this was the case.

The False One's Cleopatra too seems at some junctures to be acting in relation to an earlier dramatic instantiation of her own story, having knowledge of what will happen to her in the future when she comments about Caesar that 'Had I been old / Or blasted in my bud, he might have showed / Some shadow of dislike' (4.2.14–16). With these words, she appears eerily to anticipate Antony's insulting her several years later 'as a morsel, cold upon / Dead Caesar's trencher; nay, you were a fragment / Of Cneius Pompey's' (*Antony and Cleopatra*, 3.13.119–21) – the image of the blasted bud (which stands for her lost virginity in a similar fashion to that of the cracked ring that Petillius deploys in *Bonduca* to describe the queen's daughter) possibly echoing the idea of Cleopatra as a chewed, unappealing leftover of the Roman generals. Along the same lines, when Cleopatra, enraged at Caesar because he has ignored her during the masque (distracted as he was by the display of the wealth of Egypt), tells him that she finds 'my soft embraces / And those sweet kisses you called Elysium, / As letters writ in sand, no more remembered' (*False One*, 4.2.118–20), her questioning of Caesar's effusions of love recalls how Shakespeare's Cleopatra will express doubts about the sincerity of Antony's hyperbolic claims that 'Eternity was in our lips and eyes, / Bliss in our brows' bent; none our parts so poor / But was a race of heaven' (*Antony and Cleopatra*, 1.3.35–7).

The False One, then, exhibits the results of a stimulating conversation with Shakespeare. Presented as a prequel to *Julius Caesar* and *Antony and Cleopatra*, *The False One* crucially draws upon them for elements in the delineation of its main characters, that is, when the playwrights adjust Cleopatra's age, sexual experience, and race; for the sake of plot construction, namely when Fletcher and Massinger include the mattress scene to give Cleopatra a spectacular entrance; and for the creation of the characters' awareness of their Shakespearean predecessors. Fletcher and Massinger's Caesar and Cleopatra take Shakespeare's Caesar, Antony, and Cleopatra as examples that determine their actions, choices, and behaviour, in a way that is akin to what I have discussed in the previous sections of this chapter regarding *Valentinian* and *Bonduca*. As we shall see, this happens to an even greater extent in *The Prophetess*.

THE PROPHETESS AND JULIUS CAESAR

If the points of contact between Shakespeare's Roman plays and *Valentinian*, *Bonduca*, and *The False One* have been variously commented upon by scholars, the reworking of Shakespeare's Roman material in *The Prophetess* has instead gone completely unnoticed, possibly because scholarly discussion of the play has all but exclusively concentrated on its debt to *The*

Tempest.⁵⁶ Yet as I intend to show in the remainder of this chapter, Fletcher and Massinger's play also exhibits an organic, consistent, and flamboyant appropriation of Shakespeare's Plutarchan plays *Julius Caesar*, *Antony and Cleopatra*, and, to a lesser extent, *Coriolanus*.

The connection between *The Prophetess* and *Julius Caesar* emerges explicitly during the Romans' battle against the Persians, when Geta humorously alludes to the moment of Caesar's assassination as staged by Shakespeare: 'Shall I like Caesar fall / Among my friends? No mercy? Et tu, Brute?' (*Prophetess*, 4.5.16–17). This reprise of Shakespeare's '*Et tu, Brute?* – Then fall, Caesar' (*Julius Caesar*, 3.1.77) works in a twofold way. On the one hand, it blatantly parodies one of the most extremely heightened moments of tension in Shakespeare's oeuvre; on the other hand, it also seems to work – similarly to what occurs to Maximus with Brutus in *Valentinian*, to Bonduca with Antony in *Bonduca*, and to Caesar with Antony in *The False One* – as an example by contrast. Rather than more predictably choosing Shakespeare's Caesar as a model of how things should be done, Geta does the exact opposite: he decides not to stand still in the face of the enemies but starts fighting valorously against three Persians at once and manages to drive them off, thus even prompting one of the guards' compliments: 'O brave, brave Geta! / He plays the devil now' (*Prophetess*, 4.5.19–20).

This is a relatively rare example of comic appropriation of Shakespeare's Roman plays in a Fletcher play. While deflation of the Shakespearean precedent is fairly common in Fletcher's oeuvre outside the Roman world, in his Roman plays this tends to happen much less frequently, as though he wished to treat Shakespeare's Rome with more reverence than he did the accounts of the actual historians of classical antiquity. Significantly, for example, the comic exchange between Caesar and Scaeva in *The False One* discussed above, though connected with Shakespeare's *Antony and Cleopatra*, is not a re-enacting of a Shakespearean moment but of a Plutarchan one. To go back to *The Prophetess*, the other reminiscences of Shakespeare are indeed much more weighty than Geta's allusion to *Julius Caesar*, inasmuch as they seem decisively to contribute to Fletcher and Massinger's portrayal of Diocletian.

The Diocletian of *The Prophetess* is significantly different from the one recently depicted by Massinger himself (with Dekker) in *The Virgin Martyr* (1620). In particular, *The Prophetess* completely eschews any reference to Diocletian's persecutions of the Christians, which are central in *The Virgin Martyr*: here, argues John E. Curran, Jr, 'Diocle[t]ian presides over bustling prosperity but also savage torture of innocent Christians – he cannot understand what higher truth the martyrdoms signify.'⁵⁷ *The Virgin Martyr*'s Diocletian – appearing on stage only in the opening act and the concluding scene, both usually considered to have been written by Massinger – is indeed a more severe, firm, and cruel figure, going as far as to 'profess he is not Caesar's friend / That sheds a tear for any torture that / A Christian suffers'. In this sense, however, he seems somewhat more firmly grounded in history than Fletcher and Massinger's Diocletian, whose characterization often strays from the received accounts.[58]

This is somewhat surprising in light of the abundance of material available to the two playmakers, which almost invariably suggested an ambiguity of character that would have looked rife with dramatic potential to such consummate men of the theatre. As Curran sums up,

> the impression of Diocle[t]ian tradition had handed down was so divided as to make him seem nearly schizophrenic. As a ferocious persecutor of Christians he was supposed to be a 'wicked Tyrant', but this did not jibe with the facts of his amazing feats of prudence and benevolence. Not only had he at the summit of the empire taken steps to cooperate and share power with others, but he had willingly retired from that power and spent his last years tranquilly as a private citizen.[59]

While *The Prophetess* does loosely follow the historical trajectory of Diocletian's career from soldier to emperor to private citizen by choice, his progression through these stages does not mirror the records as closely. Beyond the aforementioned omission of the persecutions of the Christians, the play differs from the historical accounts in several further respects. First, the role of the Druidess with whom the soldier Diocles consults regarding his imperial destiny as a soldier is enlarged; second, no conflict exists between Carinus and Diocletian, nor are any mentions of Diocletian's creating the tetrarchy to be found in the play; third, the playwrights decided to place Diocletian's withdrawal earlier in his career than warranted by ancient sources and locate it in Lombardy – which they may have chosen over Salona, in present-day Croatia, by virtue of Lombardy's early modern reputation as 'The pleasant garden of great Italy' and 'the garden of the world'.[60]

Fletcher and Massinger's Diocletian seems in fact to be modelled more after Shakespeare's Antony (as portrayed in both *Julius Caesar* and *Antony and Cleopatra*) than the historical emperor, which may also partly account for the 'puzzling disjunctions of characterization in the course of the play that', argues McMullan, 'make coherent analysis difficult'.[61] The similarities between the two characters start to become apparent in Act 2, scene 2, when, before an assembly of soldiers, Diocles directly confronts Camurius regarding the murder of Numerian, an episode not to be found in the sources. Even though this seems never to have been remarked upon, this sequence – probably written primarily by Massinger, although the division of scenes between the two collaborators in this play needs to be understood, as its Cambridge editor George Walton Williams points out, as based 'on shares of work, rather than on lines of the plot or on sources, such a sharing indicating a full understanding of the entire play by each author'[62] – clearly draws upon Antony's (and, to a lesser extent, Brutus') funeral oration in *Julius Caesar*.

A political leader has just been deceitfully murdered; his body lies in the marketplace, hidden from the view of the people around it; a valiant soldier begins talking and reveals the corpse, thus prompting a violent desire for revenge in the bystanders. As Diocles begins to address the troops gathered 'I'th' marketplace' (1.3.235), his words immediately remind the audience of Shakespeare:

> What's he, that is
> Owner of any virtue worth a Roman
> Or does retain the memory of the oath
> He made to Caesar, that dares lift his sword
> Against the man that, careless of his life,
> Comes to discover such a horrid treason
> As, when you hear't and understand how long
> You've been abused, will run you mad with fury?
> I am no stranger, but, like you, a soldier,
> Trained up one from my youth, and there are some
> With whom I have served and (not to praise myself)
> Must needs confess they have seen Diocles,
> In the late Britain wars, both dare and do
> Beyond a common man. (2.2.81–94)

While the lengthy opening question that Diocles addresses to the soldiers is partly redolent of the intimidatory tone of Brutus' triplet of questions to the commoners – 'Who is here so base, that would be a bondman? ... Who is here so rude, that would not be a Roman? ... Who is here so vile, that will not love his country?' (*Julius Caesar*, 3.2.29–33) – it also becomes apparent early on in the sequence that Fletcher and Massinger rather have Antony primarily in mind, at least as soon as Diocles explains to the soldiers that discovering the truth 'will run you mad with fury', which openly echoes Antony's 'It will inflame you, it will make you mad' (*Julius Caesar*, 3.2.145), and attempts to make it even more incisive by means of entirely monosyllabic delivery. Immediately after that, Diocles proceeds to highlight the common ground he shares with his listeners ('I am no stranger, but, like you, a soldier'), which recalls in purpose, though not in form, Antony's 'I am no orator, as Brutus is, / But, as you know me all, a plain blunt man' (*Julius Caesar*, 3.2.210–11). At all events, the similarities become more and more glaring as Diocles keeps on speaking:

> *Diocles.* ... You all know with what favours
> The good Numerianus ever graced
> The provost Aper.
> *All Guards.* True.
> *Diocles.* And that those bounties
> Should have contained him, if he e'er had learned
> The elements of honesty and truth,
> In loyal duty. But ambition never
> Looks backward on desert, but with blind haste
> Boldly runs on. But I lose time. You are here
> Commanded by this Aper to attend
> The Emperor's person, to admit no stranger
> To have access to him or come near his litter,
> Under pretence, forsooth, his eyes are sore
> And his mind troubled. No, my friends, you are cozened:
> The good Numerianus now is past
> The sense of wrong or injury.
> [*He opens the litter and uncovers the dead body of* NUMERIANUS.]
> *All Guards.* How? Dead?
> *Diocles.* Let your own eyes inform you.
> *Geta.* An Emperor's cabinet?
> Faugh! I have known a charnel-house smell sweeter.
> If emperors' flesh have this savour, what will mine do
> When I am rotten?
> *1 Guard.* Most unheard-of villainy!
> *2 Guard.* And with all cruelty to be revenged.
> *3 Guard.* Who is the murderer? Name him, that we may
> Punish it in his family.
> *Diocles.* Who but Aper,
> The barbarous and most ingrateful Aper?
> His desperate poniard printed on his breast
> This deadly wound. Hate to vowed enemies
> Finds a full satisfaction in death,
> And tyrants seek no further. He, a subject,
> And bound by all the ties of love and duty,
> Ended not so, but does deny his prince –
> Whose ghost, forbade a passage to his rest,
> Mourns by the Stygian shore – his funeral rites.
> Nay, weep not; let your loves speak in your anger
> And, to confirm you gave no suffrage to
> The damned plot, lend me your helping hands
> To wreak the parricide and, if you find
> That there is worth in Diocles to deserve it,
> Make him your leader.

All Guards.   A Diocles, a Diocles!
Diocles. We'll force him from his guards. [*Exeunt all but* DIOCLES.]
                             And now, my stars,
        If you have any good for me in store,
        Show it when I have slain this fatal boar! (2.2.105-44)

'You all know with what favours / The good Numerianus ever graced / The provost Aper' holds the same communicative function as Antony's 'Brutus, as you know, was Caesar's angel' (*Julius Caesar*, 3.2.179), and while Diocles' remark that 'ambition never / Looks backward on desert, but with blind haste / Boldly runs on' rather appears to recall Brutus' remarks on Caesar's ambition during his orchard soliloquy (2.1.21-6), the moment at which the would-be emperor Diocles uncovers the dead body of Numerian is both a homage to and a re-enactment of the much more famous marketplace uncovering of the corpse of Julius Caesar by the would-be emperor Antony. The re-enactment of such a memorable theatrical moment would have been even more impressive for playgoers if Diocles was played by the same actor who played Antony in possible revivals of *Julius Caesar* in the repertory of the King's Men around 1622, when *The Prophetess* was first staged. The effect of Diocles' revelation is just as powerful as Antony's, and Diocles addresses the bystanders as 'friends', just as Antony had done: 'Friends, Romans, countrymen' (*Julius Caesar*, 3.2.74). Like Maximus with Brutus, like Bonduca with Antony and Cleopatra, like Caesar with Antony, like Caesar and Cleopatra with different versions of themselves, Diocles, in some oblique way, seems to have learned Shakespeare's Antony's lesson well: for an orator, sight is a much more powerful ally than hearing. 'Let your own eyes inform you', urges Diocles, just as Antony had commanded 'Look you here, / Here is himself, marred as you see with traitors' (*Julius Caesar*, 3.2.194-5). In a fascinating superimposition of fact and fiction, Shakespeare's retelling of the story of Caesar's murder seems to have been woven into the historical past on which the events depicted in the play are based, as Aper's decision to play for time as long as possible before revealing Numerian's death further attests: it is as though he were aware, because of such an illustrious precedent, of how irresistible the sight of a dead Caesar could be.

In addition, leaving aside the humorous and deflating remarks by Geta about the stench emanating from the rotting corpse, the guards' disconcerted reactions and their desire for revenge are in line with those of the people assembled in a ring around Antony (*Julius Caesar*, 3.2.196-200); in particular, 'We will be revenged' (3.2.198) is heightened to 'And with all cruelty to be revenged'. In *The Prophetess*, unlike *Julius Caesar*, the guards are unacquainted with the identity of the murderer, so that Diocles needs to break it to them, but his use of the deictic – 'His desperate poniard printed on his breast / *This* deadly wound' (emphasis mine) – suggests that, following the example of Antony's mapping out of the wounds inflicted on Caesar's mantle and body (*Julius Caesar*, 3.2.172–9), Diocles is pointing to the emperor's wounds, while the plosive alliteration recalls Antony's deft use of several rhetorical devices despite his disingenuous declarations about his not being a skilled orator. Interestingly, however, Fletcher and Massinger are wary in this case not to deploy any of the words used by Shakespeare except for 'wound': Shakespeare employs 'dagger' and 'steel', not 'poniard'; 'ran' and 'stabbed', not 'printed'. As implied in the Prologue to *The False One*, Fletcher and Massinger's appropriation of Shakespeare must also entail an effort to distinguish themselves from him. At the end of the speech, the guards call for 'a Diocles' as a leader, thus deploying the indefinite article with a proper noun just as in Antony's 'Here was *a* Caesar: when comes such another?' (*Julius Caesar*, 3.2.243, emphasis mine); besides, as soon as the soldiers have left, and Diocles remains alone, he rounds off his oration with the quasi-monosyllabic invocation 'And now, my stars, / If you have any good for me in store, / Show it when I have slain this fatal boar', which seems to serve a function akin to Antony's 'Now let it work. Mischief, thou art afoot: / Take thou what course thou wilt' (3.2.251–2).

All in all, even though Diocles' thirst for power emerges as much more transparent than Antony's, and although the former's speech, though effective, does not display the same rhetorical grip, poignancy, and mastery as the latter's – Diocles is not as good an orator as Antony – the similarities are unmistakable, and the differences largely depend on the fact that the situation in which Diocles operates and its implications are remarkably different: this is the Empire, not the Republic; the guards are unaware that the emperor is dead and have no clue as to who might have killed him; Diocles has no Brutus to overcome and does not need to ask for permission to speak.

THE PROPHETESS AND ANTONY AND CLEOPATRA

As the play progresses, Fletcher and Massinger's effort to model Diocletian after Antony becomes more subtle and elaborate, as reminiscences of *Antony and Cleopatra*, rather than *Julius Caesar*, begin to creep in and progressively accumulate for the audience to pick up, especially by virtue of Diocletian's association with Hercules and Mars, who are also repeatedly connected with Shakespeare's Antony. As Jonathan Bate helpfully sums up regarding Hercules,

> In Plutarch's 'Life of Marcus Antonius', Antony claims descent from Anton, son of Hercules; to Shakespeare's Cleopatra he is a 'Herculean Roman'

(1.3.84). His allegiance to the greatest of the mythical heroes is strengthened by the strange scene in the fourth act, when music of hautboys is heard under the stage and the second soldier offers the interpretation that 'the god Hercules, whom Antony loved, / Now leaves him' (4.3.21–2; in Plutarch, the music and the Antonine allegiance belong to Bacchus, to wine and revelry). The image of Antony and Cleopatra wearing each other's clothes ... may suggest not only the cross-dressing of Mars and Venus ... but also that of Hercules and Omphale, as described in the *Heroides*.[63]

Virginia Mason Vaughan adds that 'Antony's violent fury when Caesar's messenger Thidias kisses Cleopatra's hand also recalls the madness of Hercules Furens', while Janet Adelman goes so far as to consider Hercules 'the allusive center of the play', insofar as he 'functions ... as a distant and godlike figure of achieved excess: a figure who overflows every human scale'.[64]

The first, most overt element connecting Diocles to Hercules in *The Prophetess* – though unrelated to Shakespeare – is the boar hunt. At the outset of the play, Diocles is depicted as attempting to fulfil Delphia's prophecy:

> *Imperator eris Romae cum Aprum grandem interfeceris:*
> Thou shalt be emperor, O Diocles,
> When thou hast killed a mighty boar. (1.2.33–5)[65]

Unable to penetrate the surface of the message and understand the actual meaning of Delphia's words (he will in fact have to kill the man called Aper, whose name means 'boar' in Latin), since the time of the delivery of this prophecy Diocles has 'employed / Much of his life in hunting', killed 'with his own hands' several 'Hideous and fierce' boars, as portrayed in Figure 5, and brought them all to Delphia (1.2.35–8). When confronting Delphia about his frustration at not being able to catch the right boar or unveil the impenetrable mystery contained in her prophecy, Diocles describes his hunt in terms that emphasize his toil and effort: he complains because he 'Rise[s] early and sleep[s] late', 'Labour[s] and sweat[s]', 'Hunt[s] daily and sweat[s] hourly' (1.3.161, 163, 174), while Delphia 'take[s] no labour' whatsoever (1.3.169).[66] Diocles' remarks concerning his labour(s) seem further to connect him with Hercules, who had to capture the Erymanthian boar, a monstrous animal that lived on Mount Erymanthos and laid waste the farmers' fields, as part of his famous Twelve Labours. In accomplishing these deeds, Hercules was ultimately working towards the fulfilment of his father Zeus's desire to bestow immortality on him, much like Diocles is 'kill[ing] boar on boar' (1.3.175) for Delphia, whose powers are shown in the play (as seen in Chapter 2) to be unlimited like a goddess's and whom Diocles repeatedly calls 'mother'. Just as Hercules

5 Diocles exhibits a boar he has successfully hunted, while Delphia and Drusilla fly on a chariot pulled by dragons, in *The Prophetess*

was trying to please his divine father, Diocles is trying to please his goddess- and mother-like protectress.

Also connecting Diocletian to Hercules are the references in *The Prophetess* to the Titan Atlas. This time, Shakespeare comes into play as well, in that Cleopatra calls Antony 'The demi-Atlas of this earth, the arm / And burgonet of men' (*Antony and Cleopatra*, 1.5.24–5), in one of the only two occurrences of the name Atlas in the entire Shakespearean canon – the other being in Warwick's words to King Edward IV in *3 Henry VI*: 'Thou art no Atlas for so great a weight'.[67] In the passage from *Antony and Cleopatra*, 'demi-Atlas' means 'the substitute of Atlas', as Frank Kermode argues.[68] Greek mythology firmly connected Atlas with Hercules because the latter once held up the celestial heavens in the for- mer's place as part of his Twelve Labours: accordingly, in the early modern imagination the only hero who could replace Atlas was Hercules. Only Hercules had the strength to bear such weight. As mentioned in Chapter 2, *The Prophetess* is informed by a pervasive preoccupation with the oppressive burdens of power, which are recurrently described as so men- tally and physically unbearable that the strength of Atlas comes up twice in connection with Diocletian. First, upon being elected emperor, Diocletian proclaims that 'It shall be / My study to appear another Atlas, / To stand firm underneath this heaven of empire, / And bear it boldly' (2.3.73–6). In being 'another Atlas' supporting 'this heaven of empire', Diocletian will have to be a substitute for Atlas, and thus another Hercules. Later on, as the play draws to a close, while Carinus inveighs against Maximian by sharply pointing out the latter's inability to rule, he claims that he does not doubt that, on hearing of Maximian's 'overweening pride, riot and lusts' (5.2.113), Diocletian will either reclaim the title for himself 'or at least make choice / Of such an Atlas as may bear this burden, / Too heavy for these shoulders' (5.2.119–21). While in this case the connection seems less explicit, cumulatively the evidence seems to suggest that what Carinus implies is that Maximian can never possess the Atlantic/Herculean force of Diocletian or whichever substitute he might nominate.

It is precisely because of the excessive weight and the dangerous pitfalls of glory and power – together with his 'fear of the contradictions of mortality and absolutism', as McMullan notes – that Diocletian ultimately decides to relinquish the throne.[69] In disclosing his resolution to the other characters on stage, he explains:

> I know that glory
> Is like Alcides' shirt if it stay on us
> Till pride hath mixed it with our blood; nor can we
> Part with it at pleasure: when we would uncase,
> It brings along with it both flesh and sinews,

> And leaves us living monsters.
> [...]
> No. I will not be plucked out by the ears
> Out of this glorious castle; uncompelled
> I will surrender rather. Let it suffice:
> I have touched the height of human happiness
> And here I fix *nil ultra*. (4.6.57–62, 66–8)

This is perhaps the moment at which the connection between Diocletian and Antony is most profoundly and meaningfully developed. Here, Fletcher reworks the references to the story of Nessus' poisoned shirt and to the Pillars of Hercules as well as the unquenchable strivings to infinity that punctuate *Antony and Cleopatra*, with the implied comparison between Diocletian and Antony reflecting unfavourably on the latter. Antony conjures up the image of Nessus' poisoned shirt after having followed Cleopatra's retreating ships and lost the sea battle at Actium:

> The shirt of Nessus is upon me. Teach me,
> Alcides, thou mine ancestor, thy rage.
> Let me lodge Lichas on the horns o'th' moon,
> And with those hands that grasped the heaviest club
> Subdue my worthiest self. The witch shall die. (4.12.43–7)

At this point, Antony is about to commit suicide: poor judgement and unrestrainable anger have consumed him. As Vaughan contends, Antony here 'resembles Hercules at Oeta', and, adds Bate, 'The context of the allusion is decisive; immediately after flinging Lichas into the air, Hercules sets about preparing his own funeral pyre. He goes to his death rehearsing his own past glories, in the style of the stoic hero; in Antony's phrase, he "subdues his worthiest self".'[70] Antony's evocation of Hercules in this case does not point to the latter's achievements, power, or greatness; on the contrary, it recalls a rare moment of vulnerability of the demigod, which is particularly apt as an analogue for Antony's predicament. As Curran remarks,

> when Antony invokes Hercules, it is to cry out, with abject futility, his irrevocable parting from Fortune, and he calls down not Hercules' valour, patience or self-awareness but his fury ... Bereft finally of any prospect of Fortune bolstering it, Antony experiences a searing melting away of identity, but with no compensatory reasserting of Herculean amplitude; instead, we have distinctly un-Herculean impotence, all the more withering for its venting at Cleopatra.[71]

Whereas Antony is dominated by rage and has his eyes turned to an irretrievable past, Diocletian's evocation of Hercules coincides with a moment at which he confidently looks to the future, thus anticipating in tangibly trenchant terms ('flesh and sinews') the disastrous consequences that would be in store for him should he let unlimited pride and ambition get the better of him.

In contrast to Antony's experience of a scorching dissolution of identity, this seems to be a juncture at which Diocletian, at the end of what Curran describes as a 'personally edifying journey of self-discovery', in fact comes to terms with his true self, which is revealed as not needing boundlessness to find satisfaction.[72] In quoting the words Hercules supposedly carved above the pillars on the promontories that flanked the entrance to the Strait of Gibraltar – *nil ultra* – Diocletian reveals himself to be the opposite of Shakespeare's Antony, immune as he grows to the insuppressible need to cross the limits in order to find 'new heaven, new earth' that is inherent to Antony's personality.[73] Again, a Fletcherian Roman has learned a lesson from a Shakespearean one. Antony leaves Rome and loses himself in Egypt with Cleopatra in search of something beyond the simplicity of mundane concerns, and in so doing loses his mortal life while chasing a god-like, superhuman one. In contrast, Diocletian manages to attain the imperial mantle that Antony is never able to don but then decides to relinquish it *sponte sua* in order to live a simple life in the countryside with Drusilla – who may be regarded as his Octavia, in contrast to Aurelia, who represents the hollow allure of the court and might be (very) loosely seen as his Cleopatra.

The choice between two women representing two ways of life again seems to hark back to the myth of Hercules for both plays, in particular to the episode of *Hercules in bivio* ('Hercules at the crossroads'), originally narrated in Xenophon's *Memorabilia*. The story was part of the common currency of classical allusions that permeated the cultural air of the early modern age: it was frequently illustrated in the sixteenth and seventeenth centuries and was also dramatized by Jonson in his court masque *Pleasure Reconciled to Virtue* (1618). Fletcher need not have read Xenophon to have been acquainted with the story. As John Wilders usefully sums up, Hercules

> went out to a quiet place and 'sat pondering which road to take'. He was approached by two women, one modest, sober and dressed in white, the other plump, soft and dressed 'so as to disclose all her charms'. Whereas the latter, Vice, invites him to follow her, offering a life free from hardship, effortlessly devoted to the pleasures of food, drink and love, Virtue offers only the toil and hardship which lead to glory.[74]

While this mythical precedent is more straightforwardly applicable to Antony's choice between pleasure and duty, between Egypt and Rome, between Cleopatra and Octavia, it is also roughly similar to Diocletian's predicament between the seductiveness of 'The artificial court' (5.4.25) and the peace of the uncontaminated countryside, between mutability and steadfastness, between the evil Aurelia and the pure Drusilla. Like Hercules, but unlike Antony, Diocletian chooses the modest-eyed woman rather than the brazen one, even though the play repeatedly foregrounds Delphia's decisive role in Diocletian's deliberation. As McMullan synthesizes, the play concludes 'with a strong affirmation of the virtue of the country life over that of the court'.[75]

Thanks to Delphia, then, Diocletian realizes, unlike Antony, that desire need not be unbounded: there *can* be limits, and, within such limits, there *can* be satisfaction, as well as happiness and contentment with an ordinary life and the ordinary love of an ordinary wife. The other side of the coin, however, is that, although Diocletian becomes emperor, he never appears as grand as Antony, the emperor who never was. As Adelman remarks, 'If the presence of Hercules emphasizes the folly of Antony's ventures into the realm of hyperbole, it also emphasizes their grandeur.'[76] Indeed, if Diocletian has any grandeur, this seems to be all but restricted to the battlefield – he is certainly no match for Antony rhetorically, as observed above.

As briefly remarked upon in Chapter 2, *The Prophetess* makes it clear early on that Diocles is hailed as 'the bravest soldier of the Empire' (2.2.95), and, even though the audience is only allowed to catch fleeting glimpses of this, the other characters display no hesitation in associating Diocletian with Mars as a way to extol his military prowess, as Drusilla's exalted description shows:

> How god-like he appears! With such a grace,
> [...]
> The giants that attempted to scale Heaven,
> When they lay dead on the Phlegraean plain,
> Mars did appear to Jove. (2.3.25, 27–9)

In Drusilla's eye, Diocletian is a god uniting in himself 'grace' and destructive power, as the grandiose similitude with Mars in full glory after having contributed to the victory in the Gigantomachy suggests. Later, it is Niger who compares Diocletian to Mars, as already seen in Chapter 2:

> The Persians shrink; the passage is laid open;
> Great Diocletian, like a second Mars,
> His strong arm governed by the fierce Bellona,
> Performs more than a man. His shield, struck full
> Of Persian darts, which now are his defence
> Against the enemies' swords, still leads the way. (4.5.21–6)

This image too is extremely powerful. Diocletian is glorified for his martial valour as 'a second Mars' even capable of turning the enemies' arrows into his own weapon. What is especially interesting is the fact that Diocletian is described as performing 'more than a man'. As it happens, then, there is something in which Diocletian 'O'erflows the measure' (*Antony and Cleopatra*, 1.1.2), but it is his masculinity. This is also foregrounded in his aforementioned and unrelenting boar hunt. As Edward Berry helpfully summarizes,

> In his survey of the medieval conception of the boar, John Cummins calls the animal an 'archetype of unrelenting ferocity'. In both medieval and Elizabethan hunting manuals the boar is treated as the most dangerous animal hunted. The medieval writer Gaston Phoebus claims to have seen a boar 'strike a man and split him from knee to chest, so that he fell dead without a word'. In *The Noble Arte of Venerie*, [George] Gascoigne is reluctant even to recommend the boar hunt in view of its destructive effect upon dogs; the boar, he says, 'is the only beast which can dispatch a hounde at one blow'. Hunting the boar, then, is a supreme test of manhood.[77]

The contrast with Antony is further sharpened by the explicit and implicit stresses the play here puts on Diocletian's masculinity – which emerges as less compromised, problematic, or troubling than that of other leaders populating Fletcher's Roman world, especially Valentinian and, to a lesser extent, Caesar. While it is to some extent possible to argue with Bate that Antony 'is Mars-like in his combination of greatness of spirit ... and wrath, the latter manifested most vigorously in his treatment of Thidias', Antony's association with Mars seems more generally to reflect rather poorly on him, as it in fact deflates his god-like pretences.[78] Philo's comparison between Antony and 'plated Mars' (*Antony and Cleopatra*, 1.1.4) in the play's opening speech is meant to underline the fact that Antony is especially Mars-like because of his being now focused on love (i.e., Venus) rather than war, and the audience is more explicitly reminded of the connection with the gods of love and war in Act 1, scene 5, by the eunuch Mardian, who confesses to having fierce affections and to thinking 'What Venus did with Mars' (1.5.19). What is more, Antony's seems to be a more permanent, or all-encompassing, state than that of Mars.

Linking Mars to Venus meant recalling two mythical stories that were very well known in the early modern era. The first was that in which Mars and Venus were caught in bed together by Venus' husband Vulcan, who then exposed them to the laughter of the Olympian gods, an image that, suggests Bate, would seem to be 'proleptic of the lovers' downfall'.[79]

In the second story, told by Lucretius, Mars lay unarmed in Venus' lap, and this image could be interpreted in two opposite ways, either as a picture of the triumph of love over strife or as the utmost exemplification of how lust can weaken masculinity and bellicosity.[80] It is especially this second story that Shakespeare seems to have in mind. As Antony's loss of masculinity through his shameful lack of self-governance in his abandonment to pleasure with Cleopatra, together with his resulting neglect of affairs of state, is one of the main issues of the play, the associations with Hercules and Mars then seem to have the principal intent of discrediting Antony, the exact opposite of the function they have for Fletcher and Massinger's Diocletian.

In the development of the character of Diocletian, *The Prophetess* exhibits an even more telling example of the elaborate dialogue that exists between Fletcher's and Shakespeare's Roman worlds. As an *exemplum e contrario*, the memory of Antony is organic to the construction of Diocletian's personality and actions. Through its framework of Herculean allusions, it guides Diocletian through his momentous choice to abandon power and retire to the quiet of the countryside, where he can be Diocles again, in essence though not in name. Given these connections, as already remarked concerning the other potential pairings of Fletcherian and Shakespearean plays discussed above, having the same actor perform Diocles and Antony across the repertory of the King's Men at roughly the same time would have been potentially explosive.

THE PROPHETESS AND CORIOLANUS

Before concluding, there is another aspect to consider in investigating the conversation between *The Prophetess* and Shakespeare's Roman plays, namely the relationship between Diocletian and Delphia, which the play takes pains to frame as a metaphoric mother-and-son relationship and which, as a consequence, seems to recall *Coriolanus*. In the opening and concluding acts, Diocletian repeatedly calls Delphia 'mother' (1.3.154, 166, 200, 221, 251, 260, 273; 5.4.42, 49, 155), and she calls him 'son' (1.3.152, 215, 259; 5.4.41, 47, 50, 151), much like what occurs in *Coriolanus*, which dwells at length on Volumnia's and Coriolanus' actual mother–son nexus (especially on Coriolanus' side): 'good mother' (2.1.196), 'sweet son' (3.2.108), 'Mother' (3.2.132), 'the most noble mother of the world' (5.3.49), 'O, mother, mother!' (5.3.182), 'O, my mother, mother!' (5.3.185). Just as Diocletian seems to do things either under the command or for the sake of Delphia, so Coriolanus is rumoured in fact to do things for his mother's pleasure: 'Though soft-conscienced men can be content to say it was for his country, he did it to please his mother', scornfully comments a citizen (1.1.34–6).

In addition, both Martius and Diocles change their names publicly and acquire new ones ending in '-anus'. Cominius declares:

> and from this time,
> For what he did before Corioles, call him,
> With all th'applause and clamour of the host,
> Martius Caius Coriolanus! (1.9.61–4),

while Diocletian similarly proclaims:

> I will keep
> The name I had being a private man,
> Only with some small difference: I will add
> To Diocles but two short syllables
> And be called Diocletianus. (2.3.77–81)

Here, the analogy is evident, even though the differences are also important to notice. In particular, the context of the name change is different: Martius is being conferred with a toponymic *cognomen* as recognition of his exceptional courage and valour in the Roman siege of the Volscian city of Corioli, whereas Diocletian is attributing a new name to himself by enlarging his own as he is elected (co-)emperor of Rome in order to make it sound more Roman and, as it were, more emperor-like (cf. Domitianus, Aurelianus, Numerianus, etc.).

Finally, by leaving Rome for Lombardy, Diocletian goes into what amounts to a sort of voluntary exile, which might recall by opposition the forced exile of Coriolanus. At the end of *The Prophetess*, similarly to what happens to Coriolanus, people go to visit Diocletian away from Rome; yet they have different intentions and are received in different ways. While Cominius and Menenius go to Coriolanus in Antium to entreat his clemency and are haughtily refused, Maximian and Aurelia disrupt Diocletian's idyll in the countryside with the intention of killing him and, after their plan is thwarted by Delphia, they are met with Diocletian's unexpected mercy and forgiveness, which is implied to be certain to have beneficial consequences for the well-being of the Empire. Again, a Fletcherian Roman has learned a lesson from a Shakespearean one regarding how *not* to behave. All in all, while recalling two Shakespearean Roman generals and leaders, Fletcher and Massinger's Diocletian seems to be modelled against them in such a way as to emerge as a more balanced, better self-governing figure, although this also ends up making him a less tragic and less compelling character.

CONCLUSION: EXEMPLARY SHAKESPEARE AND THE FIRST FOLIO

Maximus, Bonduca, Caesar, Cleopatra, and Diocletian all provide compelling examples of the peculiar Fletcherian reworking of material taken from Shakespeare's Roman plays. Far from merely producing a pattern of sophisticated allusions to their predecessor's writings or simply parodying successful plays in the company's repertory, the Shakespearean reminiscences are so woven into the Fletcherian texts as to make those stories part of the characters' memories and decisively influence their thoughts, decisions, and actions by bestowing on them a kind of prescience of future events and an increased awareness of both the inward and the outward worlds. Maximus learns from Brutus; Bonduca from Cleopatra; Caesar from Antony and from a chronologically 'future' version of himself, like Cleopatra; Diocletian from Antony and Coriolanus; Fletcher and Massinger from Shakespeare. Harking back to *Julius Caesar*, *Antony and Cleopatra*, and *Coriolanus* enables Fletcher to create a continuity with Shakespeare, while at the same time giving a different (and often unexpected) twist to the stories the latter had so compellingly dramatized and putting them to different uses. On the one hand, this stands as a further exemplification of Fletcher's intense and multifarious engagement with Shakespeare's oeuvre; on the other, it chimes with Fletcher's treatment of ancient sources as surveyed in Chapter 1 and with his view of Roman *exempla* discussed in Chapter 3. The idea that the Roman past is in some sense superior to the early modern present seems to be foreign to the Fletcher canon, which treats past and present as though they were one: Plutarch or Tacitus do not seem to hold any more authority than Shakespeare, nor Livy's Lucrece be a better model for the plays' characters than Shakespeare's Cleopatra. As has already become clear, the ancient paradigms in the Fletcher canon are repeatedly shown to be either unreliable or inadequate.

Looking at Fletcher's engagement with the Roman Shakespeare from the broader standpoint of the activity of the King's Men opens up new ways of thinking about Fletcher's Roman plays, in particular as regards the complex interplay between character and audience memories, in that he may have taken advantage of the ghostly echoes of prior and current performances carried by both the individual roles and the actors who performed them, as described by Carlson. We have no firm evidence of combined revivals of Fletcher's and Shakespeare's Roman plays in the repertory of the King's Men, but in a period of scanty records there are likely to have been many performances for which no documentation survives. All in all, given the elaborate conversation between the two playwrights' Roman worlds that has been revealed in this chapter, it would be surprising if the King's Men did not exploit the possibility of having the same actors play different roles so as to add the players' bodily memories on stage to the textual memories that are so prominent in the construction of the Roman Fletcherian characters. The impact on audiences would have been exceptionally powerful and extraordinarily effective.

While Fletcher's conversation with Shakespeare's Roman plays spans his entire career, it intensifies in the 1619–23 period, which, on closer inspection, seems to display a near obsession with *Julius Caesar* and *Antony and Cleopatra*, ranging from verbal echoes to the re-enactment of theatrical situations. Apart from those discussed in this chapter, the examples from the non-Roman plays of the period are legion. As demonstrated in the previous chapter, *The Double Marriage* (1620–23) abundantly draws upon *Julius Caesar*. In *Sir John Van Olden Barnavelt* (1619) the rhyming couplet 'And let this Prince of Orange seat him sure, / Or he shall fall when he is most secure' (2.1.748–9) clearly echoes Shakespeare's rhyming couplet 'And after this, let Caesar set him sure, / For we will shake him, or worse days endure' (*Julius Caesar*, 1.2.320–1). In addition, as Ivo Kamps remarks, the play seems to set up 'an analogy between Shakespeare's Julius Caesar and the Prince of Orange. Eager to portray himself as the reluctant ruler, Maurice resembles Shakespeare's Caesar who repeatedly refuses the crown that he longs for with all his heart, and which he eventually intends to accept.'[81] In *The Little French Lawyer* (1619–23), *Julius Caesar* is quoted directly by La-Writ as Champernell beats him into giving up fighting and returning to his job as a lawyer: '*Et tu Brute*' (4.6.165). Lopez in *Women Pleased* (1619–23) alludes to 'Cleopatra's banquet' (1.2.10); in *A Very Woman* (1621–25), one of Leonora's waiting women mentions 'the Egyptian queen' (2.3.16), and when Almira threatens to take her own life as a retort to her father's decision to have Don John, the man she wants to marry, tortured because he is a slave (which would render that marriage socially unacceptable), she asserts:

> Death hath a thousand doors to let out life:
> I shall find one. If Portia's burning coals,
> The knife of Lucrece, Cleopatra's aspics,
> Famine, deep waters have the power to free me
> From a loathed life, I'll not an hour outlive him. (5.4.162–6)

Here, the references to the suicides of Portia by swallowing fire and of Cleopatra by applying asps to her breast, as well as the suggestion of starving oneself to death, would all seem to be references to *Julius Caesar* and *Antony and Cleopatra*. In *The Island Princess* (1619–21), the use of the adjective 'tawny' (1.1.63) is a reminiscence of Shakespeare's Cleopatra's 'tawny front' (*Antony and Cleopatra*, 1.1.6), and Rui Dias laments, 'Oh,

I have boyed myself' (*Island Princess*, 2.6.134), his words recalling Cleopatra's 'I shall see / Some squeaking Cleopatra boy my greatness' (*Antony and Cleopatra*, 5.2.218–19). *The Wild-Goose Chase* (1620–21) also features a reference to *Antony and Cleopatra*. Towards the end of the play, the Servant tells Lilia Bianca "Twill be long enough / Before ye cry, "Come Antony, and kiss me!"' (5.4.39–40). This allusion is particularly tantalizing because it seems to hint at what happened on stage in *Antony and Cleopatra*. As S. Viswanathan explains, Lilia Bianca

> is mocked at by an all too earthly servant in the course of an action which takes place with reference to two acting areas, at the upper and lower stages. The servant's words recall the prolonged and difficult process of Antony in *Antony and Cleopatra* being lifted up to the 'above', all for a kiss ... The line names Antony and recalls Cleopatra's iteration of 'come', the word repeated by her possibly as a 'yo-he-ho' expression as she pulls with effort.[82]

Was this an allusion to a recent, unrecorded performance by the King's Men? While the allusions to *Julius Caesar* and *Antony and Cleopatra* in this period of Fletcher's career result from his keen interest in Shakespeare's depiction of the transition between the Roman Republic and the Roman Empire, they might also reflect the continued presence of the two plays in the active repertory of the King's Men (as hypothesized above) or indicate that the two plays had been recently revived on stage, as the performance of another play drawing upon *The Tempest* – that is, *The Two Noble Ladies* – at the Red Bull around 1619–23 would appear to suggest.[83] Even more interestingly, however, the fact that both tragedies (as well as *Coriolanus*) were among the plays that were published in Shakespeare's First Folio in 1623 significantly seems to corroborate McMullan's argument in relation to the 'spate of rereadings of *The Tempest*' in 1621–22 in such plays as *The Island Princess*, *The Wild-Goose Chase*, *The Double Marriage*, *The Prophetess*, and *The Sea Voyage*. 'One can only assume', contends McMullan, 'that the research of fellow King's Men Heminges and Condell into Shakespeare's texts at that time had rekindled Fletcher's long-standing fascination with his erstwhile colleague's work.'[84]

Fletcher seems to have been especially attracted at this time to previously unpublished plays, and it might not be coincidental that his interest in *Julius Caesar*, *Antony and Cleopatra*, *Coriolanus*, and *The Tempest* was reawakened in 1619, when plans for the realization of Shakespeare's First Folio would seem to have been set in motion, as might be suggested by the letter the Lord Chamberlain sent to the Court of the Stationer's Company on 13 May 1619, in response to which the Court declared that 'It is thought fit and so ordered that no plays that His Majesty's players do play shall be printed without consent of some of them.'[85] If this is the case, the King's Men possibly started going through Shakespeare's plays afresh in order to gather them together in the Folio as early as 1619 – if not even soon after (or right before) Shakespeare's death – even though printing itself did not begin until early 1622 and took nearly two years.[86] Mary Edmond suggests that John Heminges's documented presence in Oxford in 1620 may be an indication of the fact that he was then travelling to Stratford-upon-Avon to retrieve more of Shakespeare's papers.[87]

Aside from the necessity of gathering the texts, it was also necessary for someone to edit them. Unlike the work of the Folio compositors, which has been studied in painstaking detail, the Folio editors, Paul Werstine remarks, 'have received almost no attention' and 'remain shadowy figures'.[88] Several candidates have been proposed over the decades, but the matter still appears far from settled. People who have been put forward as possible editors of the First Folio are, among others, Heminges and Condell themselves, the printers William and Isaac Jaggard, the publisher Edward Blount, the King's Men's book-keeper Edward Knight, the scribe Ralph Crane, Shakespeare's fellow playwright Ben Jonson, the translator and teacher John Florio, and poet and translator Leonard Digges.[89]

Despite the long list of potential candidates that have been put forward, a broader input to the editing of the Folio by playwrights working with the King's Men has not been posited so far. Given Fletcher's assiduous engagement with previously unpublished Folio plays in 1619–23, I wonder whether he was among the people who collaborated in checking (or perhaps even editing) the copy-texts for publication in the Folio. Heminges and Condell would have had regular contact with Fletcher through the King's Men, even though both seem to have retired from regular performance by this point. What kind of access did Fletcher have to playhouse manuscripts or transcripts of Shakespeare's plays? At present, it is impossible to answer this question, but it is an important one to ask.

It would take much firmer evidence, and it is beyond the scope of this book, to try to make a case for Fletcher's involvement in the making of the Folio – and, admittedly, Fletcher never manifested great interest in the publication of his own plays apart from *The Faithful Shepherdess* around 1609–10. Yet it is tantalizing to think that Fletcher might have felt particularly attracted to some of Shakespeare's yet unpublished plays at this time, and been tempted therefore to rework some of their elements in his own dramatic practice because he had been granted the opportunity to look over several of them in manuscript while the Folio was in preparation. Although at this stage such a suggestion can be little more than speculation, the possibility that Fletcher was somehow involved in the preparation of the Folio deserves further scholarly consideration as possibly shedding new light not only on his intellectual life but also on the publication of the Folio itself.

NOTES

1 Leech, *John Fletcher Plays*, 162; David L. Frost, *The School of Shakespeare: The Influence of Shakespeare on English Drama 1600–42* (Cambridge: Cambridge University Press, 1968), 238.
2 McMullan, 'Introduction', 114–15; McManus, 'Introduction', 11; Misha Teramura, 'The Anxiety of *Auctoritas*: Chaucer and *The Two Noble Kinsmen*', *Shakespeare Quarterly* 63 (2012), 544–76 (576).
3 McKeithan, *Debt to Shakespeare*, 21–2; T. W. Craik, 'Commentary', in *The Maid's Tragedy* by Francis Beaumont and John Fletcher (Manchester: Manchester University Press, 1988), 48–198 (98 n.24); Rota Herzberg Lister, 'Commentary', in *A Critical Edition of John Fletcher's Comedy The Wild-Goose Chase* (New York: Garland, 1980), 3–149 (139 n.40); Clare McManus, 'Commentary', in *The Island Princess*, 97–288 (109 n.64, 177 n.134); McKeithan, *Debt to Shakespeare*, 184–5; T. W. Craik, 'Introduction', in *The Maid's Tragedy*, 1–46, 7; Craik, 'Commentary', 49 n.10; McKeithan, *Debt to Shakespeare*, 43–4, 113, 51; Wilhelmina P. Frijlinck, 'Notes', in *The Tragedy of Sir John Van Olden Barnavelt; Anonymous Elizabethan Play, Edited from the Manuscript with Introduction and Notes* (Amsterdam: Van Dorssen, 1922), 84–111 (96 n. 748); McKeithan, *Debt to Shakespeare*, 171, 167–9, 138–9. As regards *Henry VIII*, though this seems to have escaped scholarly notice, the scene – usually acknowledged as written by Fletcher – in which 3 Gentleman relates the coronation of Anne Bullen to 1 Gentleman and 2 Gentleman (4.1.56–94) displays a few similarities to Casca's account of Antony's failed attempt at Caesar's coronation to Cassius and Brutus in *Julius Caesar* (1.2.214–86). 3 Gentleman is 'stifled / With the mere rankness of their joy' (*Henry VIII*, 4.1.58–9) and says that, when the people finally beheld the beauty of Anne Bullen, 'such a noise arose / As the shrouds make at sea in a stiff tempest, / As loud and to as many tunes. Hats, cloaks – / Doublets, I think – flew up, and had their faces / Been loose, this day they had been lost' (4.1.71–5). Such images appear redolent of the elements of noise, bad smell, and throwing pieces of clothing in the air that are found in Casca's description of how 'the rabblement hooted, and clapped their chapped hands, and threw up their sweaty nightcaps, and uttered such a deal of stinking breath' (*Julius Caesar*, 1.2.243–5) upon Caesar's triple refusal of the coronet offered to him by Antony.
4 Gossett, 'Introduction', 13; Gurr, *Shakespeare Company*, 153.
5 William W. E. Slights, 'Dower Power: Communities of Collaboration in the Jacobean Theater', *Essays in Theatre/Études Théâtrales* 19 (2000), 3–19 (15).
6 Munro, *Shakespeare in the Theatre*, xvii–xviii.
7 Marvin Carlson, *The Haunted Stage: The Theatre as Memory Machine* (Ann Arbor, MI: University of Michigan Press, 2002), 8.
8 Lisa Hopkins, 'Introduction', in *Bess of Hardwick: New Perspectives*, ed. Lisa Hopkins (Manchester: Manchester University Press, 2019), 1–17 (10, 13).
9 William Shakespeare, *The Rape of Lucrece*, in *Shakespeare's Poems*, ed. Katherine Duncan-Jones and H. R. Woudhuysen (London: Thomson Learning for Arden Shakespeare, 2007), 231–383, ll. 1366–7. All references to the poem are to this edition. Subsequent references will be incorporated parenthetically into the text.
10 Mincoff, 'Shakespeare, Fletcher and Baroque Tragedy', 6.

11 Makkink, *Philip Massinger and John Fletcher*, 70.
12 David Bevington, 'Introduction', in *Troilus and Cressida* by William Shakespeare (London: Bloomsbury Arden Shakespeare, rev. edn, 2015), 1–142 (20–1).
13 Bevington, 'Introduction', 21.
14 See Gossett, 'Introduction', 4–7; Valerie Wayne, 'Introduction', in *Cymbeline* by William Shakespeare (London: Bloomsbury Arden Shakespeare, 2017), 1–136 (48–9); and the scholarship mentioned in them.
15 Appleton, *Beaumont and Fletcher*, 55.
16 Leech, *John Fletcher Plays*, 163.
17 Leech, *John Fletcher Plays*, 165.
18 Leech, *John Fletcher Plays*, 165.
19 Leech, *John Fletcher Plays*, 166–7.
20 Leech, *John Fletcher Plays*, 166–7.
21 Alison Calder '"I Am Unacquainted with That Language, Roman": Male and Female Experiences of War in Fletcher's *Bonduca*', *Medieval and Renaissance Drama in England* 8 (1996), 211–26 (224); Bretz, '"Are you my sweet heart?"', 60.
22 Reginald Saner, '*Antony and Cleopatra*: How Pompey's Honor Struck a Contemporary', *Shakespeare Quarterly* 20 (1969), 117–20; Anon., *A Horrible, Cruel and Bloody Murder* (London, 1614), B3r; Wiggins, *Catalogue*, #1517, 5:325–31.
23 Paul D. Green, 'Theme and Structure in Fletcher's *Bonduca*', *Studies in English Literature, 1500–1900* 22 (1982), 305–16 (311 n.17), who also suggests similarities between Enobarbus and Caratach, which I do not find entirely convincing, as is the case with those that Squier, *John Fletcher*, 108, identifies between Enobarbus and Poenius.
24 Kelly Neil, 'The Politics of Suicide in John Fletcher's *Tragedie of Bonduca*', *Journal for Early Modern Cultural Studies* 14 (2014), 88–114 (112 n.17); Drabek, *Fletcherian Dramatic Achievement*, 87. The similarity had also been noted by Leonhardt, '*Bonduca*', 63. As Drabek, *Fletcherian Dramatic Achievement*, 87, adds, 'This scene also has a parallel in the final "blackmailing scene" (5.3) of *Love's Cure*.'
25 Boling, 'Fletcher's Satire', 404.
26 Frénée-Hutchins, *Boudica's Odyssey in Early Modern England*, 155.
27 Green, 'Theme and Structure', 313–14.
28 Hickman, '*Bonduca*'s Two Ignoble Armies', 166; Sarah E. Johnson, 'Pride and Gender in Fletcher's *Bonduca*', *Modern Philology* 115 (2017), 80–104 (103).
29 Calder, '"I Am Unacquainted with That Language, Roman"', 216.
30 Calder, '"I Am Unacquainted with That Language, Roman"', 218.
31 Boling, 'Fletcher's Satire', 404.
32 Johnson, 'Pride and Gender', 103.
33 Michael Neill, *Issues of Death: Mortality and Identity in English Renaissance Tragedy* (Oxford: Clarendon Press, 1997), 314.
34 Bridget Escolme, *Antony and Cleopatra: A Guide to the Text and Its Theatrical Life* (Basingstoke: Palgrave Macmillan, 2006), 92.
35 Neil, 'Politics of Suicide', 99–100.
36 Hickman, '*Bonduca*'s Two Ignoble Armies', 166.
37 Maxwell, *Studies in Beaumont, Fletcher, and Massinger*, 223.
38 On *The False One* as a prequel to Shakespeare's plays, see Michael Neill, 'Introduction', in *Antony and Cleopatra* by William Shakespeare (Oxford: Oxford University Press, 1994), 1–130 (24); Kewes, 'Julius Caesar in Jacobean England', 172–3; Sarah Hatchuel, *Shakespeare and the Cleopatra/Caesar Intertext: Sequel, Conflation, Remake* (Madison, WI: Fairleigh Dickinson University Press, 2011),

110–12. Caesar's liaison with Cleopatra had in fact been brought on stage in the anonymous *Tragedy of Caesar's Revenge* (publ. 1606), but Fletcher and Massinger seem to pretend not to be aware of this. For a more detailed examination on the relationship between *Caesar's Revenge* and *The False One*, see Lovascio, 'Introduction', in *The False One*, forthcoming.

39 Joyce Green MacDonald, *Women and Race in Early Modern Texts* (Cambridge: Cambridge University Press, 2002), 59.
40 Kim F. Hall, *Things of Darkness: Economies of Race and Gender in Early Modern England* (Ithaca, NY: Cornell University Press, 1995), 9; Ania Loomba, *Shakespeare, Race, and Colonialism* (Oxford: Oxford University Press, 2002), 60; Eva Johanna Holmberg, *Jews in the Early Modern English Imagination: A Scattered Nation* (Farnham: Ashgate, 2011), 119.
41 Farah Karim-Cooper, *Cosmetics in Shakespearean and Renaissance Drama* (Edinburgh: Edinburgh University Press, 2006), 11.
42 Ramona Wray, 'Introduction', in *The Tragedy of Mariam* by Elizabeth Cary (London: Bloomsbury Arden Shakespeare, 2012), 1–69 (38).
43 Wray, 'Introduction', 41.
44 Wray, 'Introduction', 43.
45 Kimberly Woosley Poitevin, '"Counterfeit Colour": Making Up Race in Elizabeth Cary's *The Tragedy of Mariam*', *Tulsa Studies in Women's Literature* 24 (2005), 13–34 (17).
46 Claire Jowitt, 'The Island Princess and Race', in *Early Modern English Drama: A Critical Companion*, ed. Garrett A. Sullivan, Patrick Cheney, and Andrew Hadfield (Oxford: Oxford University Press, 2005), 287–97 (294–5).
47 For an insightful discussion of the early modern English conception of 'blushing', see Sujata Iyengar, *Shades of Difference: Mythologies of Skin Color in Early Modern England* (Philadelphia, PA: University of Pennsylvania Press, 2004), 103–39.
48 Incidentally, I suggest elsewhere that *The False One* may have been designed primarily for the Blackfriars (Lovascio, 'Introduction', forthcoming). If that were the case, Fletcher and Massinger might have decided against having a black Cleopatra at least partly on the grounds that the light of candles in an indoor playhouse would have had an unsatisfactory effect on artificially blackened skin, insofar as Cleopatra's facial expressions would have been less easily intelligible as a result, thus compromising her connection with playgoers. For the problems that candlelight poses for actors of colour, see Munro, *Shakespeare in the Theatre*, 78–9, though the shifts in the casting of *Othello* that she suggests may reflect concerns about the Blackfriars in the 1630s, and not necessarily also in the late 1610s or early 1620s.
49 Hatchuel, *Shakespeare and the Cleopatra/Caesar Intertext*, 112.
50 Maxwell, *Studies in Beaumont, Fletcher, and Massinger*, 169. McKeithan, *Debt to Shakespeare*, 165–6, helpfully groups passages from Shakespeare's *Antony and Cleopatra* that expose her changeability and variety (2.2.245–6; 1.1.50–1; 1.3.3–5; 1.3.71–3; 2.5.1, 3, 9–10) – to which Hatchuel, *Shakespeare and the Cleopatra/Caesar Intertext*, 110, adds 1.2.137–40.
51 Plutarch, 'The Life of Julius Caesar', in *Lives*, 786D-E; Lucan, *Pharsalia*, 10.56–8.
52 Alexandra Shepard, *Meanings of Manhood in Early Modern England* (Oxford: Oxford University Press, 2003), 55.
53 Waith, *Pattern of Tragicomedy*, 125.
54 Lucan, *Pharsalia*, 10.65
55 Hatchuel, *Shakespeare and the Cleopatra/Caesar Intertext*, 111.
56 See McKeithan, *Debt to Shakespeare*, 173–6; Frost, *School of Shakespeare*, 225–6; McMullan, *Politics of Unease*, 183–92; Munro, *Shakespeare in the Theatre*, 140–3.

57 Curran, 'Fletcher, Massinger and Roman Imperial Character', 333.
58 Thomas Dekker and Philip Massinger, *The Virgin Martyr*, in *The Dramatic Works of Thomas Dekker*, ed. Fredson Bowers, 4 vols (Cambridge: Cambridge University Press, 1958), 3.365–480, 5.2.89–91.
59 Curran, 'Fletcher, Massinger and Roman Imperial Character', 327–8.
60 William Shakespeare, *The Taming of the Shrew*, ed. Barbara Hodgdon (London: Methuen for Arden Shakespeare, 2010), 1.1.4; John Florio, *Florio His First Fruits* (London, 1578), 31v.
61 McMullan, *Politics of Unease*, 183.
62 George Walton Williams, 'Textual Introduction', in *The Prophetess* by John Fletcher and Philip Massinger, in Bowers (gen. ed.), *Dramatic Works*, 9.223–31 (223).
63 Bate, *Shakespeare and Ovid*, 205.
64 Virginia Mason Vaughan, *Shakespeare and the Gods* (London: Bloomsbury Arden Shakespeare, 2019), 112; Janet Adelman, *The Common Liar: An Essay on Antony and Cleopatra* (New Haven, CT: Yale University Press, 1973), 135.
65 I have preserved the lineation of the Latin sentence as found in Williams's edition, but I suspect the correct lineation might in fact be '*Imperator eris Romae / Cum Aprum grandem interfeceris*', which would result in an eight- (or nine-)syllable line followed by a ten-syllable line.
66 Maximian too remarks upon Diocles' 'labour and ... danger' (1.3.91).
67 William Shakespeare, *Henry VI Part 3*, ed. Eric Rasmussen and John D. Cox (London: Thomson Learning for Arden Shakespeare, 2001), 5.1.36.
68 Frank Kermode, *Shakespeare, Spenser, Donne: Renaissance Essays* (London: Routledge and Kegan Paul, 1971), 98.
69 McMullan, *Politics of Unease*, 186.
70 Vaughan, *Shakespeare and the Gods*, 113; Bate, *Shakespeare and Ovid*, 208–9.
71 John E. Curran, Jr, 'New Directions: Determined Things: The Historical Reconstruction of Character in *Antony and Cleopatra*', in *Antony and Cleopatra: A Critical Reader*, ed. Domenico Lovascio (London: Bloomsbury Arden Shakespeare, 2019), 133–54 (146).
72 Curran, 'Fletcher, Massinger and Roman Imperial Character', 331.
73 Here, as in *The Humorous Lieutenant* (5.5.15), Hercules' phrase is not quoted in its more common form '*Nec* (or *Non*) *plus ultra*'; it is used by Fletcher in the form also mentioned in an oft-quoted passage from Thomas Heywood's *Apology for Actors* (London, 1612): 'To see, as I have seen, Hercules in his own shape hunting the boar, knocking down the bull, taming the hart, fighting with Hydra, murdering Geryon, slaughtering Diomedes, wounding the Stymphalides, killing the centaurs, bashing the lion, squeezing the dragon, dragging Cerberus in chains, and, lastly, on his high pyramids writing *nil ultra*, oh, these were sights to make an Alexander' (fol. B4r).
74 John Wilders, 'Introduction', in *Antony and Cleopatra* by William Shakespeare (London: Routledge for Arden Shakespeare, 1995), 1–84 (65); Xenophon, *Memorabilia*, trans. W. C. Marchant (London: Heinemann, 1923), 2.1.21–34. On *Hercules in bivio*, see also David Bevington, 'Introduction', in *Antony and Cleopatra* by William Shakespeare (Cambridge: Cambridge University Press, updated edn, 2005), 1–80 (9); Ernest Schanzer, *The Problem Plays of Shakespeare: A Study of Julius Caesar, Measure for Measure, Antony and Cleopatra* (London: Routledge, 1963), 155–8; John Coates, 'The Choice of Hercules in *Antony and Cleopatra*', *Shakespeare Survey* 31 (1978), 45–52; Bate, *How the Classics Made Shakespeare*, 210–31.
75 McMullan, *Politics of Unease*, 183.
76 Adelman, *Common Liar*, 135.

77 Edward Berry, *Shakespeare and the Hunt: A Cultural and Social Study* (Cambridge: Cambridge University Press, 2001), 45.
78 Bate, *Shakespeare and Ovid*, 204.
79 Bate, *Shakespeare and Ovid*, 204.
80 Lucretius, *On the Nature of Things*, trans. W. H. D. Rouse, rev. Martin F. Smith (Cambridge, MA: Harvard University Press, 1924), 1.29–40.
81 Kamps, *Historiography and Ideology*, 153.
82 S. Viswanathan, 'A Shakespeare "Gest": Bearing the Body in the Plays', *Points of View* 1 (2008), 3–16 (15).
83 Munro, *Shakespeare in the Theatre*, 130.
84 McMullan, *Politics of Unease*, 182.
85 William A. Jackson, *Records of the Court of the Stationers' Company* (London: The Bibliographical Society, 1957), 110.
86 See Eric Rasmussen, 'Publishing the First Folio', in *The Cambridge Companion to Shakespeare's First Folio*, ed. Emma Smith (Cambridge: Cambridge University Press, 2016), 18–29; John Jowett, *Shakespeare and Text* (Oxford: Oxford University Press, rev. edn, 2019), 71–98.
87 Mary Edmond, 'Heminges, John (bap. 1566, d. 1630)', *Oxford Dictionary of National Biography* (Oxford: Oxford University Press, 2004), https://www.oxforddnb.com/view/10.1093/ref:odnb/9780198614128.001.0001/odnb-9780198614128-e-12890 (accessed 8 February 2021).
88 Paul Werstine, 'Folio Editors, Folio Compositors, and the Folio Text of *King Lear*', in *The Division of the Kingdoms: Shakespeare's Two Versions of King Lear*, ed. Gary Taylor and Michael Warren (Oxford: Oxford University Press, 1983), 252. On the printing of the Folio, see Charles Hinman, *The Printing and Proof-Reading of the First Folio of Shakespeare* (Oxford: Clarendon Press, 1963).
89 On Heminges and Condell, see William B. Hunter, 'Heminge and Condell as Editors of the Shakespeare First Folio', *ANQ: A Quarterly Journal of Short Articles, Notes and Reviews* 15 (2002), 11–19; on the Jaggards, see Sidney Lee, 'An Elizabethan Bookseller', *Bibliographica* 1 (1895), 474–98, and W. W. Greg, *The Editorial Problem in Shakespeare: A Survey of the Foundation of the Text* (Oxford: Clarendon Press, 1942), 77–9; on Blount, see A. W. Pollard, *Shakespeare Folios and Quartos: A Study in the Bibliography of Shakespeare's Plays, 1594–1685* (London: Methuen, 1909), 112; on Knight, see W. W. Greg, *The Shakespeare First Folio, Its Bibliographical and Textual History* (Oxford: Clarendon Press, 1955), 78–9; on Crane, see T. H. Howard-Hill, 'Shakespeare's Earliest Editor, Ralph Crane', *Shakespeare Survey* 44 (1991), 113–29; on Jonson, see Donaldson, *Ben Jonson*, 370–6; on Florio, see Saul Frampton, 'Who Edited Shakespeare?', *Guardian*, 12 July 2013, https://www.theguardian.com/books/2013/jul/12/who-edited-shakespeare-john-florio (accessed 8 February 2021); on Digges, see Eric Rasmussen, 'Who Edited the Shakespeare First Folio?', *Cahiers Élisabéthains* 93 (2017), 70–6.

CONCLUSION
QUESTIONING THE CLASSICS

As many as five plays in the Fletcher canon contain more or less explicit allusions to a popular anecdote tracing back to around 362 BCE, in the early republican age of Rome. It is the story of an incredible act of courage by a young Roman soldier. After an earthquake, Rome faced great danger when a chasm opened on the Forum, which the Romans made multiple attempts to fill – all in vain. An oracle was consulted, and the response was that, in order to close the crevice and make the Roman nation last forever, the Romans would need to throw into it what amounted to the greatest strength of the Roman people. The Romans tried tossing several different things into the ravine, to no avail, until a young horseman named Marcus Curtius realized that nothing was more precious to the Romans than their arms and bravery. Accordingly, he decided to jump in himself, astride his horse, fully and meticulously armed and decorated. Only then did the earth close above him and was Rome saved. The story, mentioned in passing by Varro and narrated at greater length by Livy, was very popular in the Renaissance, thanks also to etchings made by such artists as Lucas Cranach the Elder (1507–08) and Hendrick Goltzius (1586).[1] Such a myth had been crucial to ancient Rome's glorification of itself as founded on the admirable ideals of honour, *virtus*, and propensity to self-sacrifice.

An examination of the ways in which the plays in the Fletcher canon deploy this story seems particularly fit as a means to draw this volume to its conclusion, in that they epitomize his overall approach to classical history and *exempla*. Towards the end of *The Double Marriage*, Sesse gives his pirates the following pep talk as they set out to assault King Ferrand in order to kill him:

> Then wait the first occasion, and, like Curtius,
> I'll leap the gulf before you, fearless leap it.
> Then, follow me like men, and, if our virtues
> May boy our country up and set her shining
> In her first state (our fair revenges taken),
> We have our noble ends or else our ashes (4.4.71–6).

Disguised as Switzers, the pirates raise the city in rebellion, and Ferrand flees to his stronghold. Sesse talks of 'liberty' from 'The Tyrant's yoke' for the people of Naples (5.1.162, 152), yet his expedition does not originate from any revolutionary yearning to set the city free from the oppression of tyranny but from all too personal motivations. As it happens, Sesse had turned pirate fourteen years previously after a falling out with Ferrand, and his desire for revenge has been exacerbated by the fact that his daughter, Martia, has now become the 'whore' (5.4.32) of Ferrand himself, who, after discovering whose daughter Martia is, even dares to boast to Sesse's face that 'To know she's thine affords me more true pleasure / Than the act gave me, when even at the height / I cracked her virgin zone' (5.3.124–6). A similar use of the Curtius story is to be found halfway through *Rollo*, when the title character tries to justify his order to execute the two senior courtiers Gisbert and Baldwin by crafting a specious narrative according to which, if Rollo had not done so,

> my mother here,
> My sister, this just lord and all had filled
> The Curtian gulf of this conspiracy,
> Of which my tutor and my chancellor
> [...] were the monstrous heads. (3.1.351–4, 356)

The truth, as the audience knows, is that Gisbert and Baldwin lost their lives for refusing to aid Rollo's fratricide and usurpation, and not because they jeopardized the state by opening a (metaphorical) dangerous ravine through the plotting of a heinous conspiracy against established authority.

In both these plays, then, the references to Curtius can be seen to carry political valence; moreover, in both cases they are put in the mouths of characters who can by no means be regarded as admirable individuals. On the one hand, moved by a thirst for personal vengeance, Sesse deploys the Curtius story in an attempt to reframe his plan to kill Ferrand as a glorious enterprise. On the other, Rollo, a bloody tyrant to the bone, ready to murder anyone who stands between him and the enjoyment of absolute power (even venturing to kill his own brother in their mother's presence), refers to Curtius with a view to sanctioning his own assassinations as acts perpetrated for the general good rather than to save his own neck. In both instances, the Curtius myth is therefore used perversely in attempts to cloak with glory enterprises that are in fact not remotely as noble or as selfless as that of Marcus Curtius had been.

Elsewhere in the canon, the Curtius anecdote is even demoted to serving primarily as the basis for humorous remarks. In *The Tamer Tamed*, as

Maria resolves not to live as a submissive wife in her marriage to Petruccio and to try instead to tame the tamer, she grandiosely claims:

> Like Curtius, to redeem my country have I
> Leaped into this gulf of marriage;
> Farewell all poor thoughts but spite and anger,
> Till I have wrought a miracle upon him. (1.2.66–9)

Maria compares marriage with the legendary crevice (and, hence, implicitly with death) and herself with Curtius, her 'country' being made up of other women. Gordon McMullan rightly points out that here 'Maria sees herself as a modern-day Curtius, developing the obviously female sexual imagery of the chasm into a challenge to the norms of sexual politics.'[2] And certainly the use of the anecdote is also a way of pointing to what is at stake in the play's representation of gender relations. It is in keeping with the way in which the play also echoes *Lysistrata* and is related to the importance that Jacobean commentators put on the household as a political structure in miniature. Gender relations matter, in part, because the authority of the husband mirrors that of the ruler, whose authority mirrors that of God – sexual politics *are* politics, on some level. Perhaps paradoxically, when a space in Fletcherian comedy is opened for assertive women to make rhetorical and strategic capital by placing themselves within a Roman tradition, the reference is to a male rather than a female model. Nonetheless, the political overtones of Maria's comparison seem less evident than the humorous connotations of her attempt to frame her barricading herself into the house on her wedding night (in order to starve Petruccio sexually so as ultimately to build a more equitable marriage relationship) as a 'miracle' worthy of comparison with Curtius' famous deed.

The appropriation of the Roman legend has even more pronouncedly humorous implications in *The Custom of the Country*, which spring from the incongruity of the application of the anecdote to Rutilio's situation and the radical difference between him and Curtius. Rutilio ends up working as a male prostitute in the brothel managed by the bawd Sulpicia after she has paid the fine for his release from prison. Rutilio quickly gains a reputation as a stallion and has to lean over backwards in order to satisfy the flocks of new clients that now crowd the brothel. In the end, completely exhausted by his unendurable sexual labours, he exclaims: 'women? Women? Oh, the devil! Women? / Curtius' gulf was never half so dangerous' (4.5.11–12). In Rutilio's lament, the gulf signifies the vagina and, by synecdoche, woman in her allegedly unquenchable sexual voracity, here construed as more perilous even than jumping to certain death in the ravine as Curtius did, which eventually leads the former womanizer Rutilio to resolve to keep away from women.[3]

Ranging from the perversion of Roman values to humorous or bawdy treatments, these four allusions cumulatively suggest that Fletcher's plays treat the Curtius story with no particular solemnity or reverence, but simply as narrative material like any other, to be manipulated and reworked at will by whoever decides to appropriate it. They thus provide a trenchant exemplification of Fletcher's overall approach to all things classical. Crucially, none of these references appear in a classical context. However, the fact that in none of these cases does Fletcher put the allusions to Curtius in the mouth of a Roman character becomes all the more telling when one looks at the only instance of a reference to the story in a Roman play. This occurs in *Bonduca*, during the preparations for the decisive battle between the Britons and the outnumbered Romans, when Petillius wonders:

> Who but fools,
> That make no difference betwixt certain dying
> And dying well, would fling their fames and fortunes
> Into this Britain gulf, this quicksand ruin,
> That, sinking, swallows us? (2.1.46–50)

Although Petillius does not openly mention Curtius, the way he describes the 'Britain gulf' as a ravine bound to devour the Romans after they have attempted to throw 'their fames and fortunes' in it does appear to suggest that he has that story in mind. His words forcefully contribute to strengthening the impression that the republican ideals have irreparably perished in Fletcher's Rome: to sacrifice one's life for Rome's sake in a battle that cannot be won, argues Petillius, is not merely useless or ill-advised, but absolutely foolish. Thus, the only instance in the Roman plays of an allusion to such a crucial myth for the glorification of republican Rome makes it mercilessly evident that probably no one in Fletcher's Rome would be willing to perform such an illustrious self-sacrifice as Curtius' – perhaps not even Aëtius, whose final suicide, as discussed in Chapter 3, is ultimately to be viewed as an extreme act of obedience to the emperor rather than a noble sacrifice for Rome as a whole.

This reworking of the Curtius story would therefore seem to confirm the general patterns that have emerged over the previous pages. The Fletcher canon repeatedly suggests that classical models and paradigms have lost their authority and effectiveness as guides for the present; accordingly, they need to be substituted and are often implicitly replaced by other examples and stories, which are often those set by the characters populating Shakespeare's Roman world rather than their real-life counterparts as presented in the historical records. The greatness of Rome, the notion of

Rome as a mythical ideal – at least in the imperial era – is treated with scepticism and suspicion, and the characters' recourse to the Roman past is revealed as being part of a rhetorical strategy rather than resulting from any profoundly meaningful engagement.

Fletcher depicts a Rome whose internal structures are dangerously on the verge of extinction and in which corruption, violence, and vice have become systemic. Abandoned by the gods and lacking dependable political leaders, Rome is prey to a sense of disorientation that is compounded by the acutely felt nostalgia for a glorious past. Looking at Fletcher's depiction of Rome, one could argue that it would be better not to be there at all; significantly, *Bonduca* is set in Britain; *The False One* is set in Egypt; *The Prophetess* moves between Rome, Persia, and Lombardy; and it seems no coincidence that the only play entirely set in Rome, *Valentinian*, undoubtedly ranks as the grimmest of Fletcher's Roman plays, featuring a rape, the murder of two emperors, the suicide of what history records as Rome's last champion against the barbarians, and an ending without a leader.

Fletcher's Roman plays seem to share some traits typical of the seventeenth-century German *Trauerspiel*. In particular, his Roman plays lack a focalizing hero and, above all, dispiritingly portray history as a mechanically aimless succession of events, and the world as a place in which there is nothing larger than the self and where no transcendent meaning is to be found. Viewing Fletcher's Roman plays in terms of the *Trauerspiel* results in a notable change in our perception of his perspective on the deep mechanisms at work in history and reality, revealing his thinking as much deeper and more sophisticated than is usually assumed, and pioneeringly framing him as a serious philosopher of history as well as a successful playwright. And there is evidence that his interest in ancient Rome also ended up influencing the value systems he created for some of the plays that he did not set there, especially in terms of his rejection of stoicism, as examined in such plays as *The Little French Lawyer*, *The Captain*, and *The Loyal Subject*, as well as his depiction of history in *Sir John Van Olden Barnavelt*.

The canon's sceptical portrayal of Rome and its paradigms seems to relate to Fletcher's egalitarian or irreverent use of classical sources, which he does not treat as worthier of consideration or as more authoritative than contemporary texts, interested as he appears to have been rather in the transition of historical accounts across times and cultures as well as in always blending the ancient and the contemporary. The Fletcher canon calls into question Rome as an unreachable model, as the supreme embodiment of liberty and *virtus*, and as a storehouse of unsurpassable knowledge that holds a sort of epistemic monopoly.

Side by side with these broader claims, this book also illuminates more localized aspects of the individual plays. In the case of *Valentinian*, I have provided more solid evidence for Fletcher's use of Martin Fumée's 1587 French translation of Procopius' *History of the Wars* and identified for the first time both Fletcher's engagement with the tradition of Italian comedy through his use of names and his deployment of Henry Savile's essay 'The End of Nero and the Beginning of Galba' as a source. I have also brought attention to the implications of his depiction of Roman women as exceptionally passive in the play, argued for a negative portrayal of stoicism, and illuminated the play's relationship with Shakespeare's *Julius Caesar*, especially as regards the construction of the character of Maximus as oddly reminiscent of the example of Brutus.

As for *Bonduca*, I have brought new elements to the discussion of the play's sceptical attitude to colonial conquest, mainly by focusing on the play's portrayal of the suicides of Bonduca and her daughters as extreme acts of defiance against foreign conquest. In this sense, I have also argued for a strong connection between the play and Shakespeare's *Antony and Cleopatra*, insofar as Bonduca's final decision to commit suicide by poison rather than by the sword frames Shakespeare's Antony and Cleopatra as *exempla e contrario*, in another example of the weird theatrical temporality that is the cipher of the relationship between Fletcher's and Shakespeare's Roman plays.

With regard to *The False One*, I have demonstrated that Fletcher and Massinger used Florus' *Epitome*, possibly in Edmund Bolton's 1619 translation, side by side with Lucan and Plutarch. I have also provided new insights on the negative attitude the play expresses regarding colonialism, reassessed Cleopatra's role in the play as much more relevant than traditionally assumed, and further spelled out the play's relationship with Shakespeare's *Julius Caesar* and, even more importantly, *Antony and Cleopatra*, mainly in terms of Fletcher and Massinger's characterization of Cleopatra as a young, white virgin whose actions are nonetheless eerily reminiscent of the future Cleopatra previously depicted by Shakespeare.

Finally, I have provided a comprehensive reassessment of the sources of *The Prophetess* by demonstrating that the play has Nicolas Coeffeteau's *Histoire romaine* as its primary source rather than *Historia Augusta*, though that could also have been consulted for details regarding the main character. I have also shed light on the stance assumed in the play towards Jacobean politics as predicated on the portrayal of the rotting body of the emperor as metaphor for the progressive decay of the Roman Empire, and I have explored the significance of Delphia's almost goddess-like agency in the play. Even more crucially, I have brought to the fore for the first

CONCLUSION   183

time the play's pervasive grappling with Shakespeare's *Julius Caesar*, *Antony and Cleopatra*, and *Coriolanus*, chiefly in terms of the characterization of Diocletian as uncannily remembering and implicitly commenting on Shakespeare's Antony and, to a lesser extent, Coriolanus.

In light of all this, the scrutiny of *Valentinian*, *Bonduca*, *The False One*, and *The Prophetess* as a group of plays that form a significant part of the largest single dramatic canon of the Jacobean era proves to be significant and fruitful in several respects. First, it has provided fresh insights into Fletcher's intellectual life by shedding new light on his *modus operandi* with classical texts as sources for his plays, as well as his conception of history and human life. Second, it has enabled the identification of a number of shared features that characterize Fletcher's imaginative reworking of the matter of Rome. Third, it has offered a clearer view of the stance that Fletcher and his collaborators adopted with regard to classical values, paradigms, and beliefs, as well as the extent to which they probed and questioned them. Fourth, it has supplied yet another instantiation of Fletcher's never-ending conversation with Shakespeare in his exuberant, dazzling, and vibrant appropriation of his predecessor's Roman world. Fifth, it has illuminated a wide array of interconnections not only within this group of plays but, even more importantly, between them and the rest of the Fletcher canon, thereby throwing into sharper relief both the unique traits of the Roman plays and the unmistakable signs of continuity between them and Fletcher's wider oeuvre. Finally, it has added a new chapter to the history of classical reception in early modern England by focusing on a sizeable and noteworthy, though still sadly under-appreciated, corpus of plays, thereby shifting attention away from Shakespeare while simultaneously debunking an all too easy equation between Shakespeare's depiction of ancient Rome and the early modern conception of ancient Rome in general.

John Fletcher read widely and eclectically, freely and unpredictably combining texts belonging to different types, genres, and traditions, moving swiftly and associatively across them, as though driven by an unceasing urge to follow his impulse to search for logical and analogical connections, with a constant alertness to analogues and parallels. In the works of Late Antiquity, Fletcher found a way of looking at history that enabled him to channel his own disheartened perception of reality in his Roman plays. Dissatisfied with the limitations he identified in classical paradigms and models, he turned to contemporary retellings of history, including those by Shakespeare, and irreverently merged old and new, thus producing a dispirited yet vibrant dramatization of the ancient Roman world that shines as a uniquely gripping instance of the reception of the classical past on the early modern stage.

Sweeping critical forays into Fletcher's oeuvre are still relatively infrequent. Much is yet unexplored, and the sheer size of the canon can appear daunting at first. But engaging with Fletcher's plays can be immensely rewarding, and I hope that *John Fletcher's Rome: Questioning the Classics* will stimulate further and wider investigations of the works of an accomplished playwright who was capable of practising in different theatrical genres confidently and successfully, his theatre invariably displaying a brisk, heartfelt, and honest dramatization of Jacobean culture, social imagination, and *Zeitgeist*.

NOTES

1 Varro, *On the Latin Language*, 5.32.148; Livy, *History of Rome*, 7.6.1–6.
2 McMullan, *Politics of Unease*, 167.
3 Gordon Williams, *A Dictionary of Sexual Language and Imagery in Shakespearean and Stuart Literature*, 3 vols (London: Athlone, 1994), 2.629–30.

BIBLIOGRAPHY

Adelman, Janet, *The Common Liar: An Essay on Antony and Cleopatra* (New Haven, CT: Yale University Press, 1973)
Agrati, Annalisa, 'Introduzione', in *La commedia Ardelia* (Pisa: Pacini, 1994), 5–61
Alemán, Mateo, *The Rogue, or, The Life of Guzman de Alfarache* (London, 1622)
Allman, Eileen, *Jacobean Revenge Tragedy and the Politics of Virtue* (Newark, DE: University of Delaware Press, 1999)
Altman, Joel B., *The Tudor Play of Mind: Rhetorical Inquiry and the Development of Elizabethan Drama* (Berkeley, CA: University of California Press, 1978)
Anon., 'Claudii Salmasii in Aelium Lampridium Notae', in *Historiae Augustae Scriptores VI. Aelius Spartianus, Vulcatius Gallicanus, Julius Capitolinus, Trebellius Pollio, Aelius Lampridius, Flavius Vopiscus. Claudius Salmasius ex veteribus libris recensuit et librum adiecit notarum ac emendationum. quib[us] adiunctae sunt notae ac emendationes Isaac Casauboni, iam antea editae adiunctae* (Paris, 1620)
Anon., *A Horrible, Cruel and Bloody Murder* (London, 1614)
Appleton, William W., *Beaumont and Fletcher: A Critical Study* (London: Allen and Unwin, 1956)
Armstrong, William A., 'The Elizabethan Conception of the Tyrant', *Review of English Studies* 22 (1946), 161–81
Ascham, Roger, *The Schoolmaster* (London, 1570)
Aubrey, John, *'Brief Lives', Chiefly of Contemporaries, Set Down by John Aubrey, between the Years 1669 & 1696*, ed. Andrew Clark, 2 vols (Oxford: Clarendon Press, 1898)
Baldwin, Thomas Whitfield, *The Organization and Personnel of the Shakespearean Company* (Princeton, NJ: Princeton University Press, 1927)
Bate, Jonathan, *How the Classics Made Shakespeare* (Princeton, NJ: Princeton University Press, 2019)
Bate, Jonathan, *Shakespeare and Ovid* (Oxford: Clarendon Press, 1993)
Bauman, Richard A., *Women and Politics in Ancient Rome* (London: Routledge, 1992)
Beaumont, Francis, and John Fletcher, *Cupid's Revenge*, ed. Fredson Bowers, in *The Dramatic Works in the Beaumont and Fletcher Canon*, ed. Fredson

Bowers, 10 vols (Cambridge: Cambridge University Press, 1966–96), 2.315–448.
Beaumont, Francis, and John Fletcher, *Filastro: azione drammatica in 5 atti*, trans. Luigi Gamberale (Agnone: Sanmartino-Ricci, 1923)
Beaumont, Francis, and John Fletcher, *La tragedia della fanciulla*, trans. Giuliano Pellegrini (Florence: Sansoni, 1948)
Beaumont, Francis, and John Fletcher, *La tragedia della fanciulla*, trans. Lorenzo Salveti and Aldo Trionfo (Bologna: Cappelli/Associazione Teatri Emilia Romagna, 1979)
Beaumont, Francis, and John Fletcher, *Philaster*, ed. Suzanne Gossett (London: Methuen for Arden Shakespeare, 2009)
Beaumont, Francis, and John Fletcher, *The Woman Hater*, ed. George Walton Williams, in *The Dramatic Works in the Beaumont and Fletcher Canon*, ed. Fredson Bowers, 10 vols (Cambridge: Cambridge University Press, 1966–96), 1.156–237
Benjamin, Walter, *Origin of German Tragic Drama*, trans. Howard Eiland (Cambridge, MA: Harvard University Press, 2019)
Bentley, G. E., *The Jacobean and Caroline Stage*, 7 vols (Oxford: Clarendon Press, 1956–68)
Berry, Edward, *Shakespeare and the Hunt: A Cultural and Social Study* (Cambridge: Cambridge University Press, 2001)
Bevington, David, 'Introduction', in *Antony and Cleopatra* by William Shakespeare (Cambridge: Cambridge University Press, updated edn, 2005), 1–80
Bevington, David, 'Introduction', in *Troilus and Cressida* by William Shakespeare (London: Bloomsbury Arden Shakespeare, rev. edn, 2015), 1–142
Bigliazzi, Silvia, 'Introduction: The Tyrant's Fear', *Comparative Drama* 51 (2017), 434–54
Blau, Herbert, 'The Absolved Riddle: Sovereign Pleasure and the Baroque Subject in the Tragicomedies of John Fletcher', *New Literary History* 17 (1986), 539–54
Bliss, Lee, 'Beaumont and Fletcher', in *A Companion to Renaissance Drama*, ed. Arthur F. Kinney (Malden, MA: Wiley-Blackwell, 2002), 524–39
Bliss, Lee, 'Introduction', in *A King and No King* by Francis Beaumont and John Fletcher (Manchester: Manchester University Press, 2004), 1–55
Boling, Ronald J., 'Fletcher's Satire of Caratach in *Bonduca*', *Comparative Drama* 33 (1999), 390–406
Braden, Gordon, 'Ovid and Shakespeare', in *A Companion to Ovid*, ed. Peter E. Knox (Malden, MA: Wiley-Blackwell, 2009), 442–54
Braden, Gordon, 'Shakespeare', in *A Companion to Plutarch*, ed. Mark Beck (Malden, MA: Wiley-Blackwell, 2014), 577–91
Bretz, Andrew, '"Are you my sweet heart?" *Bonduca* and the Failure of Chivalric Masculinity', *Research on Medieval and Renaissance Drama* 54 (2015), 59–72
Briggs, William Dinsmore, 'On the Sources of *The Maid's Tragedy*', *Modern Language Notes* 31 (1916), 502–3

Burke, Peter, 'Tacitism', in *Tacitus*, ed. T. A. Dorey (London: Routledge and Kegan Paul, 1969), 149–71

Burrow, Colin, 'Roman Satire in the Sixteenth Century', in *The Cambridge Companion to Roman Satire*, ed. Kirk Freudenburg (Cambridge: Cambridge University Press, 2005), 243–60

Burrow, Colin, *Shakespeare and Classical Antiquity* (Oxford: Oxford University Press, 2013)

Bushnell, Rebecca W., *Tragedies of Tyrants: Political Thought and Theater in the English Renaissance* (Ithaca, NY: Cornell University Press, 1990)

Cadman, Daniel, *Sovereigns and Subjects in Early Modern Neo-Senecan Drama: Republicanism, Stoicism and Authority* (Farnham: Ashgate, 2015)

Cadman, Daniel, Andrew Duxfield, and Lisa Hopkins (eds), *Rome and Home: The Cultural Uses of Rome in Early Modern English Literature*, Early Modern Literary Studies 25 (2016), special issue, https://extra.shu.ac.uk/emls/journal/index.php/emls/issue/view/15 (accessed 21 February 2021)

Calder, Alison, '"I Am Unacquainted with That Language, Roman": Male and Female Experiences of War in Fletcher's *Bonduca*', *Medieval and Renaissance Drama in England* 8 (1996), 211–26

Cantarella, Eva, *Passato prossimo. Donne romane da Tacita a Sulpicia* (Milan: Feltrinelli, 1996)

Cantor, Paul A., *Shakespeare's Roman Trilogy: The Twilight of the Ancient World* (Chicago: University of Chicago Press, 2017)

Cantor, Paul A., *Shakespeare's Rome: Republic and Empire* (Ithaca, NY: Cornell University Press, 1976)

Carlson, Marvin, *The Haunted Stage: The Theatre as Memory Machine* (Ann Arbor, MI: University of Michigan Press, 2002)

Cassius Dio, *Roman History*, trans. Earnest Cary and Herbert Baldwin Foster, 9 vols (London: Heinemann, 1914–27)

Cathcart, Charles, 'John Fletcher in 1600–1601: Two Early Poems, an Involvement in the "Poets' War", and a Network of Literary Connections', *Philological Quarterly* 81 (2002), 33–51

Catty, Jocelyn, *Writing Rape, Writing Women in Early Modern England: Unbridled Speech* (Basingstoke: Palgrave Macmillan, 1999)

Chalmers, Hero, Julie Sanders, and Sophie Tomlinson, 'Introduction', in *Three Seventeenth-Century Plays on Women and Performance* (Manchester: Manchester University Press, 2006), 1–60

Cheney, Patrick, and Philip Hardie (eds), *The Oxford History of Classical Reception in English Literature, Volume 2: 1558–1660* (Oxford: Oxford University Press, 2015)

Chernaik, Warren, *The Myth of Rome in Shakespeare and His Contemporaries* (Cambridge: Cambridge University Press, 2011)

Clark, Ira, *The Moral Art of Philip Massinger* (Lewisburg, PA: Bucknell University Press, 1993)

Clark, Sandra, *The Plays of Beaumont and Fletcher: Sexual Themes and Dramatic Representation* (Hemel Hempstead: Harvester Wheatsheaf, 1994)

Clegg, Cyndia Susan, 'Censorship and the Problems with History in Shakespeare's England', in *A Companion to Shakespeare's Works: Volume II: The Histories*, ed. Richard Dutton and Jean E. Howard (Hoboken, NJ: Wiley-Blackwell, 2003), 48–69

Coates, John, 'The Choice of Hercules in *Antony and Cleopatra*', *Shakespeare Survey* 31 (1978), 45–52

Coeffeteau, Nicolas, *Histoire romaine, contenant tout ce qui s'est passé de plus mémorable depuis le commencement de l'empire d'Auguste, jusqu'à celui de Constantin le Grand. Avec l'Épitome de Florus depuis la fondation de la ville de Rome jusques à la fin de l'empire d'August* (Paris, 1621)

Collinson, Patrick, '*De Republica Anglorum*: Or, History with the Politics Put Back', in *Elizabethan Essays* (London: Hambledon, 1994), 1–29

Collinson, Patrick, 'The Monarchical Republic of Queen Elizabeth I', *Bulletin of the John Rylands Library* 69 (1987), 394–424

Craik, T. W., 'Commentary', in *The Maid's Tragedy* by Francis Beaumont and John Fletcher (Manchester: Manchester University Press, 1988), 48–198

Craik, T. W., 'Introduction', in *The Maid's Tragedy* by Francis Beaumont and John Fletcher (Manchester: Manchester University Press, 1988), 1–46

Crawford, Julie, 'Fletcher's *The Tragedie of Bonduca* and the Anxieties of the Masculine Government of James I', *SEL: Studies in English Literature 1500–1900* 39 (1999), 357–81

Curran, John E., Jr, 'Declamation and Character in the Fletcher-Massinger Plays', *Medieval and Renaissance Drama in England* 23 (2010), 86–113

Curran, John E., Jr, 'Fletcher, Massinger, and Roman Imperial Character', *Comparative Drama* 43 (2009), 317–54

Curran, John E., Jr, 'New Directions: Determined Things: The Historical Reconstruction of Character in *Antony and Cleopatra*', in *Antony and Cleopatra: A Critical Reader*, ed. Domenico Lovascio (London: Bloomsbury Arden Shakespeare, 2019), 133–54

Curran, John E., Jr, *Roman Invasions: The British History, Protestant Anti-Romanism, and the Historical Imagination in England, 1530–1660* (Newark, DE: University of Delaware Press, 2002)

Curran, John E., Jr, 'Roman Tragedy: The Case of Jonson's *Sejanus*', in *The Genres of Renaissance Tragedy*, ed. Daniel Cadman, Andrew Duxfield, and Lisa Hopkins (Manchester: Manchester University Press, 2019), 100–14

Daileader, Celia R., and Gary Taylor, 'Introduction', in *The Tamer Tamed or, The Woman's Prize* by John Fletcher (Manchester: Manchester University Press, 2006), 1–41

Dall'Olio, Francesco, 'Xenophon and Plato in Elizabethan Culture: The Tyrant's Fear Before *Macbeth*', *Comparative Drama* 51 (2017), 476–505

Dekker, Thomas, and Philip Massinger, *The Virgin Martyr*, in *The Dramatic Works of Thomas Dekker*, ed. Fredson Bowers, 4 vols (Cambridge: Cambridge University Press, 1958), 3.365–480

Del Sapio Garbero, Maria, 'Introduction: Performing "Rome" from the Periphery', in *Identity, Otherness and Empire in Shakespeare's Rome*, ed. Maria Del Sapio Garbero (Farnham: Ashgate, 2009), 1–15

Del Sapio Garbero, Maria, 'Introduction: Shakespeare's Rome and Renaissance Anthropographie', in *Questioning Bodies in Shakespeare's Rome*, ed. Maria Del Sapio Garbero, Nancy Isenberg, and Maddalena Pennacchia (Göttingen: V&R Unipress, 2010), 13–19

Del Sapio Garbero, Maria (ed.), *Identity, Otherness and Empire in Shakespeare's Rome* (Farnham: Ashgate, 2009)

Del Sapio Garbero, Maria (ed.), *Rome in Shakespeare's World* (Rome: Storia e Letteratura, 2018)

Del Sapio Garbero, Maria, Nancy Isenberg, and Maddalena Pennacchia (eds), *Questioning Bodies in Shakespeare's Rome* (Göttingen: V&R Unipress, 2010)

Dionysius of Halicarnassus, *Roman Antiquities*, trans. Earnest Cary (London: Heinemann, 1939)

Dixon, Susan, *The Roman Mother* (London: Routledge, 1988)

Donaldson, Ian, *Ben Jonson: A Life* (Oxford: Oxford University Press, 2011)

Donaldson, Ian, *The Rapes of Lucretia: A Myth and Its Transformations* (Oxford: Clarendon Press, 1982)

Drabek, Pavel, *Fletcherian Dramatic Achievement: A Study in the Mature Plays of John Fletcher (1579–1625)* (Brno: Masarykova univerzita, 2010)

du Bellay, Joachim, *Le premier livre des antiquitez de Rome: contenant une générale description de sa grandeur et comme une déploration de sa ruine* (Paris, 1558)

Edmond, Mary, 'Heminges, John (bap. 1566, d. 1630)', *Oxford Dictionary of National Biography* (Oxford: Oxford University Press, 2004), https://www.oxforddnb.com/view/10.1093/ref:odnb/9780198614128.001.0001/odnb-9780198614128-e-12890 (accessed 8 February 2021)

Epictetus His Manual, and Cebes His Table, out of the Greek Original, trans. John Healey (London, 1610)

Escolme, Bridget, *Antony and Cleopatra: A Guide to the Text and Its Theatrical Life* (Basingstoke: Palgrave Macmillan, 2006)

Evans, John K., *War, Women and Children in Ancient Rome* (London: Routledge, 1991)

Farley-Hills, David, *A Critical Study of the Professional Drama, 1600–25* (Basingstoke: Macmillan, 1988)

Ferguson, Arthur B., 'The Historical Thought of Samuel Daniel: A Study in Renaissance Ambivalence', *Journal of the History of Ideas* 32 (1971), 185–202

Field, Nathan, John Fletcher, Philip Massinger, and Robert Daborne, *The Honest Man's Fortune*, ed. Cyrus Hoy, in *The Dramatic Works in the Beaumont and Fletcher Canon*, ed. Fredson Bowers, 10 vols (Cambridge: Cambridge University Press, 1966–96), 10.16–111

Finkelpearl, Philip J., *Court and Country Politics in the Plays of Beaumont and Fletcher* (Princeton, NJ: Princeton University Press, 1990)

Flecknoe, Richard, 'A Short Discourse of the English Stage', in *Love's Kingdom* (London, 1664)

Fletcher, John, *Bonduca*, ed. Cyrus Hoy, in *The Dramatic Works in the Beaumont and Fletcher Canon*, ed. Fredson Bowers, 10 vols (Cambridge: Cambridge University Press, 1966–96), 4.149–259

Fletcher, John, *Il domatore domato*, trans. Cristina Longo and Marco Ghelardi (Spoleto: Editoria & Spettacolo, 2020)

Fletcher, John, *The Humorous Lieutenant*, ed. Cyrus Hoy, in *The Dramatic Works in the Beaumont and Fletcher Canon*, ed. Fredson Bowers, 10 vols (Cambridge: Cambridge University Press, 1966–96), 5.303–409

Fletcher, John, *The Island Princess*, ed. Clare McManus (London: Methuen for Arden Shakespeare, 2012)

Fletcher, John, *The Mad Lover*, ed. Robert Kean Turner, in *The Dramatic Works in the Beaumont and Fletcher Canon*, ed. Fredson Bowers, 10 vols (Cambridge: Cambridge University Press, 1966–96), 5.11–98

Fletcher, John, *The Night-Walkers*, ed. Cyrus Hoy, in *The Dramatic Works in the Beaumont and Fletcher Canon*, ed. Fredson Bowers, 10 vols (Cambridge: Cambridge University Press, 1966–96), 7.531–611

Fletcher, John, *Rule a Wife and Have a Wife*, ed. George Walton Williams, in *The Dramatic Works in the Beaumont and Fletcher Canon*, ed. Fredson Bowers, 10 vols (Cambridge: Cambridge University Press, 1966–96), 6.501–77

Fletcher, John, *The Tamer Tamed or, The Woman's Prize*, ed. Celia R. Daileader and Gary Taylor (Manchester: Manchester University Press, 2006)

Fletcher, John, *The Tamer Tamed*, ed. Lucy Munro (London: Methuen, 2010)

Fletcher, John, *The Tragedy of Valentinian*, in *Four Jacobean Sex Tragedies*, ed. Martin Wiggins (Oxford: Oxford University Press, 1998), 233–328

Fletcher, John, *A Wife for a Month*, ed. Robert Kean Turner, in *The Dramatic Works in the Beaumont and Fletcher Canon*, ed. Fredson Bowers, 10 vols (Cambridge: Cambridge University Press, 1966–96), 6.355–482

Fletcher, John, *The Wild-Goose Chase*, ed. Sophie Tomlinson, in *Three Seventeenth-Century Plays on Women and Performance*, ed. Hero Chalmers, Julie Sanders, and Sophie Tomlinson (Manchester: Manchester University Press, 2006), 61–176

Fletcher, John, *Wit without Money*, ed. Hans Walter Gabler, in *The Dramatic Works in the Beaumont and Fletcher Canon*, ed. Fredson Bowers, 10 vols (Cambridge: Cambridge University Press, 1966–96), 6.10–92

Fletcher, John, *Women Pleased*, ed. Hans Walter Gabler, in *The Dramatic Works in the Beaumont and Fletcher Canon*, ed. Fredson Bowers, 10 vols (Cambridge: Cambridge University Press, 1966–96), 5.448–529

Fletcher, John, and Francis Beaumont, *The Captain*, ed. L. A. Beaurline, in *The Dramatic Works in the Beaumont and Fletcher Canon*, ed. Fredson Bowers, 10 vols (Cambridge: Cambridge University Press, 1966–96), 1.550–650

Fletcher, John, and Nathan Field, *Four Plays, or Moral Representations, in One*, ed. Cyrus Hoy, in *The Dramatic Works in the Beaumont and Fletcher Canon*, ed. Fredson Bowers, 10 vols (Cambridge: Cambridge University Press, 1966–96), 8.223–344

Fletcher, John, and Philip Massinger, *Beggars' Bush*, ed. Fredson Bowers, in *The Dramatic Works in the Beaumont and Fletcher Canon*, ed. Fredson Bowers, 10 vols (Cambridge: Cambridge University Press, 1966–96), 3.246–331

Fletcher, John, and Philip Massinger, *The Custom of the Country*, ed. Cyrus Hoy, in *The Dramatic Works in the Beaumont and Fletcher Canon*, ed.

Fredson Bowers, 10 vols (Cambridge: Cambridge University Press, 1966–96), 8.642–739

Fletcher, John, and Philip Massinger, *The Double Marriage*, ed. Cyrus Hoy, in *The Dramatic Works in the Beaumont and Fletcher Canon*, ed. Fredson Bowers, 10 vols (Cambridge: Cambridge University Press, 1966–96), 9.95–220

Fletcher, John, and Philip Massinger, *The Elder Brother*, ed. Fredson Bowers, in *The Dramatic Works in the Beaumont and Fletcher Canon*, ed. Fredson Bowers, 10 vols (Cambridge: Cambridge University Press, 1966–96), 9.469–545

Fletcher, John, and Philip Massinger, *The Elder Brother*, ed. José A. Pérez Díez (Manchester: Manchester University Press for Malone Society Reprints, forthcoming)

Fletcher, John, and Philip Massinger, *The False One*, ed. Domenico Lovascio (Manchester: Manchester University Press, forthcoming 2022)

Fletcher, John, and Philip Massinger, *The Knight of Malta*, ed. George Walton Williams, in *The Dramatic Works in the Beaumont and Fletcher Canon*, ed. Fredson Bowers, 10 vols (Cambridge: Cambridge University Press, 1966–96), 8.360–453

Fletcher, John, and Philip Massinger, *The Little French Lawyer*, ed. Robert Kean Turner, in *The Dramatic Works in the Beaumont and Fletcher Canon*, ed. Fredson Bowers, 10 vols (Cambridge: Cambridge University Press, 1966–96), 9.337–426

Fletcher, John, and Philip Massinger, *Love's Cure, or The Martial Maid*, ed. José A. Pérez Díez (Manchester: Manchester University Press, 2022)

Fletcher, John, and Philip Massinger, *The Prophetess*, ed. George Walton Williams, in *The Dramatic Works in the Beaumont and Fletcher Canon*, ed. Fredson Bowers, 10 vols (Cambridge: Cambridge University Press, 1966–96), 9.221–321

Fletcher, John, and Philip Massinger, *The Sea Voyage*, ed. Anthony Parr, in *Three Renaissance Travel Plays* (Manchester: Manchester University Press, 1995), 135–216

Fletcher, John, and Philip Massinger, *Sir John Van Olden Barnavelt*, ed. Andrew Fleck (Manchester: Manchester University Press, forthcoming)

Fletcher, John, and Philip Massinger, *The Spanish Curate*, ed. Robert Kean Turner, in *The Dramatic Works in the Beaumont and Fletcher Canon*, ed. Fredson Bowers, 10 vols (Cambridge: Cambridge University Press, 1966–96), 10.301–95

Fletcher, John, and Philip Massinger, *The Tragedy of Sir John Van Olden Barnavelt*, ed. Fredson Bowers, in *The Dramatic Works in the Beaumont and Fletcher Canon*, ed. Fredson Bowers, 10 vols (Cambridge: Cambridge University Press, 1966–96), 8.503–89

Fletcher, John, and Philip Massinger, *A Very Woman*, ed. Hans Walter Gabler, in *The Dramatic Works in the Beaumont and Fletcher Canon*, ed. Fredson Bowers, 10 vols (Cambridge: Cambridge University Press, 1966–96), 7.639–731

Fletcher, John, Philip Massinger, and Anonymous, *Rollo, Duke of Normandy, or the Bloody Brother*, ed. George Walton Williams, in *The Dramatic Works in the Beaumont and Fletcher Canon*, ed. Fredson Bowers, 10 vols (Cambridge: Cambridge University Press, 1966–96), 10.166–245

Fletcher, John, Philip Massinger, and Nathan Field, *The Queen of Corinth*, ed. Robert Kean Turner, in *The Dramatic Works in the Beaumont and Fletcher Canon*, ed. Fredson Bowers, 10 vols (Cambridge: Cambridge University Press, 1966–96), 8.10–93

Fletcher, John, and William Shakespeare, *The Two Noble Kinsmen*, ed. Lois Potter (London: Bloomsbury Arden Shakespeare, rev. edn, 2015)

Fletcher, John, et al., *Comedies and Tragedies Written by Francis Beaumont and John Fletcher* (London, 1647)

Florio, John, *Florio his First Fruits* (London, 1578)

Florus, *The Roman Histories of Lucius Julius Florus from the Foundation of Rome, Till Caesar Augustus, for above DCC. Years, & from Thence to Trajan near CC. Years, Divided by Flor[us] into IV. Ages*, trans. Edmund Bolton (London, 1619)

Frampton, Saul, 'Who Edited Shakespeare?', *Guardian*, 12 July 2013, https://www.theguardian.com/books/2013/jul/12/who-edited-shakespeare-john-florio (accessed 8 February 2021)

Fraschetti, Augusto (ed.), *Roman Women*, trans. Linda Lappin (Chicago: University of Chicago Press, 2001)

Frénée-Hutchins, Samantha, *Boudica's Odyssey in Early Modern England* (Farnham: Ashgate, 2014)

Frijlinck, Wilhelmina P., 'Notes', in *The Tragedy of Sir John Van Olden Barnavelt; Anonymous Elizabethan Play, Edited from the Manuscript with Introduction and Notes* (Amsterdam: Van Dorssen, 1922), 84–111

Frost, David L., *The School of Shakespeare: The Influence of Shakespeare on English Drama 1600–42* (Cambridge: Cambridge University Press, 1968)

Fuller, Thomas, *The History of the Worthies of England* (London, 1662)

Gentili, Vanna, *La Roma antica degli elisabettiani* (Bologna: il Mulino, 1991)

Gielen, Resi, *Untersuchungen zur Namengebung bei Beaumont, Fletcher und Massinger* (Quakenbrück: Robert Kleinert, 1929)

Gill, Roma, 'Collaboration and Revision in Massinger's *A Very Woman*', *Review of English Studies* 70 (1967), 136–48

Gossett, Suzanne, '"Best men are molded out of faults": Marrying the Rapist in Jacobean Drama', *English Literary Renaissance* 14 (1984), 305–27

Gossett, Suzanne, 'Introduction', in *Philaster* by Francis Beaumont and John Fletcher (London: Methuen for Arden Shakespeare, 2009), 1–102

Grady, Hugh, *Shakespeare and Impure Aesthetics* (Cambridge: Cambridge University Press, 2009)

Gray, Patrick, *Shakespeare and the Fall of the Roman Republic: Selfhood, Stoicism and Civil War* (Edinburgh: Edinburgh University Press, 2018)

Green, Paul D., 'Theme and Structure in Fletcher's *Bonduca*', *SEL: Studies in English Literature, 1500–1900* 22 (1982), 305–16

Greg, W. W., *The Editorial Problem in Shakespeare: A Survey of the Foundation of the Text* (Oxford: Clarendon Press, 1942)
Greg, W. W., *The Shakespeare First Folio, Its Bibliographical and Textual History* (Oxford: Clarendon Press, 1955)
Griffin, Julia, 'Cato's Daughter, Brutus's Wife: Portia from Antiquity to the English Renaissance Stage', in *The Uses of Rome in English Renaissance Drama*, ed. Domenico Lovascio and Lisa Hopkins, *Textus: English Studies in Italy* 29.2 (2016), thematic issue, 21–40
Grogan, Jane, 'Introduction', in *William Barker, Xenophon's 'Cyropaedia'* (Cambridge: MHRA, 2020), 1–67
Guardamagna, Daniela (ed.), *Roman Shakespeare: Intersecting Times, Spaces, Languages* (Bern: Peter Lang, 2018)
Gunton, Simon, *The History of the Church of Peterborough Wherein the Most Remarkable Things Concerning That Place, from the First Foundation Thereof, with Other Passages of History Not Unworthy Public View, Are Represented* (London, 1686)
Gurr, Andrew, *The Shakespeare Company 1594–1642* (Cambridge: Cambridge University Press, 2011)
Hadfield, Andrew, *Shakespeare and Republicanism* (Cambridge: Cambridge University Press, rev. edn, 2008)
Hall, Kim F., *Things of Darkness: Economies of Race and Gender in Early Modern England* (Ithaca, NY: Cornell University Press, 1995)
Hand, Molly, '"You take no labour": Women Workers of Magic in Early Modern England', in *Working Subjects in Early Modern English Drama*, ed. Michelle Dowd and Natasha Korda (Aldershot: Ashgate, 2011), 161–76
Hatchuel, Sarah, *Shakespeare and the Cleopatra/Caesar Intertext: Sequel, Conflation, Remake* (Madison, WI: Fairleigh Dickinson University Press, 2011)
Hatchuel, Sarah, and Nathalie Vienne-Guerrin (eds), *Shakespeare on Screen: The Roman Plays* (Mont Saint Aignan: Publications des Universités de Rouen et du Havre, 2009)
Hensman, Bertha, 'John Fletcher's *The Bloody Brother; or, Rollo, Duke of Normandy*', unpublished PhD thesis, University of Chicago, 1947
Hensman, Bertha, *The Shares of Fletcher, Field and Massinger in Twelve Plays of the Beaumont and Fletcher Canon*, 2 vols (Salzburg: Institut für Englische Sprache und Literatur, 1974)
Herrick, Marvin T., *Tragicomedy: Its Origin and Development in Italy, France, and England* (Urbana, IL: University of Illinois Press, 1955)
Heywood, Thomas, *An Apology for Actors* (London, 1612)
Hicklin, Christopher, 'A Critical Modern-Spelling Edition of John Fletcher's *Rule a Wife and Have a Wife*', unpublished PhD thesis, University of Toronto, 2010
Hickman, Andrew, '*Bonduca*'s Two Ignoble Armies and *The Two Noble Kinsmen*', *Medieval and Renaissance Drama in England* 4 (1989), 143–71
Hila, Marina, 'Dishonourable Peace: Fletcher and Massinger's *The False One* and Jacobean Foreign Policy', *Cahiers Élisabéthains* 72 (2007), 21–30

Hila, Marina, '"Justice shall never heare ye, I am justice": Absolutist Rape and Cyclical History in John Fletcher's *The Tragedy of Valentinian*', *Neophilologus* 91 (2007), 745–58
Hinman, Charles, *The Printing and Proof-Reading of the First Folio of Shakespeare* (Oxford: Clarendon Press, 1963)
Historical Manuscripts Commission Report on the Manuscripts of the late Reginald Raudon Hastings, Esq., ed. Francis Bickley (London: HM Stationery Office, 1930)
Holinshed, Rafael, *The First and Second Volumes of Chronicles* (London, 1587)
Holland, Peter (ed.), *Shakespeare and Rome*, Shakespeare Survey 69 (2016), special issue
Holmberg, Eva Johanna, *Jews in the Early Modern English Imagination: A Scattered Nation* (Farnham: Ashgate, 2011)
Honigmann, E. A. J., 'Shakespeare's Plutarch', *Shakespeare Quarterly* 10 (1959), 25–33
Honigmann, E. A. J., and Susan Brock (eds), *Playhouse Wills: 1558–1642* (Manchester: Manchester University Press, 1993)
Hope, Jonathan, *The Authorship of Shakespeare's Plays: A Socio-Linguistic Study* (Cambridge: Cambridge University Press, 1994)
Hopkins, Lisa, *The Cultural Uses of the Caesars on the English Renaissance Stage* (Aldershot: Ashgate, 2008)
Hopkins, Lisa, *From the Romans to the Normans on the English Renaissance Stage* (Kalamazoo, MI: Medieval Institute Publications, 2017)
Hopkins, Lisa, 'Introduction', in *Bess of Hardwick: New Perspectives*, ed. Lisa Hopkins (Manchester: Manchester University Press, 2019), 1–17
Howard-Hill, T. H., 'Shakespeare's Earliest Editor, Ralph Crane', *Shakespeare Survey* 44 (1991), 113–29
Hoy, Cyrus, 'Massinger as Collaborator: The Plays with Fletcher and Others', in *Philip Massinger: A Critical Reassessment*, ed. Douglas Howard (Cambridge: Cambridge University Press, 1985), 51–82
Hoy, Cyrus, 'The Shares of Fletcher and His Collaborators in the Beaumont and Fletcher Canon', *Studies in Bibliography* 8 (1956), 129–46; 9 (1957), 143–62; 11 (1958), 85–106; 12 (1959), 91–116; 13 (1960), 77–108; 14 (1961), 45–67; 15 (1962), 71–90
Hunter, G. K., 'A Roman Thought: Renaissance Attitudes to History Exemplified in Shakespeare and Jonson', in *An English Miscellany: Presented to W. S. Mackie*, ed. Brian S. Lee (Cape Town: Oxford University Press, 1977), 93–115
Hunter, William B., 'Heminge and Condell as Editors of the Shakespeare First Folio', *ANQ: A Quarterly Journal of Short Articles, Notes and Reviews* 15 (2002), 11–19
Ide, Arata, 'John Fletcher of Corpus Christi College: New Records of His Early Years', *Early Theatre* 14 (2011), 63–77
Innes, Paul, *Shakespeare's Roman Plays* (London: Palgrave, 2015)
Iyengar, Sujata, *Shades of Difference: Mythologies of Skin Color in Early Modern England* (Philadelphia, PA: University of Pennsylvania Press, 2004)

Jackson, William A., *Records of the Court of the Stationers' Company* (London: The Bibliographical Society, 1957)

Jensen, Freyja Cox, 'Reading Florus in Early Modern England', *Renaissance Studies* 23 (2009), 659–77

Jensen, Freyja Cox, *Reading the Roman Republic in Early Modern England* (Leiden: Brill, 2012)

Jensen, Freyja Cox, 'What Was Thomas Lodge's Josephus in Early Modern England?', *Sixteenth Century Journal* 49 (2018), 3–24

Johnson, Sarah E., 'Pride and Gender in Fletcher's *Bonduca*', *Modern Philology* 115 (2017), 80–104

Jonson, Ben, *Discoveries*, ed. Lorna Hutson, in *The Cambridge Edition of the Works of Ben Jonson*, ed. David Bevington, Martin Butler, and Ian Donaldson, 7 vols (Cambridge: Cambridge University Press, 2012), 7.495–596

Jonson, Ben, *Sejanus His Fall*, ed. Tom Cain, in *The Cambridge Edition of the Works of Ben Jonson*, ed. David Bevington, Martin Butler, and Ian Donaldson, 7 vols (Cambridge: Cambridge University Press, 2012), 2.212–391

Jonson, Ben, *The Staple of News*, ed. Joseph Loewenstein, in *The Cambridge Edition of the Works of Ben Jonson*, ed. David Bevington, Martin Butler, and Ian Donaldson, 7 vols (Cambridge: Cambridge University Press, 2012), 6.15–157

Jowett, John, *Shakespeare and Text* (Oxford: Oxford University Press, rev. edn, 2019)

Jowitt, Claire, 'Colonialism, Politics, and Romanization in John Fletcher's *Bonduca*', *SEL: Studies in English Literature, 1500–1900* 43 (2003), 475–94

Jowitt, Claire, '*The Island Princess* and Race', in *Early Modern English Drama: A Critical Companion*, ed. Garrett A. Sullivan, Patrick Cheney, and Andrew Hadfield (Oxford: Oxford University Press, 2005), 287–97

Kahn, Coppélia, *Roman Shakespeare: Warriors, Wounds and Women* (London: Routledge, 1997)

Kamps, Ivo, *Historiography and Ideology in Stuart Drama* (Cambridge: Cambridge University Press, 1996)

Kantorowicz, Ernest H., *The King's Two Bodies: A Study in Mediaeval Political Theology*, ed. William Chester Jordan (Princeton, NJ: Princeton University Press, 1997)

Karim-Cooper, Farah, *Cosmetics in Shakespearean and Renaissance Drama* (Edinburgh: Edinburgh University Press, 2006)

Kelliher, Hilton, 'Francis Beaumont and Nathan Field: New Records of their Early Years', in *English Manuscript Studies 1100–1700: Volume 8: Seventeenth-Century Poetry, Music and Drama*, ed. Peter Beal (London: British Library, 2000), 1–42

Kennedy, Gwynne, 'Gender and the Pleasures of Revenge', in *Feminism and Early Modern Texts: Essays for Phyllis Rackin*, ed. Rebecca Ann Bach and Gwynne Kennedy (Selinsgrove, PA: Susquehanna University Press, 2010), 152–71

Kermode, Frank, *Shakespeare, Spenser, Donne: Renaissance Essays* (London: Routledge and Kegan Paul, 1971)

Kernan, Alvin B., 'From Ritual to History: The English History Plays', in *The Revels History of Drama in English: Vol. 3: 1576-1613*, ed. J. Leeds Barroll, Richard Hosley, Alvin B. Kernan, and Alexander Leggatt (London: Methuen, 1975), 262-99

Kewes, Paulina, 'Henry Savile's Tacitus and the Politics of Roman History in Late Elizabethan England', *Huntington Library Quarterly* 74 (2011), 515-51

Kewes, Paulina, 'History and Its Uses', in *The Uses of History in Early Modern England*, ed. Paulina Kewes (San Marino, CA: Huntington Library, 2006), 1-30

Kewes, Paulina, 'Julius Caesar in Jacobean England', *Seventeenth Century* 17 (2002), 155-86

Kewes, Paulina (ed.), *Ancient Rome in English Political Culture, ca. 1570-1660*, *Huntington Library Quarterly* 83.3 (2020), special issue

King, Jane, and Trevor Elliott, *Mortarboards & Mitres: The Headmasters of the King's School, Peterborough, since 4th September 1541* (Peterborough: The King's School, 2017), https://www.kings.peterborough.sch.uk/attachments/download.asp?file=114&type=pdf (accessed 13 July 2020)

Kirk, Florence Ada, 'Introduction', in *The Faithful Shepherdess* by John Fletcher (New York: Garland, 1980), iii-ci

Lambert, Jean, *Teachers in Early Modern English Drama: Pedagogy and Authority* (London: Routledge, 2019)

Leach, A. F., 'Schools', in *The Victoria History of the County of Northampton: Volume Two*, ed. R. M. Serjeantson and W. Ryland D. Adkins (London: [Archibald Constable], 1906), 201-88

Lee, Sidney, 'An Elizabethan Bookseller', *Bibliographica* 1 (1895), 474-98

Leech, Clifford, *The John Fletcher Plays* (Cambridge, MA: Harvard University Press, 1962)

Leonhardt, Benno, '*Bonduca*', *Englische Studien* 13 (1889), 36-63

Levy, F. J., 'Hayward, Daniel and the Beginnings of Politic History in England', *Huntington Library Quarterly* 50 (1987), 1-34

Lister, Rota Herzberg, 'Commentary', in *A Critical Edition of John Fletcher's Comedy The Wild-Goose Chase* (New York: Garland, 1980), 3-149.

Livy, *History of Rome*, trans. Rev. Canon Roberts, 2 vols (New York: Dutton, 1912)

Loomba, Ania, *Shakespeare, Race, and Colonialism* (Oxford: Oxford University Press, 2002)

Lord, Louis E., *Aristophanes: His Plays and His Influence* (New York: Cooper Square, 1963)

Loughlin, Marie H., *Hymeneutics: Interpreting Virginity on the Early Modern Stage* (Lewisburg, PA: Bucknell University Press, 1997)

Lovascio, Domenico, 'Introduction', in *The False One* by John Fletcher and Philip Massinger (Manchester: Manchester University Press, forthcoming 2022)

Lovascio, Domenico, 'Julius Caesar's "just cause" in John Fletcher and Philip Massinger's *The False One*', *Notes and Queries* 62 (2015), 245-7

Lovascio, Domenico, 'She-Tragedy: Lust, Luxury and Empire in John Fletcher and Philip Massinger's *The False One*', in *The Genres of Renaissance Tragedy*, ed. Daniel Cadman, Andrew Duxfield, and Lisa Hopkins (Manchester: Manchester University Press, 2019), 166–83

Lovascio, Domenico, *Un nome, mille volti. Giulio Cesare nel teatro inglese della prima età moderna* (Rome: Carocci, 2015)

Lovascio, Domenico (ed.), *Roman Women in Shakespeare and His Contemporaries* (Kalamazoo, MI: Medieval Institute Publications, 2020)

Lovascio, Domenico (ed.), *Shakespeare: Visions of Rome, Shakespeare* 15.4 (2019), special issue

Lovascio, Domenico, and Lisa Hopkins (eds), *The Uses of Rome in English Renaissance Drama, Textus. English Studies in Italy* 29.2 (2016), thematic issue

Lucan, *Pharsalia sive De Bello Civili Caesar et Pompeii Libri X*, ed. Thomas Farnaby (London, 1618)

Lucretius, *On the Nature of Things*, trans. W. H. D. Rouse, rev. Martin F. Smith (Cambridge, MA: Harvard University Press, 1924)

MacCallum, Mungo William, *Shakespeare's Roman Plays and Their Background* (London: Macmillan, 1910)

MacDonald, Joyce Green, *Women and Race in Early Modern Texts* (Cambridge: Cambridge University Press, 2002)

MacLachlan, Bonnie (ed.), *Women in Ancient Rome: A Sourcebook* (London: Bloomsbury, 2013)

'Madon, King of Britain', *Lost Plays Database*, ed. Roslyn L. Knutson, David McInnis, Matthew Steggle, and Misha Teramura (Washington, DC: Folger Shakespeare Library, 2009–), https://lostplays.folger.edu/Madon,_King_of_Britain (accessed 6 July 2020)

Makkink, H. J., *Philip Massinger and John Fletcher: A Comparison* (Rotterdam: Nijgh & Van Ditmar, 1927)

Malin, Peter, *Revived with Care: John Fletcher's Plays on the British Stage, 1885–2020* (London: Routledge, 2020)

Marlowe, Christopher, *Doctor Faustus: A- and B- texts (1604, 1616)*, ed. David Bevington and Eric Rasmussen (Manchester: Manchester University Press, 1993)

Marvell, Andrew, *The Poems of Andrew Marvell*, ed. Nigel Smith (Harlow: Pearson, 2007)

Massinger, Philip, *The Renegado*, ed. Michael Neill (London: Methuen for Arden Shakespeare, 2010)

Masten, Jeffrey, *Textual Intercourse: Collaboration, Authorship, and Sexualities in Renaissance Drama* (Cambridge: Cambridge University Press, 1997)

Maxwell, Baldwin, *Studies in Beaumont, Fletcher, and Massinger* (Chapel Hill, NC: University of North Carolina Press, 1939)

McKeithan, Daniel Morley, *The Debt to Shakespeare in the Beaumont-and-Fletcher Plays* (Austin, TX: privately printed, 1938)

McLuskie, Kathleen, *Renaissance Dramatists* (Hemel Hempstead: Harvester Wheatsheaf, 1989)

McManus, Clare, 'Commentary', in *The Island Princess* by John Fletcher (London: Methuen for Arden Shakespeare, 2012), 97–288

McManus, Clare, 'Introduction', in *The Island Princess* by John Fletcher (London: Methuen for Arden Shakespeare, 2012), 1–95

McMillin, Scott, and Sally-Beth MacLean, *The Queen's Men and Their Plays* (Cambridge: Cambridge University Press, 1998)

McMullan, Gordon, 'Fletcher, John (1579–1625), playwright', in *The Oxford Dictionary of National Biography* (Oxford: Oxford University Press, 2004), https://www.oxforddnb.com/view/10.1093/ref:odnb/9780198614128. 001.0001/odnb-9780198614128-e-9730 (accessed 3 November 2019)

McMullan, Gordon, 'Introduction', in *King Henry VIII (All Is True)* by William Shakespeare and John Fletcher (London: Methuen for Arden Shakespeare, 2000), 1–199

McMullan, Gordon, *The Politics of Unease in the Plays of John Fletcher* (Amherst, MA: University of Massachusetts Press, 1994)

McMullan, Gordon, 'The Strange Case of Susan Brotes: Rhetoric, Gender, and Authorship in John Fletcher's *The Tamer Tamed*, or How (Not) to Identify an Early Modern Playwright', *Renaissance Drama* 47 (2019), 177–200

Mellows, W. T. (ed.), *Peterborough Local Administration: The Foundation of Peterborough Cathedral: A.D. 1541* (Northampton: Northamptonshire Record Society, 1941)

Miller, Anthony, *Roman Triumphs and Early Modern English Culture* (Basingstoke: Palgrave Macmillan, 2001)

Mincoff, Marco, 'Fletcher's Early Tragedies', *Renaissance Drama* 7 (1964), 70–94

Mincoff, Marco, 'Shakespeare, Fletcher and Baroque Tragedy', *Shakespeare Survey* 20 (1967), 1–15

Miola, Robert S., '*Julius Caesar* and the Tyrannicide Debate', *Renaissance Quarterly* 38 (1985), 271–89

Moul, Victoria, *Jonson, Horace and the Classical Tradition* (Cambridge: Cambridge University Press, 2010)

Munro, Lucy, *Archaic Style in English Literature, 1590–1674* (Cambridge: Cambridge University Press, 2013)

Munro, Lucy, 'Beaumont's Lives', *Early Theatre* 20 (2017), 141–58

Munro, Lucy, *Children of the Queen's Revels: A Jacobean Theatre Repertory* (Cambridge: Cambridge University Press, 2005)

Munro, Lucy, 'Introduction', in *The Tamer Tamed* by John Fletcher (London: Methuen, 2010), vii–xxv

Munro, Lucy, 'Plotting, Ambiguity and Community in the Plays of Beaumont and Fletcher', in *Community-Making in Early Stuart Theatres: Stage and Audience*, ed. Anthony W. Johnson, Roger D. Sell, and Helen Wilcox (London: Routledge, 2017), 255–74

Munro, Lucy, *Shakespeare in the Theatre: The King's Men* (London: Bloomsbury Arden Shakespeare, 2020)

Munro, Lucy, 'Virolet and Martia the Pirate's Daughter: Gender and Genre in Fletcher and Massinger's *The Double Marriage*', in *Pirates? The Politics of*

Plunder, 1550–1650, ed. Claire Jowitt (Basingstoke: Palgrave Macmillan, 2007), 118–34

Munro, Lucy, 'Writing a Play with Robert Daborne', in *Rethinking Theatrical Documents in Shakespeare's England*, ed. Tiffany Stern (London: Bloomsbury Arden Shakespeare, 2020), 17–32

Neil, Kelly, 'The Politics of Suicide in John Fletcher's *Tragedie of Bonduca*', *Journal for Early Modern Cultural Studies* 14 (2014), 88–114

Neill, Michael, 'Introduction', in *Antony and Cleopatra* by William Shakespeare (Oxford: Oxford University Press, 1994), 1–130

Neill, Michael, *Issues of Death: Mortality and Identity in English Renaissance Tragedy* (Oxford: Clarendon Press, 1997)

Nocentelli, Carmen, 'Spice Race: *The Island Princess* and the Politics of Transnational Appropriation', *Publications of the Modern Language Association* 125 (2010), 572–88

Nolan, Bernard Joseph, 'A Critical Edition of John Fletcher's *Bonduca*', unpublished MA thesis, University of Liverpool, 1951

Oliphant, E. H. C., *The Plays of Beaumont and Fletcher: An Attempt to Determine their Respective Shares and the Shares of Others* (New Haven, CT: Yale University Press, 1927)

Owens, Margaret E., *Stages of Dismemberment: The Fragmented Body in Late Medieval and Early Modern Drama* (Newark, DE: University of Delaware Press, 2005)

Oxley, Philip, 'Textual Introduction', in *The Humorous Lieutenant* by John Fletcher (New York: Garland, 1987), 1–80

Paleit, Edward, *War, Liberty, and Caesar: Responses to Lucan's Bellum Ciuile, ca. 1580–1650* (Oxford: Oxford University Press, 2013)

Park, Judy H., 'The Tragicomic Moment: Republicanism in Beaumont and Fletcher's *Philaster*', *Comparative Drama* 49 (2015), 23–47

Parker, Barbara L., *Plato's Republic and Shakespeare's Rome: A Political Study of the Roman Works* (Newark, DE: University of Delaware Press, 2004)

Paster, Gail Kern, *The Body Embarrassed: Drama and the Disciplines of Shame in Early Modern England* (Ithaca, NY: Cornell University Press, 1993)

Pasupathi, Vimala C., 'The King's Privates: Sex and the Soldier's Place in John Fletcher's *The Humorous Lieutenant* (ca. 1618)', *Research Opportunities in Medieval and Renaissance Drama* 47 (2008), 25–50

Pasupathi, Vimala C., 'Shakespeare, Fletcher and "the gain o'th' martialist"', in *Shakespeare and Fletcher*, ed. Clare McManus and Lucy Munro, *Shakespeare* 7 (2011), special issue, 297–309

Pearse, Nancy Cotton, *John Fletcher's Chastity Plays: Mirrors of Modesty* (Lewisburg, PA: Bucknell University Press, 1973)

Pennacchia, Maddalena, *Shakespeare intermediale. I drammi romani* (Spoleto: Editoria & Spettacolo, 2012)

Perry, Curtis, *Shakespeare and Senecan Tragedy* (Cambridge: Cambridge University Press, 2020)

Plutarch, *The Lives of the Noble Grecians and Romans Compared Together by That Grave Learned Philosopher and Historiographer, Plutarch of Chaeronea;*

Translated out of Greek into French by James Amyot ...; and out of French into English, by Thomas North (London, 1579)
Plutarch, *Parallel Lives*, trans. Bernadotte Perrin, 11 vols (London: Heinemann, 1914–26)
Poitevin, Kimberly Woosley, '"Counterfeit Colour": Making Up Race in Elizabeth Cary's *The Tragedy of Mariam*', *Tulsa Studies in Women's Literature* 24 (2005), 13–34
Pollard, A. W., *Shakespeare Folios and Quartos: A Study in the Bibliography of Shakespeare's Plays, 1594–1685* (London: Methuen, 1909)
Potter, Lois, 'Introduction', in *The Two Noble Kinsmen* by John Fletcher and William Shakespeare (London: Bloomsbury Arden Shakespeare, rev. edn, 2015), 1–170
Potter, Ursula Ann, 'Pedagogy and Parenting in English Drama, 1560–1610: Flogging Schoolmasters and Cockering Mothers', unpublished PhD thesis, University of Sydney, 2011
Procopius, *Histoire des guerres faictes par l'Empereur Iustinian contre les Vandales, et les Goths. Escrite en Grec par Procope, & Agathias, et mise en François per Mart[in] Fumee* (Paris, 1587)
Rabelais, François, *Œuvres*, ed. Francois-Henri-Stanislas de L'Aulnaye, 3 vols (Paris: Louis Janet, 1823)
Rasmussen, Eric, 'Publishing the First Folio', in *The Cambridge Companion to Shakespeare's First Folio*, ed. Emma Smith (Cambridge: Cambridge University Press, 2016), 18–29
Rasmussen, Eric, 'Who Edited the Shakespeare First Folio?', *Cahiers Élisabéthains* 93 (2017), 70–6
Reid, Lindsay Ann, 'Beaumont and Fletcher's Rhodes: Early Modern Geopolitics and Mythological Topography in *The Maid's Tragedy*', *Early Modern Literary Studies* 16.2 (2012), 1–28, http://purl.org/emls/16-2/reidrhod.htm (accessed 28 January 2021)
Ronan, Clifford J., *'Antike Roman': Power Symbology and the Roman Play in Early Modern England: 1585–1635* (Athens, GA: University of Georgia Press, 1995)
Salmon, J. H. M., 'Stoicism and Roman Examples: Seneca and Tacitus in Jacobean England', *Journal of the History of Ideas* 50 (1989), 199–225
Samson, Alexander, '"Last thought upon a windmill?": Cervantes and Fletcher', in *The Cervantean Heritage: Reception and Influence of Cervantes in Britain*, ed. J. A. G. Ardila (Leeds: Legenda, 2009), 223–33
Saner, Reginald, '*Antony and Cleopatra*: How Pompey's Honor Struck a Contemporary', *Shakespeare Quarterly* 20 (1969), 117–20
Savile, Henry, *The End of Nero and the Beginning of Galba. Four Books of the Histories of Cornelius Tacitus. The Life of Agricola* (London, 1591)
Schanzer, Ernest, *The Problem Plays of Shakespeare: A Study of Julius Caesar, Measure for Measure, Antony and Cleopatra* (London: Routledge, 1963)
Severn, John R., '"Then turn tail to tail and peace be with you": John Fletcher's *The Woman's Prize, or The Tamer Tamed*, Menippean Satire, and Same-Sex Desire', in *New Directions in Early Modern English Drama: Edges, Spaces,*

Intersections, ed. Aidan Norrie and Mark Houlahan (Kalamazoo, MI: Medieval Institute Publications, 2020), 199–218

Shakespeare, William, *Antony and Cleopatra*, ed. David Bevington (Cambridge, Cambridge University Press, updated edn, 2005)

Shakespeare, William, *Coriolanus*, ed. Peter Holland (London: Bloomsbury Arden Shakespeare, 2013)

Shakespeare, William, *Cymbeline*, ed. Valerie Wayne (London: Bloomsbury Arden Shakespeare, 2017)

Shakespeare, William, *Henry VI Part 3*, ed. Eric Rasmussen and John D. Cox (London: Thomson Learning for Arden Shakespeare, 2001)

Shakespeare, William, *Julius Caesar*, ed. David Daniell (Walton-on-Thames: Nelson for Arden Shakespeare, 1998)

Shakespeare, William, *Julius Caesar*, ed. John Jowett, in *The Oxford Shakespeare: The Complete Works*, ed. Stanley Wells and Gary Taylor (Oxford: Oxford University Press, 2nd edn, 1986), 627–54

Shakespeare, William, *Julius Caesar*, ed. Sarah Neville, in *The New Oxford Shakespeare: The Complete Works: Modern Critical Edition*, ed. Gary Taylor, John Jowett, Terri Bourus, and Gabriel Egan (Oxford: Oxford University Press, 2016), 1607–75

Shakespeare, William, *Othello*, ed. Michael Neill (Oxford: Oxford University Press, 2006)

Shakespeare, William, *The Rape of Lucrece*, in *Shakespeare's Poems*, ed. Katherine Duncan-Jones and H. R. Woudhuysen (London: Thomson Learning for Arden Shakespeare, 2007), 231–383

Shakespeare, William, *The Taming of the Shrew*, ed. Barbara Hodgdon (London: Methuen for Arden Shakespeare, 2010)

Sharpe, Will, 'Authorship and Attribution', in *William Shakespeare and Others: Collaborative Plays*, ed. Jonathan Bate and Eric Rasmussen, with Jan Sewell and Will Sharpe (Basingstoke: Palgrave Macmillan, 2013), 641–745

Shirley, James, *The Duke's Mistress* (London, 1638)

Slights, William W. E., 'Dower Power: Communities of Collaboration in the Jacobean Theater', *Essays in Theatre/Études Théâtrales* 19 (2000), 3–19

Smuts, Malcolm R., 'Court-Centred Politics and the Uses of Roman Historians, c.1590–1630', in *Culture and Politics in Early Stuart England*, ed. Kevin Sharpe and Peter Lake (Basingstoke: Macmillan, 1994), 21–43

Spencer, T. J. B. 'Shakespeare and the Elizabethan Romans', *Shakespeare Survey* 10 (1957), 27–38

Spenser, Edmund, *Complaints: Containing Sundry Small Poems of the World's Vanity* (London, 1588)

Squier, Charles L., *John Fletcher* (Boston, MA: Twayne, 1986)

Stanivukovic, Goran, '"The Blushing Shame of Souldiers": The Eroticism of Heroic Masculinity in John Fletcher's *Bonduca*', in *The Image of Manhood in Early Modern Literature: Viewing the Male*, ed. A. P. Williams (Westport, CT: Greenwood Press, 1999), 41–54

Starks-Estes, Lisa S., *Violence, Trauma and Virtus in Shakespeare's Roman Poems and Plays: Transforming Ovid* (Basingstoke: Palgrave Macmillan, 2014)

Steffen, William, 'Grafting and Ecological Imperialism in John Fletcher's *Bonduca*', *Journal for Early Modern Cultural Studies* 17 (2017), 68–96

Suetonius, *The History of Twelve Caesars Emperors of Rome: Written in Latin by C. Suetonius Tranquillus, and Newly Translated into English, with a Marginal Gloss, and Other Brief Annotations Thereupon*, trans. Philemon Holland (London, 1606)

Suetonius, *The Lives of the Twelve Caesars*, trans. J. C. Rolfe (London: Heinemann, 1913)

Tacitus, *The Annals of Cornelius Tacitus. The Description of Germany*, trans. Richard Greenway (London, 1598)

Tannenbaum, Samuel A., 'A Hitherto Unpublished John Fletcher Autograph', *Journal of English and Germanic Philology* 28 (1929), 35–40

Taunton, Nina, 'Biography, a University Education, and Playwriting: Fletcher and Marlowe', *Research Opportunities in Renaissance Drama* 33 (1994), 63–97

Taunton, Nina, 'Did John Fletcher the Playwright Go to University?', *Notes and Queries* 235 (1990), 170–2

Taylor, A. B. (ed.), *Shakespeare's Ovid: The Metamorphoses in the Plays and Poems* (Cambridge: Cambridge University Press, 2000)

Taylor, Archer, 'Proverbs in the Plays of Beaumont and Fletcher', *Southern Folklore Quarterly* 24 (1960), 77–100

Taylor, Gary, and John Jowett, *Shakespeare Reshaped, 1606–1623* (Oxford: Clarendon Press, 1993)

Teramura, Misha, 'The Anxiety of *Auctoritas*: Chaucer and *The Two Noble Kinsmen*', *Shakespeare Quarterly* 63 (2012), 544–76

Teramura, Misha, 'Archival Reflection: The Fortunes of Fletcher's "Against Astrologers"', *Modern Philology* 118 (2020), 130–57

Thucydides, *The Peloponnesian War*, trans. Martin Hammond (Oxford: Oxford University Press, 2009)

Tilley, Morris P., *A Dictionary of the Proverbs in England in the Sixteenth and Seventeenth Centuries* (Ann Arbor, MI: University of Michigan Press, 1950)

Toffanin, Giuseppe, *Machiavelli e Tacitismo* (Padua: Draghi, 1921)

Turner, Robert Kean, '*The Tragedy of Valentinian*: Textual Introduction', in *The Dramatic Works in the Beaumont and Fletcher Canon*, ed. Fredson Bowers, 10 vols (Cambridge: Cambridge University Press, 1966–96), 4.263–75

Turner, Robert Kean, '*The Tragedy of Valentinian*: Textual Notes', in *The Dramatic Works in the Beaumont and Fletcher Canon*, ed. Fredson Bowers, 10 vols (Cambridge: Cambridge University Press, 1966–96), 4.381–92

Turner, Robert Y., 'Responses to Tyranny in John Fletcher's Plays', *Medieval and Renaissance Drama in England* 4 (1989), 123–41

Ulrich, Otto, *Die pseudohistorischen Dramen Beaumonts und Fletchers: Thierry and Theodoret, Valentinian, The Prophetess und The False One und ihre Quellen* (Straßburg: Neuesten Nachrichten, 1913)

Varro, *On the Latin Language*, vol. 1, trans. Roland G. Kent (London: Heinemann, 1938)

Vaughan, Virginia Mason, *Shakespeare and the Gods* (London: Bloomsbury Arden Shakespeare, 2019)

Velissariou, Aspasia, 'Female Fetishised Deaths in Jacobean Tragedy', *Gender Studies* 12 (2013), 194–212

Viswanathan, S., 'A Shakespeare "Gest": Bearing the Body in the Plays', *Points of View* 1 (2008), 3–16

Waith, Eugene M., 'The Death of Pompey: English Style, French Style', in *Shakespeare and Dramatic Tradition*, ed. William R. Elton and William B. Long (Newark, DE: University of Delaware Press, 1989), 276–85

Waith, Eugene M., *The Pattern of Tragicomedy in Beaumont and Fletcher* (New Haven, CT: Yale University Press, 1952)

Wall-Randell, Sarah, 'What Is a Staged Book? Books as "Actors" in the Early Modern English Theatre', in *Rethinking Theatrical Documents in Shakespeare's England*, ed. Tiffany Stern (London: Bloomsbury Arden Shakespeare, 2020), 128–52

Wayne, Valerie, 'Introduction', in *Cymbeline* by William Shakespeare (London: Bloomsbury Arden Shakespeare, 2017), 1–136

Werstine, Paul, 'Folio Editors, Folio Compositors, and the Folio Text of *King Lear*', in *The Division of the Kingdoms: Shakespeare's Two Versions of King Lear*, ed. Gary Taylor and Michael Warren (Oxford: Oxford University Press, 1983), 247–312

Wiggins, Martin, *Shakespeare and the Drama of His Time* (Oxford: Oxford University Press, 2000)

Wiggins, Martin, in association with Catherine Richardson, *British Drama, 1533–1642: A Catalogue*, 9 vols (Oxford: Oxford University Press, 2012–18)

Wilders, John, 'Introduction', in *Antony and Cleopatra* by William Shakespeare (London: Routledge for Arden Shakespeare, 1995), 1–84

Williams, George Walton, '*The Prophetess*: Textual Introduction', in *The Dramatic Works in the Beaumont and Fletcher Canon*, ed. Fredson Bowers, 10 vols (Cambridge: Cambridge University Press, 1966–96), 9.223–31

Williams, George Walton, '*The Woman Hater*: Textual Introduction', in *The Dramatic Works in the Beaumont and Fletcher Canon*, ed. Fredson Bowers, 10 vols (Cambridge: Cambridge University Press, 1966–96), 1.147–55

Williams, Gordon, *A Dictionary of Sexual Language and Imagery in Shakespearean and Stuart Literature*, 3 vols (London: Athlone, 1994)

Williams, M. E., 'Field, Nathan (bap. 1587, d. 1619/20)', in *Oxford Dictionary of National Biography* (Oxford: Oxford University Press, 2004), https://doi.org/10.1093/ref:odnb/9391 (accessed 26 January 2021)

Womack, Peter, 'The Tyrant's Vein: Misrule and Popularity in the Elizabethan Playhouse', *Review of English Studies* 72 (2021), 61–84

Womersley, David, 'Sir Henry Savile's Translation of Tacitus and the Political Interpretation of Elizabethan Texts', *Review of English Studies* 42 (1991), 313–42

Woolf, Daniel R., 'From Hystories to the Historical: Five Transitions in Thinking about the Past, 1500–1700', in *The Uses of History in Early Modern England*, ed. Paulina Kewes (San Marino, CA: Huntington Library, 2006), 31–67

Woolf, Daniel R., *The Idea of History in Early Stuart England: Erudition, Ideology, and 'The Light of Truth' from the Accession of James I to the Civil War* (Toronto: University of Toronto Press, 1990)

Worden, Blair, 'Ben Jonson among the Historians', in *Culture and Politics in Early Stuart England*, ed. Kevin Sharpe and Peter Lake (Basingstoke: Macmillan, 1994), 67–89

Worden, Blair, 'Historians and Poets', in *The Uses of History in Early Modern England*, ed. Paulina Kewes (San Marino, CA: Huntington Library, 2006), 69–90

Wray, Ramona, 'Introduction', in *The Tragedy of Mariam* by Elizabeth Cary (London: Bloomsbury Arden Shakespeare, 2012), 1–69

Wright, Gillian, 'What Daniel Really Did with the *Pharsalia*: *The Civil Wars*, Lucan, and King James', *Review of English Studies* 55 (2004), 210–32

Xenophon, *Memorabilia*, trans. W. C. Marchant (London: Heinemann, 1923)

INDEX

Literary works can be found under authors' name, except for the plays in the Fletcher canon, which are listed as main entries.

Adelman, Janet 159, 164, 175
'Against Astrologers' 86
Agrati, Annalisa 58
Alemán, Mateo 31
All Is True, or King Henry VIII 11
Allman, Eileen 57, 63, 79, 100, 102, 111, 130
Altman, Joel B. 53
Appian 3
Appleton, William W. 56, 104, 140, 173
Aristophanes
    Ecclesiazusae 50
    Lysistrata 32, 50, 179
Aristotle 49
Armstrong, William A. 58
Ascham, Roger 129
Atlas 161
Aubrey, John 31

Baldwin, Thomas Whitfield 109, 130
Bate, Jonathan 53, 158, 162, 165, 175–6
Beaumont, Francis 1, 11–15, 32, 46–7, 51, 69, 82, 98, 129, 134
Beggars' Bush 51
Benjamin, Walter 8–9, 17, 21, 62, 93, 103
    see also Trauerspiel
Berry, Edward 165, 176

Bess of Hardwick 136
Bevington, David 99–100, 139, 173, 175
Bigliazzi, Silvia 58
Blackfriars 10, 174
Blau, Herbert 94, 103
Bliss, Lee 32, 54, 58
Blount, Edward 171, 176
Boccaccio, Giovanni, *Decameron* 51
Boling, Ronald J. 68, 100, 142–3, 173
Bolton, Edmund 32, 34–5, 50, 182
Bonduca 2, 6–10, 15–16, 19–20, 34, 51, 56, 65, 72–3, 77–8, 81, 83, 97–9, 102–3, 106, 117, 121–2, 134–5, 152–3, 157, 168, 173, 180–3
    Antony and Cleopatra and 141–5, 151
    Coriolanus and 141
    Cymbeline and 140–1
    depiction of female characters 115–16
    distance of the gods 87
    Julius Caesar and 141
    negative depiction of the Romans 67–70
Bowers, Fredson 15
Bretz, Andrew 117, 131, 141, 173
Brewer, Antony
    Lovesick King, The 55
Briggs, William Dinsmore 55
Buc, George 90

INDEX

Burrow, Colin 53
Bushnell, Rebecca W. 65, 100

Caesar, Gaius Julius 3, 8, 80
Caesar's Revenge 34, 174
'Caesars Tragedye' 139
Cain, Tom 132
Calder, Alison 141, 143, 173
Caligula, Roman Emperor 51–2, 80, 112
Camden, William 29
Cantor, Paul A. 90, 103
Captain, The 19, 69, 80, 126, 135, 181
Caracalla, Roman Emperor 6, 33, 55
'Cardenio' 12
Carlson, Marvin 136, 168, 172
Cary, Elizabeth, *The Tragedy of Mariam* 148
Casaubon, Isaac 38
Cassius Dio 33, 35, 44, 49–51, 55, 76
Cathcart, Charles 31, 54
Catty, Jocelyn 116, 118, 131
Cervantes, Miguel de 50
Chances, The 135
Chaucer, Geoffrey 51
Cicero, Marcus Tullius 49
Clark, Ira 48, 59, 120–1, 131
Clark, Sandra 23, 66, 100, 121–2, 131–2
Clegg, Cyndia Susan 23
Clytemnestra 48
Coeffeteau, Nicolas 16, 36–9, 50, 56–7, 182
collaboration 10–15, 21, 134
Condell, Elizabeth 51
Condell, Henry 51, 170–1, 176
Cotton, Robert 29
Craik T. W. 172
Cranach, Lucas 177
Crane, Ralph 171, 176
Crawford, Julie 23, 102
Cromwell, Oliver 71
Cupid's Revenge 82, 86, 118

Curran, John E., Jr 2, 6, 22–3, 53, 84–5, 96, 102–3, 122–4, 131–2, 153–4, 162–3, 175
Curtius, Marcus 21, 177–80
Custom of the Country, The 50, 68, 130, 179–80

Daborne, Robert 12, 51
Daileader, Celia R. 32, 54
Dall'Olio, Francesco 58
Daniell, David 100
Daniel, Samuel 4, 22
Dekker, Thomas, and Philip Massinger
  Virgin Martyr, The 120, 153
Devereux, Robert, 2nd Earl of Essex 81
'Devil of Dowgate, The' 12
Dickinson, Robert 29
Digges, Leonard 171, 176
Dionysius of Halicarnassus 71
Donaldson, Ian 53, 118, 131, 176
Double Marriage, The 18–19, 26, 78, 106, 121–2, 128, 134–5, 169–70, 177–8
  Julius Caesar and 118–20
Drabek, Pavel 56, 87, 103, 142, 173
Drayton, Michael 51
du Bellay, Joachim, *Les Antiquités de Rome* 72–3, 101
Duchesne, André 55
Duncan-Jones, Katherine 172
D'Urfé, Honoré, *L'Astrée* 16, 33, 39–41, 50, 107, 110–11
Dutton, William 51
Dyce, Alexander 54

Edmond, Mary 171, 176
Elder Brother, The 47–9, 51
Elizabeth I, Queen 9, 40
Elizabeth, Princess 97
English, Simon 29, 46
Epictetus 126–7, 132
Escolme, Bridget 144, 173
Euripides, *Alcestis* 32

INDEX

Fair Maid of the Inn, The 12, 53
Faithful Shepherdess, The 42, 55, 58, 171
False One, The 2, 6–10, 15–16, 19, 23, 50, 54, 56, 65, 72, 80–1, 83–4, 88, 91–2, 96, 101, 106, 109, 113, 115, 130, 134–5, 153, 158, 173, 181–3
   Antony and Cleopatra and 147–52
   Julius Caesar and 74–5, 151
   criticism of colonialism 73–4
   sources 32, 34–5, 125–6
   treatment of Cleopatra's race 148–9, 174
Farley Hills, David 75, 101–2
Farnaby, Thomas 32, 50
Field, Nathan 1, 12, 32, 55, 103, 130, 132
Finkelpearl, Philip J. 52, 60, 65, 82, 100, 102, 105, 124–5, 129, 132
Flecknoe, Richard 129, 133
Fletcher, Giles 49
Fletcher, John 1–2, 4, 6–23, 26, 55, 57–9, 61–2, 182–4
   attitude to stoicism 123–7
   conception of history 93–9
   depiction of non-Roman women 113–16
   depiction of Rome
      distance of the gods 85–9
      leaders 81–5, 89–93
      martial prowess 75–81
      politics 62–75
      women 107–13
   education 27–32
   First Folio 10, 13, 39, 134
   portrayal of education 45–9
   relationship with Shakespeare
      Antony and Cleopatra 135–6, 141–2, 144–5, 147–52, 153–4, 158–67, 168–9
      Coriolanus 135, 141, 153, 166–8
      Cymbeline 140–1
      Julius Caesar 135–40, 141, 144, 147, 149, 151, 152–8, 168–9
      potential involvement in the editing of First Folio 169–72
      Rape of Lucrece, The 137
      Tempest, The 153
   Second Folio 8, 73, 115, 134
   scepticism towards the classics 49–52, 116–22, 127–9, 177–81
   use of the classics 26–7, 32–45
Fletcher, Nathaniel 31, 49, 51
Fletcher, Richard 31
Florio, John 171, 176
Florus, Lucius Julius 32, 34–6, 50, 83, 182
Ford, John 12
Frederick V, Elector Palatine 97
Frénée Hutchins, Samantha 23, 102, 142–3, 173
Frijlinck, Wilhelmina P. 172
Frost, David L. 134, 172, 174
Fuller, Thomas 13–14, 25
Fumée, Martin 39–40, 107, 182

Garrick, David 141
Gentili, Vanna 22
Gentillet, Innocent 33–4, 50, 55
Gielen, Resi 57
Gill, Roma 55
Goltzius, Hendrick 177
Gossett, Suzanne 12, 24, 111, 130–1, 135, 172–3
Grady, Hugh 103
Greg, W. W. 176
Griffin, Julia 119, 131
Grogan, Jane 54
Guarini, Giovanni Battista 42, 55
Gunton, Simon 29, 53
Gurr, Andrew 10, 14–15, 24–5, 135, 172

Hadfield, Andrew 82–3, 102
Hall, Kim F. 148, 174
Hand, Molly 89, 103, 115, 131

INDEX

Hastings, Elizabeth Stanley, Countess of Huntingdon 81, 105
Hastings, Henry, Earl of Huntingdon 51, 81, 105
Hatchuel, Sarah 149, 151, 173–4
Healey, John 126–7, 132
Hecuba 137, 147
Heminges, John 170–1, 176
Henry Frederick, Prince 97–8
Henslowe, Philip 51
Hensman, Bertha 12, 24, 53–6
Hercules 20, 158–66, 175
Herodian 6, 33, 35, 49–50, 55
Herodotus 32, 50
Heywood, Thomas 111, 175
Hicklin, Christopher 78, 102
Hickman, Andrew 68–9, 100, 143, 173
Hila, Marina 23, 41, 58, 66, 96, 100, 103, 107, 110, 112, 130
Hinman, Charles 176
Historia Augusta 36–9, 49–50, 56–7, 182
Holinshed, Raphael 34, 51, 70, 78, 101, 115, 140
Holland, Peter 100
Holland, Philemon 32, 101
Holmberg, Eva Johanna 148, 174
Homer 129, 147
Honest Man's Fortune, The 132
Honigmann, E. A. J. 53
Hope, Jonathan 12, 24
Hopkins, Lisa 2, 22, 172
Horace 26, 53, 129
Horrible, Cruel, and Bloody Murder, A 141, 173
Hoy, Cyrus 12, 24, 59, 100, 102, 120, 130–2
Humorous Lieutenant, The 1, 32, 65, 69, 107–8, 175
Hunter, G. K. 22

Ide, Arata 31, 54
Island Princess, The 78, 135, 149, 169–70
Iyengar, Sujata 174

Jaggard, Isaac 171
Jensen, Freyja Cox 22, 35, 56
'Jeweller of Amsterdam, The' 12
Johnson, Sarah E. 143–4, 173
Jonson, Ben 1, 6, 26, 44, 51–3, 90, 163, 171, 176
  Catiline His Conspiracy 2, 134
  Devil Is an Ass, The 4
  Discoveries 74
  Poetaster, or His Arraignment 2
  Sejanus His Fall 2, 124
  Staple of News, The 74
Josephus 33, 35, 49, 56
Jove 126
Jowett, John 55, 101, 176
Jowitt, Claire 2, 22–3, 69, 100, 174
Justin 36, 49–50, 56
Juvenal 26

Kahn, Coppélia 2, 22
Kamps, Ivo 23, 95–6, 103–4, 169, 176
Kantorowicz, Ernest H. 100
Karim-Cooper, Farah 148, 174
Kelliher, Hilton 31, 54
Kennedy, Gwynne 111–12, 130
Kermode, Frank 161, 175
Kernan, Alvin 96, 103
Kewes, Paulina 22–3, 102, 173
King and No King, A 32, 50, 54, 80, 135
King's Men 20, 41, 51, 87, 135, 157, 166, 168–71
Kirk, Florence Ada 58
Knight, Edward 171, 176
Knight of Malta, The 32, 40
Knolles, Richard 51

Lambert, Jean 48, 59
Late Antiquity 16, 27, 33, 49–50, 183
Laws of Candy, The 12, 53
Leach, A. F. 29, 53–4
Leech, Clifford 14–15, 23, 25, 86, 88, 102–3, 134, 140–1, 172–3

Leonhardt, Benno 56, 173
Lily, William 47
Lister, Rota Herzberg 172
Little French Lawyer, The 19, 123, 135, 169, 181
Livy 3, 48–50, 71, 137, 168, 177
Lodge, Thomas 56
Longus 42
Loomba, Ania 148, 174
Lope de Vega 51, 55
Loughlin, Marie H. 41, 58, 110, 124, 130–2
Lovascio, Domenico 23, 56, 101, 130–1, 174–5
Lovers' Progress, The 135
Love's Cure, or The Martial Maid 122, 173
Loyal Subject, The 19, 26, 80, 127, 181
Lucan 32, 34–5, 50, 83, 91, 150–1, 182
Lucrece 18, 66, 106, 110–12, 116–18, 130, 136–7, 168–9
Lucretius 166

Mabbe, James 31, 51, 111
MacCallum, Mungo William 53
MacDonald, Joyce Green 148, 174
McKeithan, Daniel Morley 119, 131, 172, 174
MacLean, Sally-Beth 4, 22
McLuskie, Kathleen 10, 24, 127, 133
McManus, Clare 52, 56, 60, 101, 134, 172
McMillin, Scott 4, 22
McMullan, Gordon 2, 10–11, 14–15, 22–5, 46–7, 59, 82, 102, 105, 115–17, 129, 131, 134, 154, 161, 164, 170, 172, 174–6, 179, 184
Mad Lover, The 33, 35, 46, 50, 78, 80, 86
'Madon, King of Britain' 11
Maid in the Mill, The 130
Maid's Tragedy, The 1, 11, 32, 135
Makkink, H. J. 86, 102, 138, 173

Marlowe, Christopher 31
 Doctor Faustus 61
Mars 20, 75, 158–9, 164–6
Marvell, Andrew 71, 101
Massinger, Philip 1–2, 11–12, 15, 18–20, 26, 32, 34–5, 46–7, 50–1, 67, 74–5, 84, 90, 95, 106, 119–20, 122–3, 125, 130–1, 134–5, 147–55, 158, 166–8, 174, 182
 Believe as You List 5–6, 33
 Roman Actor, The 6, 120, 138
Masten, Jeffrey 24
Maximus, Valerius 32
Maxwell, Baldwin 23, 147, 173–4
Middleton, Thomas 12
 Second Maiden's Tragedy, The 111
Mincoff, Marco 21, 40, 57, 86, 102–3, 111, 130, 137, 172
Miola, Robert S. 58
Moseley, Humphrey 11
Moul, Victoria 53
Munro, Lucy 15, 25, 42, 51–2, 57–60, 89, 103, 113, 121, 127, 131, 133, 135, 172, 174, 176

Neil, Kelly 142, 145, 173
Neill, Michael 57, 144, 173
Nero, Roman Emperor 8, 44–5, 51–2, 68, 80, 83, 112
Neville, Sarah 101
Nice Valour, The 12
Nocentelli, Carmen 56, 60
Nolan, Bernard Joseph 56, 69, 100

Oliphant, E. H. C. 12, 24
Ovid 26, 40, 51, 53
Owens, Margaret E. 8, 23, 92, 103
Oxley, Philip 55

Painter, William 51
Paleit, Edward 22–3, 54, 83, 91, 102–3
Paster, Gail Kern 131
Pasupathi, Vimala 79–80, 102

Patrick, Simon 33
Peacham, Henry 46
Pearse, Nancy Cotton 55, 111–12, 116, 119–20, 122, 130–2
Pérez Díez, José A. 59, 132
Petrarch, *Triumphs* 151
Philaster 82, 96, 135, 140
Pilgrim, The 51
Plautus, *Curculio* 32
Plutarch 3, 26, 32, 34, 39, 44, 50–1, 53, 76, 90, 150, 168, 182
Poitevin, Kimberly Woosley 148, 174
Poliziano, Agnolo 55
Pollard, A. W. 176
Portia (wife of Brutus) 106–7, 117–18
Potter, Lois 13, 24, 59
Potter, Ursula Ann 46, 59
Pownall, Nathaniel 49
Priam 147
Procopius, *The History of the Wars* 16, 39–41, 49–50, 57, 107, 182
Prophetess, The 2, 6–10, 15–17, 19, 24, 27, 35, 61–3, 66–7, 71–2, 76, 82, 88–9, 92, 97, 106, 108–9, 113, 134–5, 170, 181–3
  Antony and Cleopatra and 158–66
  Coriolanus and 166–7
  Julius Caesar and 152–8
  sources 36–9, 50, 57

Queen of Corinth, The 1, 26, 119, 130–1

Rackin, Phyllis 130
Ralegh, Walter 98–9
Rasmussen, Eric 99, 175–6
Red Bull Theatre 170
Reid, Lindsay Ann 11, 24
Rollo, or The Bloody Brother 6, 11, 33, 35, 50, 55, 119, 125, 128, 132, 178

Ronan, Clifford J. 5, 22–3
Rowley, William 12, 130
Rule a Wife and Have a Wife 66, 78, 100, 102

Sallust 50
Samson, Alexander 52, 56, 60
Saner, Reginald 173
Saumaise, Claude 38
Savile, Henry 16, 44–5, 50, 58, 182
Scambler, Edmund 30
Schanzer, Ernest 175
Scornful Lady, The 51
Sea Voyage, The 46, 170
Seneca 125–9
  Hercules Furens 159
Seneca the Elder 26–7, 33, 53
Shakespeare, William 1, 6–8, 10–12, 21, 26, 53, 81–2, 86, 90, 129
  Antony and Cleopatra 2, 19–20, 62, 74, 93, 106, 121, 135–6, 141–2, 144–5, 147–52, 153–4, 158–67, 168–70, 182–3
  Coriolanus 2, 20, 62, 68, 78, 106, 135, 141, 153, 166–8, 170, 183
  Cymbeline 2, 19, 40, 140–1
  First Folio 20, 74, 136, 170–2
  Julius Caesar 2, 19–20, 62, 74, 76, 82, 84, 92–3, 106, 119–20, 131, 135–40, 141, 144, 147, 149, 151, 152–8, 168–70, 182–3
  Othello 38, 57, 174
  Rape of Lucrece, The 137
  Taming of the Shrew, The 134
  Tempest, The 20, 153, 170
  Titus Andronicus 2, 106
  Troilus and Cressida 139
Sharpe, Will 24
Shepard, Alexandra 174
Shirley, James 12, 47, 58
  Gentleman of Venice, The 55

Sir John Van Olden Barnavelt 11, 55, 80, 90, 95–6, 135, 169, 181
Smith, Emma 176
Spanish Curate, The 67, 79, 125
Spenser, Edmund
  Faerie Queene, The 51
  Ruins of Rome, The 72
Squier, Charles 80, 102, 173
Stanivukovic, Goran 23
Steffen, William 23
stoicism 7, 19, 21, 94, 107, 122–6, 137, 181–2
Suetonius, Gaius Tranquillus 32, 34, 44, 50, 76, 130
Susenbrotus, Joannes 46–7

Tacitus, Gaius Cornelius 3, 26, 44, 50–2, 70, 78, 124, 168
Tamer Tamed, The 32, 40, 46, 50, 54, 127, 134, 178–9
Tannenbaum, Samuel A. 102
Tarquin, Sextus 18, 66, 116–18, 136
Tasso, Torquato 55
Taunton, Nina 31, 54
Taylor, Gary 32, 55
Teramura, Misha 86, 103, 134, 172
Terence 39, 78
Thierry and Theodoret 11, 32, 80
Thorne, Henry 29
Thucydides 78
Tiberius, Roman Emperor 44, 80
Toffanin, Giuseppe 132
Tomlinson, Sophie 131, 133
Trauerspiel 9, 17, 21, 62, 93–5, 181
Triumph of Death, The 86, 116
Turner, Robert Kean 40, 57–9, 100, 103, 131–2
Turner, Robert Y. 23
Two Noble Kinsmen, The 47

Ulrich, Otto 16, 34, 36, 39–40, 54, 56–7, 103

Valentinian 2, 6–10, 15–17, 19, 21, 27, 35, 63–6, 72, 81–3, 85–8, 90–1, 93, 95–8, 115, 122, 124–5, 128, 130, 134–5, 145, 151–3, 165, 181–3
  corruption of Rome 63–6, 79–80
  depiction of women 106–13
  Julius Caesar and 137–40
  Rape of Lucrece, The and 136–7
  sources 39–45, 50, 58
Varro 177
Vaughan, Virginia Mason 159, 162, 175
Velissariou, Aspasia 63, 100
Venus 159, 165–6
Vergil, Polydore 3
Very Woman, A 32, 46, 124–6, 132, 169
Virgil 26, 129, 147
Viswanathan, S. 170, 176
Vopiscus, Flavius see Historia Augusta

Waith, Eugene M. 53, 92, 103, 150, 174
Wall-Randell, Sarah 51, 59
Wayne, Valerie 58, 173
Webster, John 12
Weever, John 31
Werstine, Paul 171, 176
Wife for a Month, A 117
Wiggins, Martin 4, 11–12, 22, 24, 55, 57–9, 132, 173
Wilders, John 163, 175
Wild Goose-Chase, The 117, 135, 170
Williams, George Walton 56, 58–9, 100, 132, 155, 175
Williams, Gordon 184
Womack, Peter 58
Woman-Hater, The 32, 46, 57, 59, 135

Women Pleased 78, 169
Womersley, David 44, 58
Woolf, Daniel R. 22–3, 35, 56, 98, 104
Worden, Blair 22, 53
Wotton, Henry 51
Wray, Ramona 148, 174

Xenophon 50, 54
  Cyropaedia 32
  Hiero 43, 58
  Memorabilia 163

Zonaras, Joannes, *Epitome Historiarum* 44

Lightning Source UK Ltd.
Milton Keynes UK
UKHW021311230322
400501UK00004B/33